The Masters Speak

The Masters Speak

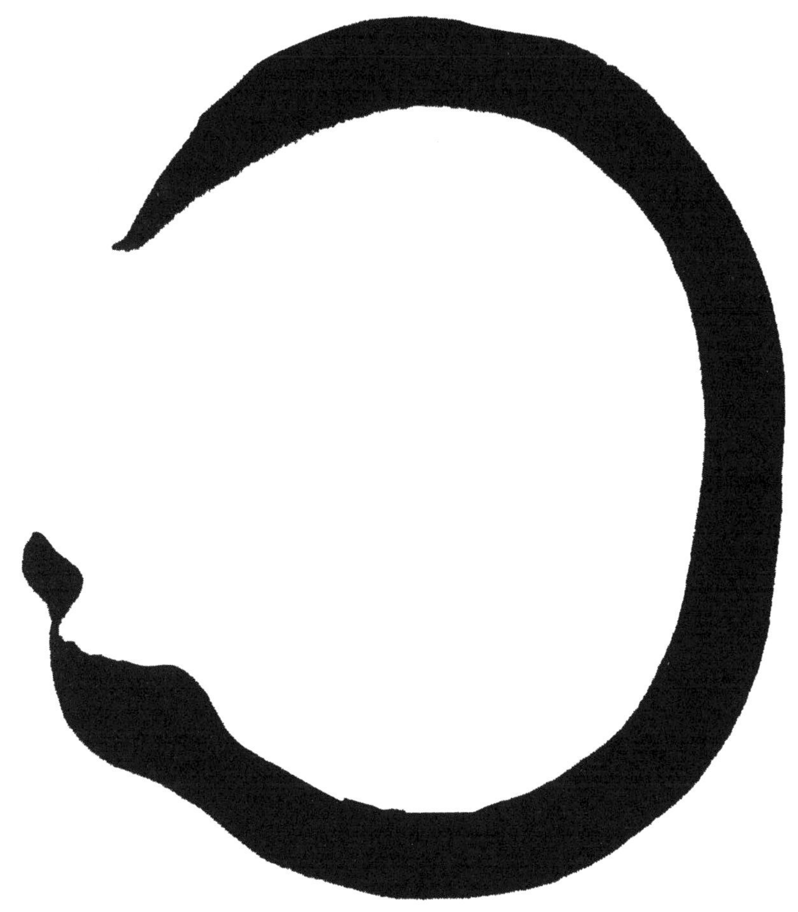

Jose M. Fraguas

UNIQUE PUBLICATIONS
Burbank, California

Disclaimer

Please note that the author and publisher of this book are NOT RESPONSIBLE in any manner whatsoever for any injury that may result from practicing the techniques and/or following the instructions given within. Since the physical activities described herein may be too strenuous in nature for some readers to engage in safely, it is essential that a physician be consulted prior to training.

First published in 2001 by Unique Publications.

Library of Congress Catalog Number: 2001 132410
ISBN: 0-86568-195-3

Unique Publications
4201 Vanowen Place
Burbank, CA 91505
(800) 332–3330

First edition
05 04 03 02 01 00 99 98 97 1 3 5 7 9 10 8 6 4 2

Printed in the United States of America.

Editor: Todd Hester
Design: Patrick Gross
Cover Design: George Chen

"Art washes away from the soul the dust of everyday life. Often while reading a book one feels that the author would have preferred to paint rather than to write; one can sense the pleasure he derives from describing a landscape of a person, as if he were painting what he is saying, because from deep in his heart he would have preferred to use brushes and colors. Art is not the application of a canon but what the instinct and the brain can conceive beyond any canon."

—Pablo Picasso (1881–1973)
Spanish painter and sculptor

Dedication

This book is dedicated to the memory of those who tragically died in New York City during the terrorist attack on September 11, 2001.

Acknowledgments

The sources of kind assistance to me in collecting material for this book are too numerous to individually acknowledge, but I would like to gratefully mention a few specific individuals who generously contributed their time and experience to the preparation of this work, above and beyond the call of duty.

At the top of my list is Todd Hester, the editor of the work. Also of particular assistance were Ed Ikuta (one of the world's greatest martial arts photographers); Germany's Norbert Schiffer (editorial director of *Satori-Verlag* and *Budo* magazine); Greg Rhodes of London (a long-time friend, martial artist, and photographer), John Steven Soet (director, and writer); Ed Parker Jr. of Pasadena, California; escrima master Tony Somera of Stockton, California; Andre Lima (martial arts instructor, writer, and photographer); James William Holzer (writer and photographer); Yves Andre David (photographer); Kali guro Steve Baishiki; Terry O'Neil (editor of England's Fighting Arts International); and finally Curtis Wong, who has carried martial arts in America on his shoulders for 30 years and made everything possible. I would further like to give my most heartfelt gratitude to all the masters appearing in this book. Not only did they generously give me an enormous amount of personal time for the long interviews, but they also provided me with wonderful photographs to illustrate the book as well.

I also want to acknowledge the constant support and encouragement of my mother. She is an extraordinary person of endless compassion, quiet and unending forgiveness, deep understanding, and limitless giving and patience. Over the years she has needed to use all those qualities—and then some—in dealing with my martial arts addiction.

I would be remiss if I did not recognize the many writers, philosophers, and martial arts masters whom I have read about but whom I have never met. Through books, their lives and spirits have greatly impacted me and brought vast insights into my life. These people are treasures to me, and my life is far richer because of them.

I also need to give thanks to one final, special individual. As Federico Garcia Lorca used to say, "al moreno de luna verde." This modest person, born in Málaga, Spain and whose privacy I wish to respect by not naming him here, is an example of how it is possible to reach excellence in any area of life by setting high standards and refusing to back away from them—and at the same time be a human being of the highest magnitude. You know who you are. Your generous spirit and natural wisdom are deeply admired and greatly appreciated.

—Jose M. Fraguas

About the Author

Born and raised in Madrid, Spain, Jose "Chema" Fraguas began his martial arts studies with judo, in grade school, at age 9. From there he moved to taekwondo and then to kenpo karate, earning a black belt in both styles. During this same period he also studied shito-ryu karate under Japanese masters Masahiro Okada and Yashunari Ishimi, eventually receiving a fifth-degree black belt. He began his career as a writer at age 16 by serving as a regular contributor to martial arts magazines in Great Britain, France, Spain, Italy, Germany, Portugal, Holland, and Australia. Having a black belt in three different styles allows him to better reflect the physical side of the martial arts in his writing: "Feeling before writing," Fraguas says.

In 1980, he moved to Los Angeles, California. His open-minded mentality helped him to develop a realistic approach to the martial arts. Seeking to supplement his previous training, he researched other disciplines such as kali, jiu-jitsu and muay Thai. In his first struggling years he managed to meet numerous martial arts greats such as Gene LeBell, Jun Chong, Wally Jay, and Dan Inosanto.

In 1986, Fraguas founded his own book and magazine company in Europe, authoring dozens of books and distributing his magazines to 35 countries in three different languages. His reputation and credibility as a martial artist and publisher became well known to the top masters around the world. Considering himself a martial artist first and a writer and publisher second, Fraguas feels fortunate to have had the opportunity to interview many legendary martial arts teachers. He recognizes that much of the information given in the interviews helped him to discover new dimensions in the martial arts. "I was constantly absorbing knowledge from the great masters," he recalls. "I only trained with a few of them, but intellectually and spiritually all of them have made very important contributions to my growth as a complete martial artist."

However there were some drawbacks to his position as a publisher, Fraguas acknowledges, that directly affected his personal martial arts development. "Of course, some people taught me because of my position as a publisher and not because who I was as a person. Even though I recognize that, I'm still grateful for the knowledge they shared with me."

Steeped in tradition yet looking to the future, Fraguas understands and appreciates martial arts history and philosophy and feels this rich heritage is a necessary stepping stone to personal growth and spiritual evolution. His desire to promote both ancient philosophy and modern thinking provided the motivation for writing this book. "If the motivation is just money, a book cannot be of good quality," Fraguas says. 'If the book is written to just make people happy, it cannot be deep. I want to write books so I can learn as well as teach."

Originally from Madrid, Spain, the author is currently living in Los Angeles, California where he is the General Manager of CFW Enterprises, the world's leading martial arts publishing company.

Introduction

I've been both lucky and fortunate. Some of my best days were spent interviewing and meeting the masters appearing in this book. There is little I enjoy more than "gnawing" on a great interview while time slows and sometimes even seems to stop. Having the opportunity to meet and interview the most relevant and prestigious martial artists of the past four decades is something that every martial artist doesn't have the chance to do. Hopefully, in some small way, this will help make up for that.

Meeting the masters and having long conversations with them that were published in magazines around the world allowed me to do more than simply "scratch the surface" of the technical aspects of their respective styles, but to also research and analyze the human beings behind the teachers. Some of the dialogues and interviews began by simply commenting about the superficial techniques of fighting, and ended up turning into a very uncommon spiritual conversation about the philosophical aspects of the martial arts.

Interestingly enough, none of the men behind the masters were interested in being the best fighters, or in trying to prove their style was the best—it was just the opposite. The essence of their whole message was very far from that. These teachers are most interested in fostering, through their teachings, the development of good human beings. They are trying to pass along a culture, a discipline, and an education to the generations to follow. Being better than someone or something else is simply something they don't care about. Although they are all very different, considering their respective styles and backgrounds, they all share a common thread of the traditional values such as discipline, respect, positive attitude, dedication, and etiquette.

For the last 25 years I've faced the long odds of interviewing these masters, one-on-one, face-to-face, and with no place to run if I asked a stupid question. Many times, it was a real challenge to not just make contact with them, but also how to make the interview interesting enough to bring out the knowledge that resided inside them. In every interview I tried to absorb as much knowledge as I could, ranging from their training methods, to their fighting methods, and to their philosophies about life itself.

Their different origins and cultural backgrounds heavily influenced them but never prevented them from analyzing, researching, or modifying anything that they considered appropriate. They always kept an open mind to improving both their arts and themselves. From a formal philosophical point of view many of them follow the wisdom of Zen and Taoism—others just use common sense.

Years before anyone ever heard of any of them, they devoted themselves to their arts, often in solitude, sometimes to the exclusion of other pursuits most of us take for granted. They worked themselves into extraordinary physical condition and stayed there. They ignored distractions and diversions and brought to their training a great deal of concentration. The best of them got as good as they could possibly get at performing and teaching their chosen art, and the rest of us watched them and, leading our "balanced lives," wondered how good we might have gotten at something had we devoted ourselves to whatever we did as ferociously as these masters embraced their arts. In that respect they bear our dreams.

It would be wonderful to find a single martial artist who combined all the great qualities of these masters—but that's impossible. That, however, was one of the things that inspired me to write this book. I wanted to preserve some things that were said a long time ago, of which not many people today are aware.

If you read carefully between the lines, you'll see that none of these men were trying to become a "fighting machine" or training in order to create the most devastating martial arts system known to man. They focused, rather, on how to use the martial arts to become a better person. Nothing more, nothing less. Of course, the functionality of their systems was and is something they care about, but it is not the focal point of their lives or their training. Eastern and Western mentality is very different—like night and day. Fortunately, there are many links that, once discovered, open a wide spectrum of possibilities not only to martial arts but to a better existence as human beings.

The interviews often lasted as long as three or four hours of non-stop talking. I would begin at their school and finish the conversation at a restaurant or coffee shop. A lot of information in these interviews had been never published before and some had to be trimmed either at the master's request or edited to avoid creating senseless misunderstandings later on. It is not the questions that make an interview. An interview is either good or bad depending on the answers given. Considering the masters in this book, I had an easy job. My goal was to make these masters comfortable talking about their life and training—especially those who trained under the founders of original systems. In modern time, there are not many who have had the privilege of living and learning under the legendary founders.

"The masters are gone," many like to say. But as long as we keep their teachings in our heart, they will live for ever. To understand the martial arts properly it is necessary to take into account the philosophical and psychological methods as well as the physical techniques. There is a deep distinction between a fighting system and a martial art, and a general feeling in the martial arts community is that the roots of the martial arts have been de-emphasized, neglected, or totally abandoned. Martial arts are not a sport—they are very different. Someone who chooses to devote themselves to a sport such as basketball, tennis, soccer, or football, which is based on youth, strength, and speed chooses to die twice. When you can no longer do a certain sport, due to the lack of any one of those attributes, waking up in the morning without the activity and purpose that has been the center of your day for twenty-five years is spooky. Martial arts can and should be practiced for life. They are not sports, they are a "way of life."

A true martial arts practitioner—like an artist of any other kind—be this a musician, a painter, a writer or an actor, is expressing and leaving part of himself in every piece of his craft. The need for self-inspection and self-realization of "who" he is becomes the reason for a journey in search of that perfect technique, that great melody, that inspiring poetry, that amazing painting or that Academy Award performance. It is this motivation to reach that "impossible dream," that allows a simple individual to become an exceptional "artist" and "master" of his craft.

Many of the greatest teachers of the budo arts share a commonly misunderstood teaching methodology. They know the words that could be used to pass their personal experience to their students have little or no meaning. They know that to try "self-discovery" in scientific or alchemical terms is a useless task. A great deal of knowledge and wisdom (the ability to use knowledge in a proper and correct way) comes from what is called the "oral traditions," which martial arts, like every other cultural aspect, has. These oral traditions have been always reserved for a certain kind of student and have been considered "secrets." I believe these secrets are such because only few very special students, perspicacious and with a keen sense of introspection, have the minds to attain them. As Alexandra David-Neel wrote: "It is not on the Master that the secret depends but on the hearer. Truth learned from others is of no value, the only truth which is effective and of value is self-discovered... the teacher can only guide to the point of discovery." In the end "The only secret is that there is no secret," or as Kato Tokuro, probably the greatest potter of the last century, and a great art scholar and teacher of Spanish painter and sculptor Pablo Picasso (1881–1973), said: "The sole cause of secrets in craftsmanship is the student's inability to learn!"

Martial arts have always been a large part of my life and I draw inspiration from them, both spiritually and philosophically. I really don't know the 'how' or the 'why' of their affect on me, but I feel their influence in even my most mundane activities. It's not a complex thing where I have to look deep into myself to find their influence. All human beings have sources or principles that keep them grounded, and martial arts is mine. I believe that is when the term 'way of life' becomes real.

I don't believe that great books are meant to be read fast. I've always thought that really good writing is timeless, and that time spent reading doesn't detract anything from your life, but rather adds to it. So take your time. Approach the reading of this book with either the Zen 'beginner's mind' or 'empty cup' mentality and let the words of these great teachers help you to grow not only as a martial artist but as a human being as well. ↄ

Contents

합기도

Bong Soo Han

The Snow Tiger Roars

He is considered by many to be the most celebrated hapkido practitioner in the world. He has spent over four decades refining one of the deadliest martial arts known to man. His training began in Seoul, Korea, under one of the country's most famous fighting masters; later, his study continued in the seclusion of a Korean Buddhist monastery. There he learned fighting techniques never before seen outside the temple walls. Between 1956 and 1959 he traveled to Hwa Chu, Kwan Wong province, where he trained in the art of tae kyun, under the late master Bok Yong Lee. Bong Soo Han incorporated these techniques into a system of his own and began training U.S. military forces—which included the Green Berets. Upon coming to the United States, he began to work in films as a chorographer, a stunt double, and then acting roles in feature films. There is a quiet authority about Bong Soo Han—no movement or word is wasted. Students find a session with him to not only be a workout, but a lesson in life as well. This masterful technician currently teaches in Santa Monica, California, advancing his art and offering his pupils all aspects of his considerable martial arts knowledge and insight.

Q: What are the strengths of your art?
A: The strength of hapkido is its internal power; it is a style of nonresistance. Its circular movements permit the redirecting of the opponent's force to be used against him, but at the same time there are more kicks in the style than in any other system. The kicks are an intricate part of the self-defense aspects of the art.

Q: What is the purpose of hapkido?
A: Self-defense is hapkido's purpose. All self-defense is situationally unique. Some people believe they can defend themselves by relying on two or three techniques—I do not believe that. Think how many different situations you can find yourself in. What if you are confronted in a phone booth? There will not be room to even swing your arms. Space is too limited. Or you may

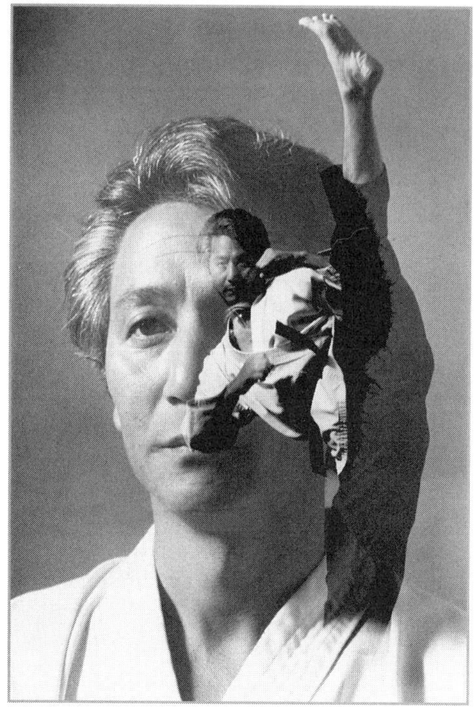

"All self-defense tactics depend on the situation—and the ability to read the opponent's intentions. You should never look down on an opponent and never be overconfident. If you are overconfident your awareness is not there."

find yourself confronted in a parking lot. There is plenty of space to maneuver, and you can use kicking techniques effectively in such a situation. After all, the leg is the longest and the strongest part of the body. In any kind of situation you must determine the opponent's weakness—mental and physical—and attack it. All self-defense tactics depend on the situation—and the ability to read the opponent's intentions.

Q: What about a situation where you face more than one opponent?

A: Sparring, of course, is part of the training. This aspect adds new information and insight to the self-defense applications. First of all, the most important thing you must realize is how to manipulate the opponent psychologically. Second, I always face the attacker. No matter how many opponents there are, I will always be facing one of them. The third aspect is to see who the leader is—and then to move-in decisively and hurt him. When you do it, do it—no hesitation, no analysis. When you have made up your mind, go for it. No hesitation and no doubt—either run or attack. That is the essence of self-defense. Of course, there is always a problem with overconfidence. If you are overconfident, your opponent has an opening.—and if he is experienced he will use it. There will be no second chance. That is why mental discipline is so important and is always stressed in all martial arts. You should never look down on an opponent and never be overconfident. If you are overconfident your awareness is not there.

Q: What kind of mental approach should a martial artist have in a street situation?

A: "Mental attitude" is a very common term used by martial artists to show that they are ready to fight. But in real applications the most dangerous opponents are not the ones with formal dojo training, but those who have experience in streetfighting. A streetfighter is tough and never gives you a chance or an opening. There is no hesitation—he is committed from the very start.

Q: Why does hapkido stress circular movements?
A: One of the main principles of the art is its emphasis on circularity and deflection in order to 'flow' with an opponent. This is the water principle, so-called because of its linkage to the character of water—being soft and flowing in nature, but of considerable power. The water principle is the most beautiful thing we learn in hapkido. Never resist an opponent. Flow with him and redirect his force. It is the principle of yin and yang. If you attack me—you are yang, aggressive. But your punch will reach a point of richness and extension. Then yang becomes yin. If I have flowed with the opponent, at that very moment when the yang is transformed to yin, I am in a position to become yang—aggressive. I counter and flow in harmony with the opponent. Go around him. Redirect his force and use it against him. That's the water principle.

"The water principle is the most beautiful thing we learn in hapkido. Never resist an opponent. Flow with him and redirect his force. It is the principle of yin and yang."

Q: Does that include sidestepping?
A: If you sidestep an attack, you may be too far away to counter effectively. But if you go around the opponent, you are in a position to counter and he is helpless. There is an old saying: "To catch a tiger, you must go to the tiger's lair." So in defense, to be effective, you must flow with the opponent. You must read his force—this will let you know what force you must apply as the appropriate counter. Then, because you have stayed with the opponent, the counter is ready and quick.

"There are 360 major pressure points you can strike with effectiveness. Whether a person is big or small, we all have bodies that function the same way. Size becomes unimportant."

Q: How do you apply that in a real confrontation?

A: There are several applications of the principle. If your counter is going to be strong and hard, look at your position. If you have gone around the opponent, his back and side are exposed to you. You can strike swiftly to vital points. If you are going to lock the opponent and have flowed around his motion—you can easily apply a joint lock—or you can throw the opponent with little force because he is already moving. You add a little strength to the movement and redirect it—and the opponent will go flying.

Q: Are hapkido's principles more suitable for big individuals?

A: No. There are many approaches to the same style of martial art. By learning the principles of leverage and working the joints, you can redirect and defeat an opponent who is larger than you. It may take more effort, but it can be done. In many styles, hard blocking is encouraged. This works well against someone of your own style who is your size. But what happens if you meet someone who is stronger? There can be problems right away. Is your force sufficient to block his blow? If yes, fine; but if not, you are in trouble because you lack of any other formula to solve the problem. But if you redirect the opponent—it doesn't matter what his size is. This also applies to pressure points There are 360 major pressure points you can strike with effectiveness. Whether a person is big or small, we all have bodies that function the same way. Size becomes unimportant.

Q: Do you focus on one particular aspect of the art?

A: I try to teach all the various fundamentals. After that, the students develop 18 individual techniques and learn how to expand and adapt them to situations. Of course, a great deal of stretching and flexibility exercises are called for—even to kick. What good does it do to kick if you injure yourself and the technique has no power? There are also questions of developing speed, timing, balance, focus and reading the opponent as you flow with him. Then comes holds—defending against chokes and locks—how to escape using the wrist and the shoulder—using leverage to unbalance the attacker and redirect ing his own weight against him. Hapkido is endless and after more than 40 years of training I feel I am just beginning to learn it.

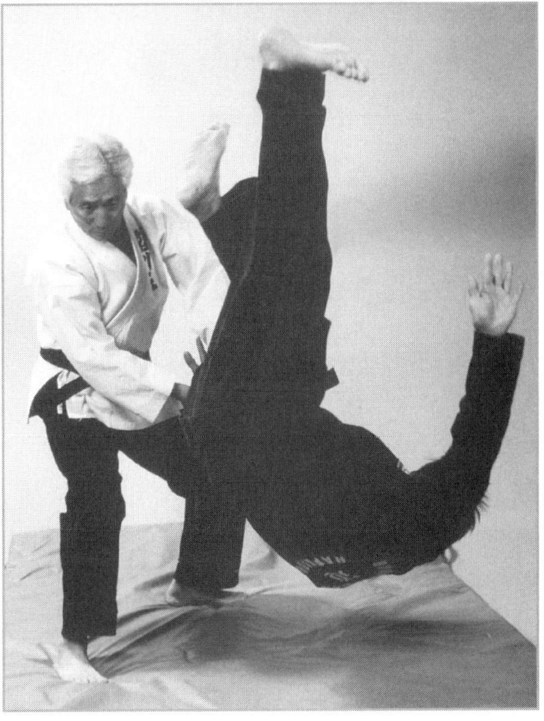

"There are no superior styles of martial arts. This point has been made many times by many people. Styles are merely growth. The benefit of all martial arts is in your approach to the art and to the training. It is something you have to learn."

Q: Do you think any style is superior to another?

A: There are no superior styles of martial arts. This point has been made many times by many people. Styles are merely growth. They develop because of people's race, and the geographical area in which they lived and what they saw and mimicked from others. And there is always the question of the individual. Some prefer using their hands and other their feet. But no martial art is better than another. The benefit of all martial arts is in your approach to the art and to the training. It is something you have to learn.

Q: Why was hapkido not included in the formulation of modern taekwondo by the Korean government?

A: In Korea there were several different names for taekwondo. Everyone learned a different method and then started teaching under that name. After the Korean War the president gave it one name—taekwondo. But there was an exception to this and it was hapkido. The reason was that the techniques were so different that they didn't fit into the taekwondo format.

"In hapkido, technique is conditional—the tactics are determined by the situation, by the available fighting space, and by the nature of the opponent. Combinations fit the appropriate conditions."

Q: Why do aikido and hapkido share so many common principles?

A: Yong Shui Choi, the founder of hapkido and Morihei Ueshiba, founder of aikido, both studied daito-ryu aiki-jutsu in Japan. Ueshiba combined his studies with judo, Shinto and Buddhist principles and Choi mixed the material he learned with the earlier Korean kicking art of tae kyun. Of course, they are different but there are still many similarities in the foundations of both systems. Many people think hapkido is an outgrowth of aikido but this is not the case. It just happens that they share a number of common elements, but it doesn't mean they are the same. For instance, in a throw might look similar in both, but in concept they might be immensely different. They both utilize the opponent's attack but while the aikido approach is peaceful disorientation, the hapkido plan is disorientation with minimal effort followed by a disabling attack. Philosophically, they are very divergent.

Hapkido bears striking similarities to aikido and jiu-jitsu through its use of joint locks, throws, chokes, and pressure-points attacks. Viewed from another perspective, it is the very epitome of a hard style with forceful kicking techniques similar to taekwondo. Indeed, hapkido embodies those two terms so often used in describing martial arts: soft and hard. In hapkido, technique is conditional—the tactics are determined by the situation, by the available fighting space, and by the nature of the opponent. Combinations fit the appropriate conditions. This is what I love about the art, it is so broad and offers so many choices for self-defense.

In some ways hapkido shares many common principles with taekwondo, also with tai chi chuan. In aikido, focus means flowing with the opponent and turning his force against him. In tai chi, one stays with the opponent, flowing with his motion until the opponent is overextended and off balance—the point of richness. Hapkido shares much of the same philosophy—flowing with the opponent and redirecting his motion. But they are also like day and night. Aikido is more passive and it lacks the hard counters and the kicks. The counter in hapkido is hard most of the time. It depends on what you want to do, of course. You can throw your opponent, lock his joints, stun him with a pressure-point attack, and then immobilize him with a wrestling hold. You can also kick or punch, which we stress most of the time. We like to deflect the opponent's force, go around him before he can recover, and then counter hard.

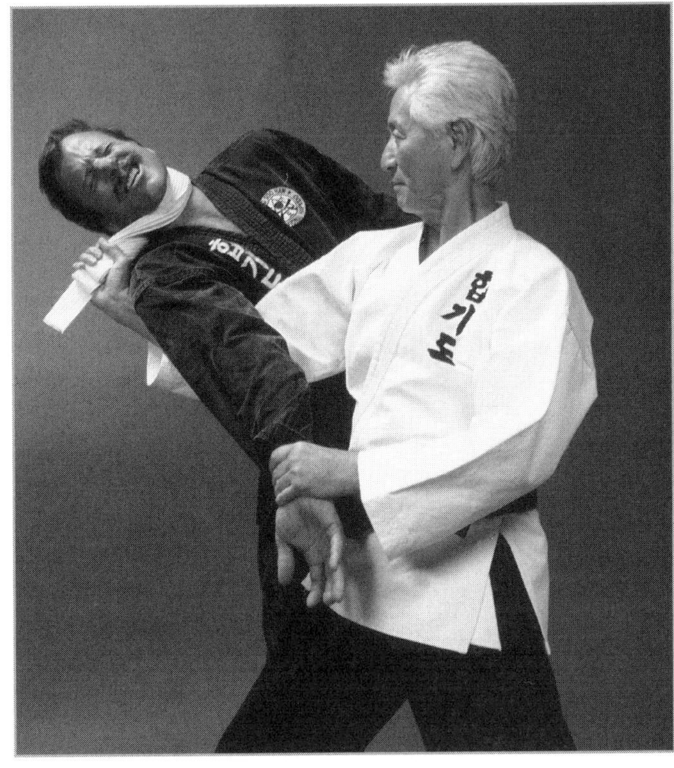

"My style and training methods are very traditional but I'm open to teach anyone and I try to explain the art from a very scientific point of view. I suppose that this is not a traditional approach per se."

Q: Do you consider yourself a traditionalist or modernist?

A: All the masters from the past took the knowledge handed down to them by their teachers and modified or adapted it, incorporating their own point of view and truths. If we take their teachings and only crystallize it, we are being no more than a human Xerox copy machine. There is no way the art can live through the non-creative individual because there is no self-expression. My style and training methods are very traditional but I'm open to teach anyone and I try to explain the art from a very scientific point of view. I suppose that this is not a traditional approach per se. The art of hapkido has

"My teaching method is altered to conform to the abilities of the individual student, so that even the handicapped can achieve some degree of competency. Martial arts are a lifetime endeavor. It is body and mind as one."

been streamlined with many of the outmoded or repetitious movements eliminated. Other moves have been modified to adjust to the modern way of fighting, thus permitting the art to be effectively used throughout the world. My teaching method is altered to conform to the abilities of the individual student, so that even the handicapped can achieve some degree of competency.

Q: How has modern society influenced the practice of the martial arts?

A: First of all you have to accept the fact that our time is very different from the past, and people have different goals and different lifestyles. This influences the approach to life itself and, of course, martial arts training as well. Interestingly enough, however, if someone wants to become a master in the arts, there is only one way to achieve this regardless of the time you live in: dedication, discipline, perseverance and hard training. This is the only formula I know. No matter if you live in the year 1800 or the year 2100, the requirements are the same.

Q: What do the martial arts mean to you?

A: Martial arts are a lifetime endeavor. It is body and mind as one. For example, you train your kicks—train for years both mentally and physically. The final goal is spontaneous movement—instinctive and beyond hesitation or analysis. When someone attacks, you go back to the kick training—you feel the opening your opponent has made and before you can think, you feel the kick sliding in and landing. It is spontaneous action—mental and physical discipline in instinctive action. That's the ultimate goal in martial arts, that kind of action, that unity. Yet we must be aware that of all the individuals who are striving for that goal, only a very few will attain it. I don't know if I have attained it or ever will—who knows?

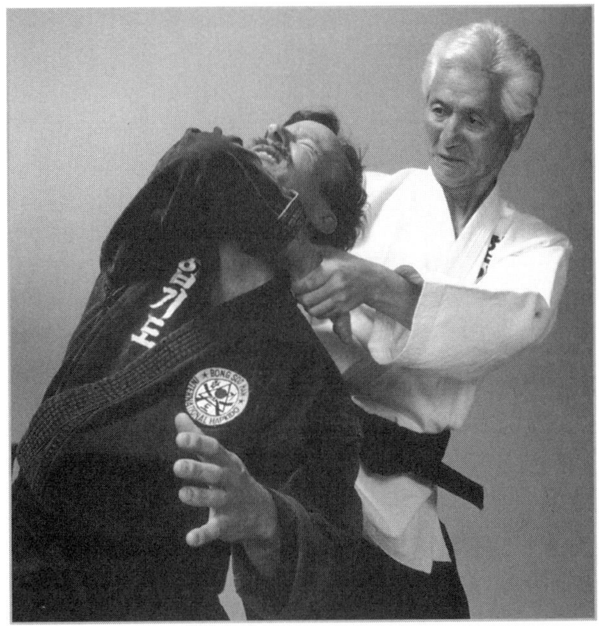

"My personal goal is to share with my students the martial knowledge from the past, and also my experiences in both the arts and in life."

We hear of our ancestors being capable of such feats, of attaining such a goal. But we must remember that life was simpler in the past. To survive, one had to train with that single mindedness of purpose. Our lives today and our society is more complex and complicated. Even if one is in the profession of the martial arts, there are many other necessary things one must do to support oneself. And among students today, one must recognize that the art is only a part, not the whole focus, of their lives. There is only a slim chance of attaining the perfection we seek.

But if we benefit from the self-control, the mental and physical discipline, the calmness, analytical ability, and spirituality we have accomplished a great deal. I do not believe there is any other method outside of the martial arts that can bring so many great benefits. My personal goal is to share with my students the martial knowledge from the past, and also my experiences in both the arts and in life. If I help one single person to become a better human being then I'll be happy.

(1) Master Bong Soo Han faces his opponent. (2) The opponent starts the attacking movement (3) that Master Han blocks with the newspaper, (4) unbalancing the aggressor to strike back with a double slash to the face (5 & 6).

Master Han faces off his aggressor (1) who attacks him with a straight punch to the face (2). Han blocks (3) and delivers a straight hit with the newspaper to the opponent's throat (4).

Master Han faces his opponent and holds a business card in his hand (1). The aggressor starts a approach (2) but Master Han begins to react (3) and delivers a slashing motion (4) to the aggressor's neck (5).

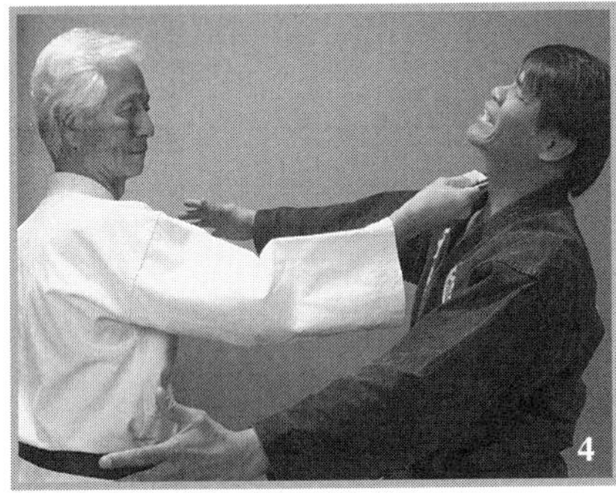

Master Han holds a belt in his right hand (1). The aggressor tries to hit him (2) and Han blocks the punch and moves to the side of the opponent to apply a choke with the belt (3).

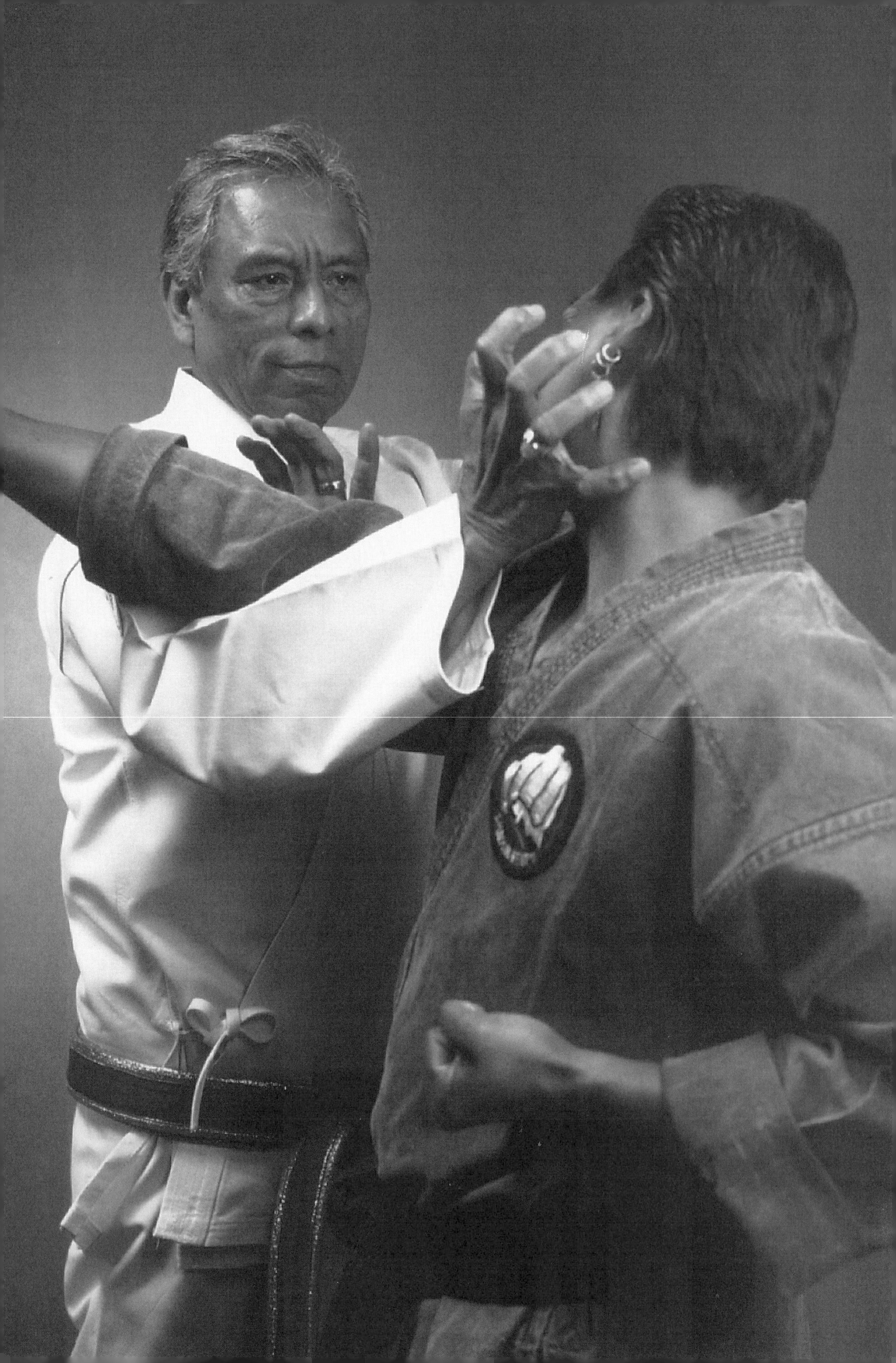

Ralph Castro

The Shaolin Way

Ralph Castro is one of professor William Kwai Sun Chow's original students in Hawaii. Castro began his training in boxing under his father, who was highly respected in Hawaiian boxing circles. In 1958 he began teaching kenpo in San Francisco. Since the opening of his school, Castro has gained a worldwide reputation as one of the most knowledgeable teachers of Professor Chow's original techniques and philosophies. All of his children hold the rank of black belt in the Shaolin kenpo system. He is the founder of the International Shaolin Kenpo Association, with headquarters in Daly City, California. Professor Castro worked hard to keep the art as it was taught to him by Master Chow.

Q: How did you start martial arts?
A: I began in 1955, training kenpo under Master William Kwai Sun Chow in Hawaii. I moved to mainland in 1958 and became pretty good friends with the late Ed Parker. At that time Mr. Parker was already teaching kenpo. For 28 years we were affiliated and worked together.

Q: How did you get started in Shaolin kempo?
A: After a while, I decided that it was the right time for me to move on and start my own association. Professor Chow told me that I should promote the Shaolin kenpo system that he had developed in Hawaii and which had Chinese roots. There were a lot of problems between Chinese kenpo and the Japanese kenpo. Mr. Chow told me that since his father and grandfather were trained in kung-fu, I should name the system Shaolin kenpo. Mr. Parker kept his American kenpo karate and a little bit later founded the International Kenpo Karate Association.

Q: How was your training under Professor Chow?
A: I remember that I had the opportunity to meet him. He was really impressive with his big knuckles. He had an extreme amount of power in his movements and from a student's point of view I can tell you that he never

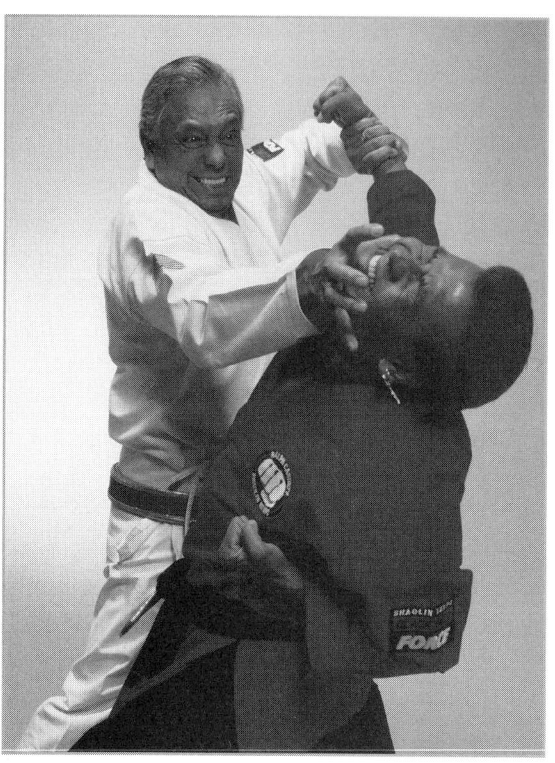

"Kenpo is a very complicated system. We evolved it with the knowledge we had and developed ourselves further as individual martial artists."

taught the same technique twice. My training with him was very intense. Almost every single day I was with him learning and learning. Of course, my wife wasn't very happy about it but I know she understood. In fact, she always encouraged me to pursue new goals in my life and improve in everything I do. She was the one who really pushed me into opening my own school. My good friend Ed Parker helped me with the business side of it. He was pleased that my style was different than his method. It was Ed Parker who gave me the black belt, because at that time I didn't know if I'd ever see Professor Chow again. Interestingly enough, when I saw him again in 1970 he gave me my grand master certificate. And it was in 1981, during a visit of Professor Chow to Hawaii, that I officially originated the style of Shaolin kenpo with his approval.

Q: All of Professor Chow's students created their own systems. Why?
A: Kenpo is a very complicated system. We evolved it with the knowledge we had and developed ourselves further as individual martial artists. Adriano D. Emperado created kajukenbo, Ed Parker had America karate, et cetera. Some schools have added judo or jiu-jitsu locks to the art and others have brought more Japanese influence to kenpo. I simply tried to keep it as Professor Chow taught it to me.

Q: Describe Shaolin kenpo?
A: Just as it is possible to use a gun for many different purposes, Shaolin kenpo has been structured to serve several purposes such as self-defense, sport competition, et cetera. It is a well-rounded fighting system.

Q: How did Professor Chow structure his Hawaiian classes?

A: We never practiced or learned forms. The training was strictly based on techniques. He used to teach a lot of material in one single class. If you missed one you had to learn the material from the other students. He seldom, if ever, repeated information.

Q: Have you modified or made any innovations to the system?

A: I have an open mind, so I like to look at different styles to see what are they doing. My father, Boss Castro, taught me how to box, so I incorporated some elements to be able to efficiently defend against a boxer. My personal experiences gave me a great amount of knowledge to add. On other hand, I never subtracted anything from the techniques and philosophy I was taught. I did come up with a method that formally structured and trained the techniques. I incorporated the techniques in various fixed patterns I developed, called "key dances."

"My personal experiences gave me a great amount of knowledge to add. I never subtracted anything from the techniques and philosophy I was taught."

Q: Did you like boxing?

A: Yes and no. If you practice boxing you know you're gonna get hit. It doesn't matter how good you are. So I got hit a lot with I first started. So even today I like to keep my distance in a fight and not get hit!

Q: How did you meet Professor Chow for the second time?

A: After many years I went to train under Mr. Chow and sponsored a seminar for him where he taught basic techniques. Everything he taught was automatically incorporated into the Shaolin kenpo system that I was teaching at the time. Mr. Chow introduced the thunderbolt set, which is a requirement today for my black belts.

"Every high ranking instructor in my system is in charge of a particular form given to them to preserve that form in the traditional way. This is a very big responsibility."

Q: Who holds the highest rank in your system?
A: My son Robert Castro. He is my successor. So on the day I die there will be no problems. My association is already established and everybody know who holds the highest rank and where to go for knowledge. Every high ranking instructor in my system is in charge of a particular form given to them to preserve that form in the traditional way. This is a very big responsibility.

Q: Are the concepts you use the same that Ed Parker used in his system?
A: Yes, the only difference is that I gave them different names—that's all. We developed the same principles using different names.

Q: Do you use weapons in the art of Shaolin kenpo?
A: Yes, of course we use weapons! In fact, I adapted the use of the *tonfa* for kenpo techniques. It's important that the students know how to use anything within their reach. But they must remember that is not correct to depend on weapons for self-defense—only your body. When someone attacks my students with a weapon, they know they have to react with total commitment. It's either him or the weapon!

Q: Do you have any pre-arranged two-person weapon sets in Shaolin kenpo?
A: No, we don't. I truly believe that this kind of training does not strengthen the student's natural responses.

Q: Do you have pre-planned two-person empty-hand sets?

A: Yes, we do. A strong defense is only as good as a strong offense and vice versa. This is the reason the students have to learn both side of the sets—defensive and offensive.

Q: How does kenpo do against other styles in a fight?

A: Let me tell you this: if a kenpo practitioner fights against a kick-boxer using kickboxing rules, the kenpo man will be defeated. But if the kenpo man fights his way, then he will win. Every system has its own way—the important thing is to make your opponent fight your way. Then you are the one making the rules!

"Every system has its own way—the important thing is to make your opponent fight your way. Then you are the one making the rules!"

Q: What is the difference between Shaolin kenpo and other kenpo systems?

A: The differences are immense. Our stances are unmistakably Chinese, not Japanese. The way we move to avoid the attack is not the Japanese tactic of meeting attacks with a solid frontal defense. We like to circle, quickly bombarding the opponent with an onslaught of blows to find or create an opening in the defense. This maneuver is typical Chinese. Our foot techniques are also very similar to those used in kung-fu. We use the hand like a kenpo man, of course, but we emphasize kung-fu hand movements such as leopard, tiger, eagle, dragon styles, et cetera. Of course, there are many other principles but it would take the whole day to describe them.

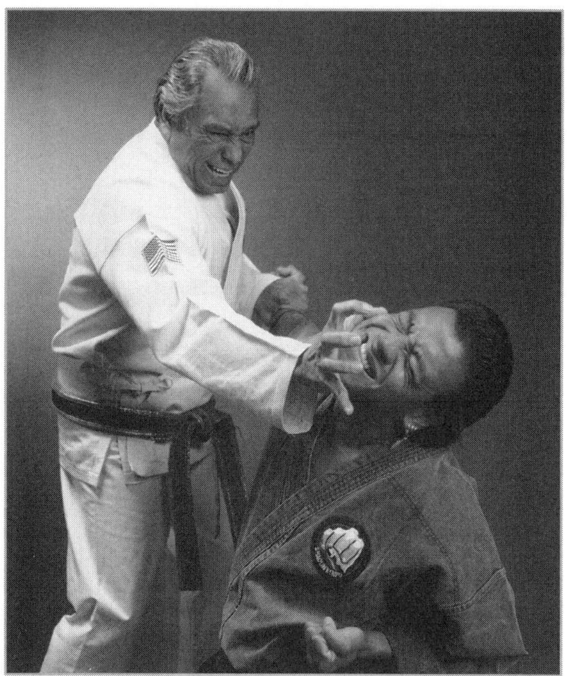

"I understand that a master sometimes has to adopt a student in order to assure his succession and the future of the art. But in my case I have a son that I personally trained since he was a child."

Q: Can you explain the internal training in your art?

A: The internal conditioning in Shaolin kenpo is developed through breathing exercises.

Q: Did you know Bruce Lee?

A: Yes, I did. He was a great person and had a lot of respect for me, my family, and my art. After he became famous I didn't see any difference in his character. I recall him asking me of I wanted to learn from him. He had a lot to offer but what I had it was very good too, so I decided that I'd rather be his friend instead of his student. I respected him first for who he was as a person, not for his martial arts skills.

Q: What is your primary concern these days?

A: My goal is to keep martial arts simple, direct, and traditional, and Shaolin kenpo fulfills that desire. I have been in the art for a long time and I acknowledge that some mistakes have been made along the way. But I believe mistakes are natural in life, and that we should learn from them. Over the years, I have seen some of my good friends go away and their organizations with them. I tried to prevent this by setting up a line of succession in my Shaolin Kenpo Association. I wanted to do the things the right way—not only for today but for future generations as well. This is the reason I delegated all duties to my son, Rob Castro. I understand that a master sometimes has to adopt a student in order to assure his succession and the future of the art. But in my case I have a son that I personally trained since he was a child. He has a complete knowledge and understanding of the art and has maintained respect for the system and for himself. He already has a reputation of excellence, so either you support Grandmaster Rob Castro or you move on.

Q: What is your advice for future generations?

A: I truly hope people take martial arts training in their lives. The martial arts teach far more than fighting. They involve other aspects of human behavior and teach confidence, respect, dedication, and peace. All these qualities are necessary to build a better world.

"The martial arts teach far more than fighting. They involve other aspects of human behavior and teach confidence, respect, dedication, and peace."

Master Castro faces the opponent (1). He deflects the aggressor's first attack (2) and, closing the distance, nullifies the second punch (3), to apply a inside sweep (4) followed by a hit to the neck (5), a strike to the back (6) and a kick to the chest (7) that finishes his opponent (8).

Castro squares off with his opponent (1). He intercepts the opponent's motion defending and countering simultaneously (2), applies an elbow strike to the ribs (3), followed by a new hit to the body (4), a new attack to the face with his left hand (5) that opens the angle to use his right hand on the inside (6) to grab the aggressor (7) and send him to the ground (8). There he finishes with a new hit (9) and covers himself afterwards (10).

The aggressor is in front of Castro holding a club (1). Castro blocks the attack with his left hand (2) and delivers a front kick to the groin (3) followed by a palm strike to the chin (4) and a control to the left arm that holds the weapon (5).

Castro faces the aggressor (1). The attacker moves in and Castro blocks the hit with his left hand (2), followed by a hit to the ribcage (3) a control of the attacking arm for a quick disarm (4) followed by a hit (5) to the opponent's head (6).

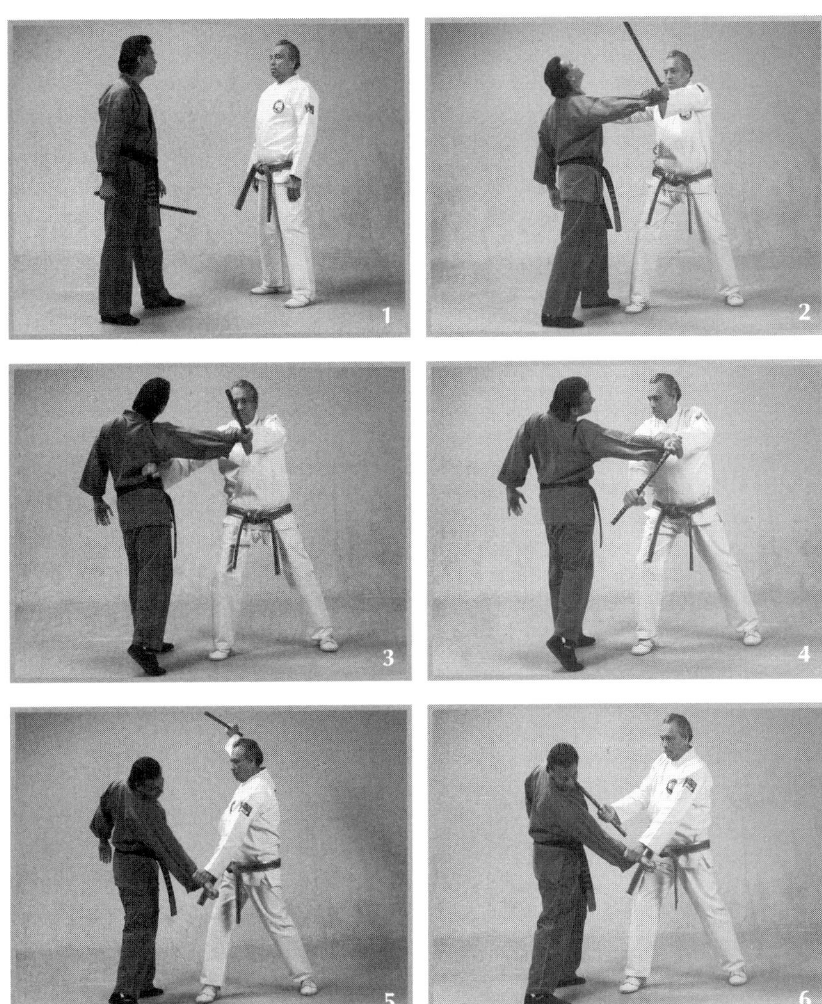

Hee Il Cho

A Man of Contrasts

He is one of the most renowned taekwondo masters in the world. In the highly competitive taekwondo community—where there are more kickers than pro football has punters—Cho's reputation lands him right at the top of the pack. His open mind and flexible sentiments about full-contact karate and boxing, along with his unorthodox teaching methodology, put a black mark on him among traditional taekwondo instructors—but attracted flocks of students who were interested in learning the true essence of martial arts. After decades of sharing his knowledge and experience with students from all over the world, Master Cho still trains every day and is living proof of an everlasting youth that can be obtained through dedication and attention to training. Fittingly, his trademark is the most powerful spinning back-kick the world of martial arts has ever known. Hee Il Cho would have it no other way.

Q: How did growing up during the Korean War affect you?
A: I'm the eldest of three brothers and after the war times were very hard and tough. I still remember going hungry and scrounging around for a bowl of white rice. Yet today I consider that experience extremely valuable, because I'm very conscious of whatever I have, and always thankful for it.

Q: Why did you start taking martial arts?
A: I began my training in a typical fashion. At a local fair I was beaten by five other youths, and I was black and blue for days. The worst was not the physical pain but the humiliation I felt. As soon as I recovered I began my training in tang soo do. The classes were absolutely grueling. We trained for five or six hours a day and only the strong survived. My instructor was incredibly rigid—we never questioned anything and we treated him like a god. I remember that after classes I would sometimes have to wash his feet, and he still didn't even speak to me for the first year. After training for three years I received my black belt. After that, I moved with my family to Inchon,

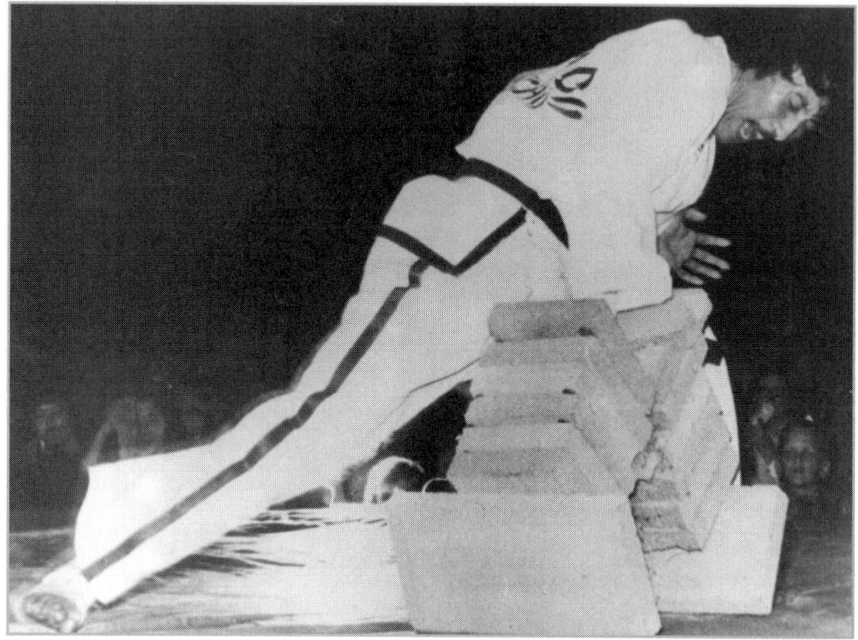

"I came here as part of a demonstration team and I found the country to be a place where you could achieve anything you wanted to with hard work and dedication."

near Seoul. While living in Inchon I realized that martial arts were my destiny in life.

Q: When did you join the military?
A: When I was 21. At the time I was already a fourth-degree black belt. I taught taekwondo to the servicemen and continued my studies under general Choi Hong Hi. It was through his federation that I had the opportunity to teach in India, Germany, and finally the United States. I came here as part of a demonstration team and I found the country to be a place where you could achieve anything you wanted to with hard work and dedication. I spent time in South Bend, Indiana, then in Milwaukee, Wisconsin and finally in New York City. I was living at the YMCA because I had no money, and my weight was down to something like 115 pounds. I didn't know what to do with my life, but I knew I was not going to do it in New York. So I took off again and moved to Providence, Rhode Island. Just when I was ready to quit the martial arts, a sympathetic landlord offered me six months free rent

on a small building. With the last of my money I took out a tiny ad in the local newspaper—two days later I had 50 students! From then on I never looked back.

"There is a reason why full contact and kickboxing fighters use boxing and not karate punches—it's because boxing works better!"

Q: When did you move to California?

A: I just felt that there was something more in store for me. So in 1976 I sold my schools and headed for California, where I purchased a Chuck Norris school on Santa Monica Boulevard and opened Cho's Taekwondo Studio. California was like a foreign country to me. People were very different. They still are different and I am not sure why—perhaps it has something to do with the climate and the easy lifestyle—but students aren't as disciplined; they are softer. Today, I have adapted my methods somewhat to accommodate their lifestyle, but back then I was still quite strict. I had students sparring with no protective gear, full-contact. Also, I didn't recognize the belts they'd gained under previous instructors. Of course, some parents thought my teaching methods were too harsh. I was also criticized by my brethren in the Korean martial arts community because I was teaching boxing in my classes, and I didn't have my students attired in white gi's.

Q: Why did you break with tradition?

A: I don't like to live in the past. The original reason for the white gi's was because in the old days, the only material available was that color. But that's got nothing whatsoever to do with the present. Do you If you want to know why I started boxing, just look where the best physical conditioning is, and look where the money is. There is a reason why full contact and kickboxing fighters use boxing and not karate punches—it's because boxing works better! Although I agree it is not for everyone, martial artists can still learn a lot from boxing even if they still prefer their own art. And when the two are truly blended, taking the best from each, the result is very effective. That blend is the martial art of the future. How do the old masters expect their students to respect them when they are stuck in the past? Half of the

"In the tournaments at that time, with the exception of punches to the face, the blows were rarely pulled—which was fine with me."

time they are just a bunch of fat old men who sit back and say, "I am great." I don't think any martial arts teacher deserves respect unless he can back up his teaching. I still tell my students that action is what's important, not some mystical or metaphysical mumbo-jumbo.

Q: Don't you think that inner peace can be attained through the study of martial arts?

A: If there is, you are not going to find it by going off on some mountain-top and sitting for three hours in a cross-legged position. No, the only way you are going to find it is through actions—because life *is* action.

Q: You competed in the United Sates during your early years. Why?

A: I believe that you will never know how good you are if you don't test your skills against other martial artists. When I came here from Korea I saw that the American fighters were doing things differently from what I was used to. I had to see if the way I trained really worked. Of course, I did lose once in a while but that was mostly from excessive contact. I knocked a lot of people out. In the tournaments at that time, with the exception of punches to the face, the blows were rarely pulled—which was fine with me. Back in Korea when we fought in a tournament it was with no protective gear and we went at it full-out. That's the way it should be, because if you practice pulling the blow, that's the way you are going to react out on the street.

Q: Were you impressed with the masters you met here when you first arrived?

A: It was funny, in a way, because when I first came to United States I was very rigid. I adhered strictly to tradition. But gradually I came to see that the masters were really just people who had a little more knowledge than I did; they certainly weren't gods, though there was a time when I regarded them as such. But that was a long, long time ago.

"If there is a superior way of teaching or developing techniques, I want to know about them and adapt that way into the methods I have established."

Q: What point have you reached in your personal martial arts journey?

A: I have reached a moment in my life where much disturbs me about the martial arts. The time has arrived for the fresh air of change to sweep away the static insular attitudes and exchange them for new ideas and rejuvenation. This needs to be a porous acceptance of change within all aspects of the various systems of martial arts, especially from the martial artists themselves.

Each today is the only true reality. We may be the sum total of our past, and the pasts of millions who lived before us, but life is what we are doing, thinking, feeling, and creating now—at this moment. That is reality. I cannot live captured by the ideals of the past or in fear of my future. Neither am I afraid to admit change into my life, especially within my teachings of taekwondo.

If there is a superior way of teaching or developing techniques, I want to know about them and adapt that way into the methods I have established. The future of all systems of martial arts depends on continual growth. While holding onto our noble traditions we should explore new concepts and training methods.

My martial arts' ancestors may curl up and cringe at my ideas, but I am interested in analyzing and exploring the most effective scientific methods for developing techniques. The great masters of the past were indeed excellent teachers but, surrounded as we are today by new technology and innovative research into new training methods, there may be better ways of developing certain techniques. I therefore do not feel guilty nor compelled to stick to one method formulated many years ago.

"I have only trained in taekwondo and believe it to be one of the finest systems of martial arts. But I will adopt a technique from any other style if I see that technique is more effective than my own method."

Q: What's your opinion on full-contact karate and kickboxing?

A: Full-contact karate has definitely put pressure on traditional martial arts and questioned its effectiveness. Often, when matched with an experienced full-contact fighter, the traditional stylist gets slaughtered. I don't want to compare a full-contact fighter to a martial art and say which is better. I kickboxing is beneficial for developing physical strength, endurance, and prowess. But it is a sport and not a martial art. Full-contact kickboxing is very competitive, and should only be done by those who wish to make a tremendous commitment to the sport. Why, though, have the Americans so successfully dominated the full-contact and point tournaments? Because they have usually not limited themselves to training solely within one system. They carefully observe many different systems and take the best each has to offer, putting the various techniques together to suit themselves. I am not by any means advocating that a student jump from one style to another. However, I do think it is important for instructors to analyze the success of these types of fighters. I have only trained in taekwondo and believe it to be one of the finest systems of martial arts. But I will adopt a technique from any other style if I see that technique is more effective than my own method.

Q: Some people say that traditional martial arts not effective against kickboxing.

A: You can't really talk about full-contact and kickboxing—which are sports—the same way you can talk about traditional martial arts. People are always saying that traditional methods are ineffectual, and that if you put a taekwondo or karate man in a ring and put gloves on him he's going to look bad. That may be true to a certain extent; but on the street traditional systems are more effective. You can finish a fight with one blow if you know what you are doing.

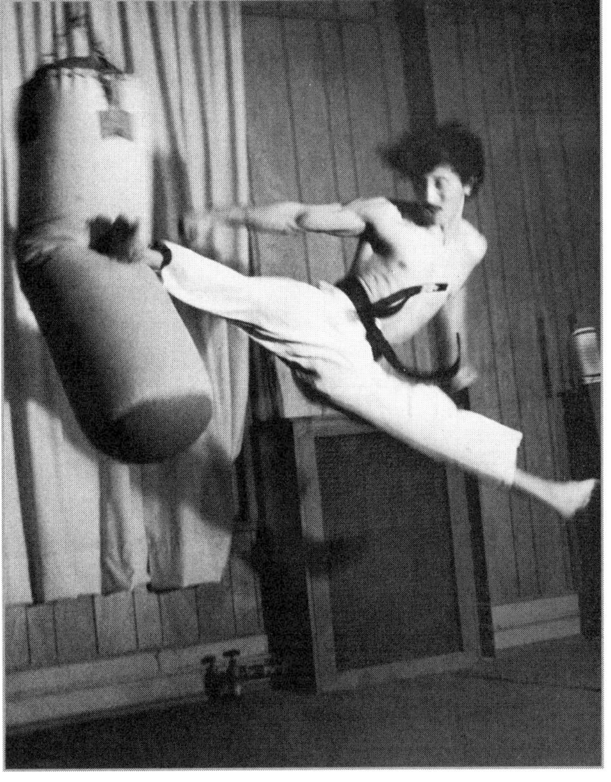

"Each system has its own diverse and unique set of principles and rules, which could never merge. What we should do is learn more from each other with open minds."

Q: Have you made changes in the art?

A: I have incorporated basic boxing techniques into my advanced classes. I trained as a boxer in Korea and realize that my knowledge of boxing definitely helped me become a successful fighter. Boxing is scientifically designed to generate the most power possible from each motion executed; additionally, it teaches good avoidance techniques, which is vital to any fighter. My students' fighting has vastly improved and the results from our tournaments are excellent. There's no use hiding beneath the precarious umbrella of our so-called mystical past, which sanctions the belief that one blow will finish a fight every time. Rather, we should accept change and be open to other options and outcomes. I don't want to give the impression that I am hoping for an amalgamation of all systems—I'm not. I hope, rather, for an adaptation and acceptance of all styles. Taekwondo is a great kicking style; Japanese karate masters have some of the fastest hands; Chinese systems are designed more for the aesthetic aspects of the martial arts. Each system has its own diverse and unique set of principles and rules, which could never merge. What we should do is learn more from each other with open minds. Personally, I have put extra emphasis on weight training and increased intensity during workouts, and I have added boxing techniques to the training regimen as

"The pressures of life and the stifling atmosphere of over-populated cities mount against us. The restless tiger of our competitive society throttles the weak and frightens the young. The martial arts provide a much-needed release."

well. The weight training program should be a specific routine in order to meet the individual's needs; however, it is a supplementary training for a martial arts workout, not a substitute for it.

Q: Do you consider yourself a non-traditionalist?

A: I see myself as a traditionalist and non-traditionalist. I follow the mental, ethical, and moral principles of traditional martial arts, which includes self-control, perseverance, and indomitable spirit. As a non-traditional master, I have adapted my training regimen to my students, and will incorporate new techniques to benefit them. As I said, I maintain an open mind to all styles of fighting and recognize the benefits of each discipline.

Q: What is your opinion of all the jealousy in martial arts?

A: It is arrogant egotism that has created bad feelings between martial artists. The days when instructors strutted about, puffed-up with their feeling of importance, are long gone I hope. Because all that nonsense gets in the way of presenting martial arts to the public for what it is: a physical and mental art form that gives students a deeper understanding of themselves and a greater capacity toward achieving self-fulfillment.

During this increasingly violent age that we all have to cope with and live within, the martial arts have more to offer than ever before. The pressures of life and the stifling atmosphere of over-populated cities mount against us. The restless tiger of our competitive society throttles the weak and frightens the young. The martial arts provide a much-needed release. They strengthen us mentally and physically, unifying our minds and bodies, enabling us to face any challenges life presents us. The martial arts have taken our feisty young, shaking their fists at the world and bubbling with insecurities, away from the streets and channeled all that anger and negative energy, reforming it into positive energy. Martial arts forms a silent bridge—a harbor to rest fears—a place to come and gain much-needed mental strength and self-respect. By working together we can give more and be part of building a society with more quality, less violence, and deeper understanding of each other.

We are bound only by the limitations we place upon ourselves. People spend more time saying, "I can't," and giving excuses than they ever do thinking, "I can." I hear excuses all the time: "I can't do this Master Cho because..." and so it goes. I am no superman, but I always say to myself first, "I can and I will," and then I work backwards to success from there.

"By working together we can give more and be part of building a society with more quality, less violence, and deeper understanding of each other."

Q: How do you approach fighting?

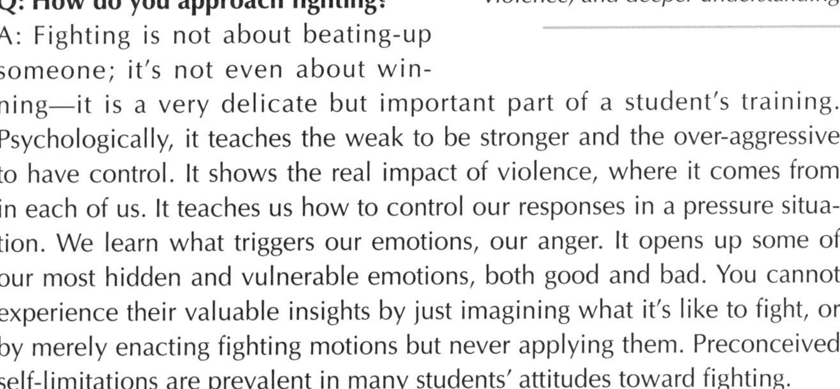

A: Fighting is not about beating-up someone; it's not even about winning—it is a very delicate but important part of a student's training. Psychologically, it teaches the weak to be stronger and the over-aggressive to have control. It shows the real impact of violence, where it comes from in each of us. It teaches us how to control our responses in a pressure situation. We learn what triggers our emotions, our anger. It opens up some of our most hidden and vulnerable emotions, both good and bad. You cannot experience their valuable insights by just imagining what it's like to fight, or by merely enacting fighting motions but never applying them. Preconceived self-limitations are prevalent in many students' attitudes toward fighting.

"Mr. Cho, do I have to fight? I just can't. It's not my nature. I may get hurt."

"Yes, you do have to fight," I say.

"But why?"

"By fighting, one learns to cope with our society and daily life. It is a terrific proving ground."

"Because I want to know what fear you have inside yourself, that makes you so sure you can't face an opponent here in the safety of our studio, protected by equipment. When I know why you have that fear and where it came from, then I will talk to you again. Together we can erase that weakness. That is a part of becoming a martial artist."

By fighting, one learns to cope with our society and daily life. It is a terrific proving ground.

Q: How important is forms training in your teaching?

A: Students often ask why I teach forms, and how does performing a *hyung* benefit them? On a very simple level, performing forms has been compared to learning the letters of the alphabet. Put the letters together and you have a word; the words can then be made into a sentence. Another example is likening forms to the walls that support a roof; without them the roof would collapse.

It takes a tremendous amount of self-discipline, well-practiced techniques, and mental concentration to perform a form well. We start with the simplest forms, containing only a few simple movements. Gradually, we build up a repertoire of more complicated forms with increasingly varied and complex techniques. The practice of forms helps develop precision, controlled timing, breath control, balance in movement, focus, and much more.

From the instructor's point of view, forms also provide a perfect vehicle to enable the instructor to evaluate a student's progress on many different levels. Forms also provide a means to physically illustrate the aesthetic aspect of a particular style and a student's personal interpretation of that style. Styles that don't have forms, to my way of thinking, lack in depth and miss an important part of the arts.

"Styles that don't have forms, to my way of thinking, lack in depth and miss an important part of the arts."

Q: Do you follow a particular diet?

A: I do. I try to eat balanced meals and supplement these with vitamins and minerals. I strongly recommend fresh vegetables, seafood, and unprocessed fruits and vegetables with no preservatives. For those training very heavy, rigorous workouts, plenty of red meat and protein are essential.

Q: What is your expectation for the future of the arts?

A: It is my hope that the future will bring martial artists closer together, and that the childish egotism of the past will become a thing of the past. I eagerly await the prospect of change within the arts, of exciting new training methods, and the further prosperity of the martial arts all over the world.

Q: Do you agree with the description that "Hee Il Cho is a man of contrasts?"

A: Yes, I guess it's true. I am a man of action, but I also admit to having many contrasts. Like many Koreans, I am quiet, reserved, and introspective. And yet I insist on being open to change and to throwing-out what is unessential. If one hopes to improve their art and their life then that is an absolute necessity. Life is change.

Master Cho faces his opponent (1), as the knife enters the zone (2), the defender slides back and drop both palms down on the weapon hand in a pressing motion (3). Balancing on the left foot (4), Master Cho steps in counterclockwise with the right foot (5), simultaneously lifts the opponent's arm (6), then steps through and behind the opponent, with the option of stabbing the aggressor on his way through (7-9). Close up (10).

Master Cho squares off with an opponent who holds a club (1). As the opponent attempts to strike Master Cho, he simultaneously slides in toward the attack (2) and applies an uprising block. He then brings his right arm through the opening and grabs the opponent's wrist (3-5) Close up (6). He crosses over with his right foot (7) and sweeps (8). He can control his opponent's arm with a takedown, which can be followed by a punch to the face (9).

When fighting a grappler the idea is that you must move fast. From a ready position (1), the attacker lunges for Master Cho's legs (2). Assuming a fighting posture, Master Cho brings his left foot back into a parallel stance and palm strikes to the shoulders or head (3). This is followed by an elbow strike to the back of the spine (4-5) and a hook to the kidney (6).

1

The attacker grabs Master Cho's right hand with his right hand (1). Master Cho takes the back of his attacker's hand (2). Close up (3). He then steps forward with his left foot clockwise (4) 180 degrees and moves in front of his opponent (5). He lifts up his opponent's arm and slams it down on his left shoulder (6) with a sharp jerking motion (7).

2

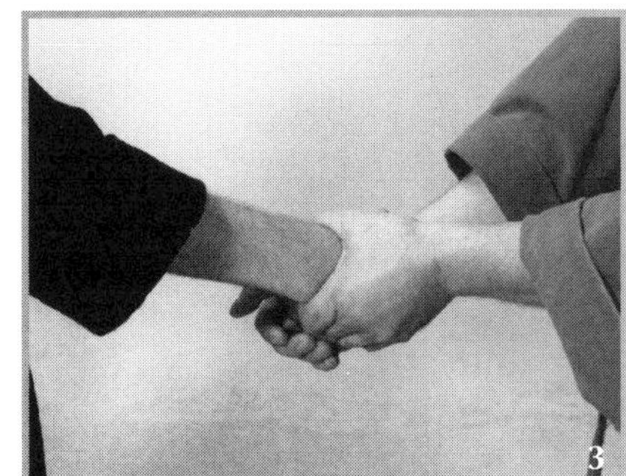
3

4

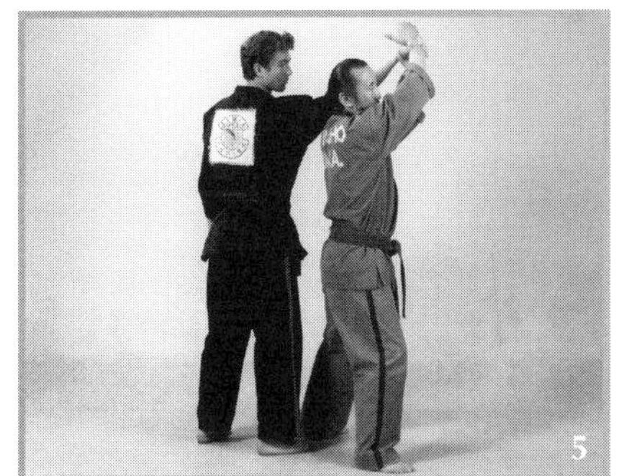
5

6

7

Jun Chong

A Dedication to Excellence

He is a role model to the entire martial arts world. Devoted to the arts and to his students, Master Chong is one-of-a-kind individual. Shy during his teen years in Korea, he managed to beat the odds and blossom as a tough competitor in junior high and high school. Immigrating to the United States changed his whole life. His career evolved into different areas and he became extremely successful—opening several studios in Southern California and getting involved in the movie business. With thousand of students in his system and several successful films to his credit, Master Chong still trains several hours per day. He can usually be found every night at a different school, teaching classes as much as possible and explaining the history, philosophy, and techniques of the art he devoted his entire life to.

Q: What prompted you to get involved in martial arts?

A: I wanted to learn how to defend myself from the big guys. I was always small as a kid—and even now I'm only 5'6" tall. I was raised by my mother, without a father to take care of me. I had no family support outside of my mother. She encouraged me to take martial arts. The training was very hard and I was shy and had a weak mind at first. When I was ten years old, I got injured: my arm was cracked from a side kick. So I quit for three or four months. My mother was very supportive. I was scared by the injury, but she encouraged me to continue. She set up private lessons two times a week, for several years. Through this individualized instruction, I got physically stronger and also developed a stronger self-image and character.

At that time there were no international federations of any kind. When I trained, all the different Kwans were active. My master was from Song Moo Kwan—Master Kim Il Sung. My mother, who was a single parent, wanted me to know how to protect myself because I was an only child. During that particular time, right after the Korean War, things could get a little rough. Many people did not have money and there were some hard times in Korea. At first, I was a bit hesitant, but I needed some discipline. I may have been a lit-

"My teacher taught me how to spar and convinced me to compete. He gave me confidence in everyday life, not just in martial arts. Even today, I use his methods when I teach."

tle bit scared too, but that may have stemmed from a lack of confidence. Initially, I went five days per week. Of course when my arm was broken I got scared and didn't want to train anymore. I thought the sport was too rough.

Eventually, my skill and confidence grew. My teacher taught me how to spar and convinced me to compete. He gave me confidence in everyday life, not just in martial arts. Even today, I use his methods when I teach. At the time we did non-contact sparring, so this really helped my coordination, balance, timing, speed, and strategy. This also enabled me to use more techniques because it was non-contact. If you go with contact, you have to limit your techniques. We used to train outside in the yard, even during the winter. We used to practice in the rain and snow for hours. I still remember those types of things.

Q: Was it difficult to practice in such bad weather?

A: Well, we did not wear shoes so it was pretty slippery and cold. However, once we got going and got sweaty, the cold did not bother us. When it snowed hard, sometimes it was hard to focus, at least at first. Eventually, my focus improved. In fact, training in the snow enabled me to strengthen my focus and concentration skills. If I could focus during that, I was confident that I could focus through anything—including a fight. Training during the rain made the practices slippery and uncomfortable because water splashed into my face, but it was fun. We also hung a heavy bag from a tree and threw kicks for 30 to 40 minutes almost every practice. Eventually, those trees started to die.

After several years, Mr. Cho went into military, and I never saw him after that. I did learn to not go into the snow to practice the martial arts (laughing). Seriously, I think it's important for beginners to start with non-contact sparring. This enables them to become very natural in their techniques once they do contact sparring. I also learned that even when you are angry, you should not hurt your opponent. The purpose of the martial arts is to provide balance and control.

Q: What was the most important thing you learned from Mr. Cho?
A: He taught me many things, but I think enjoying training and believing in myself were the most important things. He also taught me strategy in combat. After class, we would sit and talk. He always told me to look at my opponent's face. He said that the eyes tell everything. I should be able to look at my opponent's face and determine what he's going to do.

"There was a taekwondo team at our school, and I trained almost eight hours per day. Sometimes, I would think about how to fight on the way home on the bus and other times I'd just fall asleep because I'd be so tired."

Q: Did you ultimately get back into formal training?
A: Yes. There was a taekwondo team at our school, and I trained almost eight hours per day. I would get up at 6 a.m. and do a two-hour workout, I'd do an hour at lunch, more time after school, and then I would train from 6 p.m. to 9 p.m. in the *dojang* (training hall). I'd finally get home about 10:30 p.m. Sometimes, I would think about how to fight on the way home on the bus and other times I'd just fall asleep because I'd be so tired. I had six years of that routine.

Q: Do you have an orientation toward the traditional aspects of martial arts?
A: I think traditional is the right way to teach. In high school in Korea, I got into tournament competition. They were not like tournaments today. In those days, tournaments were very physical and there were no limitations on techniques. You could have many techniques, like punching to the face, sweeps, and grabs. Today, there are many rules. I think martial arts have to allow more varied ways of defense and use every possible situation of a real fight. I think this is very important and should not be limited. In the 1970's tournaments, even though they allowed more techniques, they were con-

"Nowadays, competitors wear no uniforms, carry a radio, do not bow, and show no respect. It is foolish to make a tournament like that. I think students should avoid these kinds of tournaments."

trolled in other ways. Tournaments had respect and a sense of beauty. Nowadays, competitors wear no uniforms, carry a radio, do not bow, and show no respect. It is foolish to make a tournament like that. I think students should avoid these kinds of tournaments. I'm afraid my students will go and learn bad attitudes! In my studio, we teach how to respect. There are a lot of big names in tournaments and the Olympics, but in the long run this is limited. They may kick well, but they are leaving out most everything else which is important to the martial arts.

Q: Did you always want to come to the United States?

A: Not really. Actually, I was going to go into the military. Later, however, I had a chance to come to America, which is what I did. After high school, in 1966, an American family adopted me. I was 18, but they reduced my age for the adoption to 15. I moved with them to Olympia, Washington. My mother approached them because she felt there was no future in Korea. She worked on a United States military base and met a man and wife who did not have kids. She recommended that they adopt me. To be honest, at first I didn't like it. After I thought about it, though, I thought it might be a good chance to make a living in America. At that time, Korea was a poor country and there were times when we had to fight for food. These people, Mr. and Mrs. Graf, were very nice people.

Q: What did you tell your mom when you left?

A: I told her I would be back to bring her to America some day. She said she would wait. When I was flying to America, I cried the whole time. It was quite sad. But I kept my word and she came over three years later. She was very happy that I did not forget her—as if I could. She did so much for me.

We didn't have a lot of money and times were very hard for us in Korean, but she always made sure there was money for private lessons and education for me.

"I still have my school on Wilshire Boulevard in Beverly Hills, and I think that one of the reasons we're successful is that I give hard martial arts to my students. They accept that and appreciate it."

Q: Los Angeles is a big place for a young man on his own.

A: After graduating from high school and coming to the United States, I studied with hapkido founder Sea Oh Choi for four years. He taught me the real knowledge of the martial arts. Hapkido is pure knowledge: knowledge of throwing techniques, kicking techniques, and punching techniques. During those four years I learned from him spiritually, too. I also looked for a taekwondo school that needed an instructor. I met Mr. Choi in Gardena, California and I asked him for a job. That was in 1968, and I stayed with him until 1972. I stayed in the studio and slept there and cleaned the school. I tried to go to college but it didn't work out so I did martial arts full-time. Then I opened my own school in Rosemead, California in 1972. Three years later I bought Chuck Norris' school on Wilshire Boulevard in Los Angeles. I had 200 students within two years and 400 within four years. I still have my school on Wilshire Boulevard in Beverly Hills, and we offer 11 classes per day, and are open seven days a week. I think that one of the reasons we're successful is that I give hard martial arts to my students. They accept that and appreciate it.

"I truly believe that the only formula for success is hard work. I think it also helps that we blend taekwondo and hapkido. These two arts give students a balance in class, and that is how I teach."

Q: What do you mean by "hard" martial arts?

A: The students are very focused and there is plenty of strong, physical work. There may not always be contact, but there is lots of kicking and punching combinations, lots of time devoted to practicing techniques, and the action is non-stop. I truly believe that the only formula for success is hard work. I think it also helps that we blend taekwondo and hapkido. With taekwondo, the students get a lot of kicking and punching—they sweat a lot and spar a lot. On the other hand, hapkido is calm with its hand grabs, take-downs, and joint locks. These two arts give students a balance in class, and that is how I teach. After they are sweating from the kicking and punching, we stop and do some hapkido movements. Once they've had a chance to cool down while doing hapkido movements, we start with some hard kicks. The balance is good for the class. I think it's also because we provide flexible hours. We have many professionals who train here and time is a concern—therefore we have flexible hours.

Q: You have trained in many other systems. Why?

A: I just want to know what tai chi was, what aikido was, and what shotokan was. I wondered what the difference was between aikido and hapkido, and so I found out for myself instead of asking someone. Aikido is more graceful and more precise with each lock. Hapkido is more powerful and more physical. It's graceful too, but it has more power. Tai chi has very soft power. I always get stiff after tai chi workouts because there is no training quite like it. In taekwondo, we stretch ourselves to our utmost physical limits and totally put ourselves mentally and physically into it. Tai chi, on the other hand, is very slow. Dan Lee always says how tai chi is different from taekwondo. Of course they are different—but that doesn't mean one is good and one is bad. Everybody is different. For some people, tight is good and for others tight is bad. So for some people taekwondo is good and for others it is not. All styles are different and none is the best for everybody.

Q: Do you favor the idea of cross-training in different styles?

A: Definitely—but you have to be careful what you are doing. You need to find elements or styles that directly improve what you are already doing, and not jump from one style to another just for the sake of learning something new. You need to have a direction and a purpose in your research and training—otherwise, you may end up with a combination of many styles that do not bring anything good to yourself as a martial artist. If you practice taekwondo, you can learn shotokan or boxing to improve your hand technique—this makes sense. You should look to improve and complement what you have.

"You need to have a direction and a purpose in your research and training—otherwise, you may end up with a combination of many styles that do not bring anything good to yourself as a martial artist."

Q: Do you do full-contact sparring at your school?

A: We do contact always, but we have to pull back, like in shotokan. And we do totally controlled kicking. We also teach two-against-one and three-against-one. But this type of sparring must be no-contact because of the possibility of many injuries. Two-on-one sparring is very tiring and requires tough mental discipline. Three-on-one, the way I teach it, is only one minute long—one quick round. To fight three-on-one you must use a defensive concept: never think attack, think defense. You will automatically lose if you start a fight one-against-three, no matter how good you are!

Q: What is your teaching methodology?

A: I think the master must have strong discipline to be at the school every day. No matter how many students come, I teach—even if it is only one student. I give sincere teaching, with the philosophy that one student will bring

"In taekwondo, punching and kicking is more focused, with many different varieties of punches and kicks. We combine everything together. After black belt, we teach weapons like the nunchaku, bo *and* sai.*"*

ten students later. When beginners first walk-in, I make it very loose, very relaxed. I teach them a relaxed meditation for five minutes, Then I teach yoga stretches and breathing, combined with taekwondo stretches for about 15 minutes. Next we do punching techniques, somewhat like shotokan punches, and we perform a routine of blocks. Then we start kicking—stretch kicks and kicks. After a little more stretching, we do *hyungs* or forms.

Q: Which hyungs do you teach?
A: We do Palgwe *hyungs*, though I changed them a little. The traditional Palgwes were designed by old instructors and they are a little stiff. They look more complicated to learn, but they are more challenging that way. Then I teach how to fall. The traditional taekwondo doesn't usually teach how to fall. We also teach self-defense against grabs—how to deal with somebody who grabs the neck, or from behind, et cetera. Students love the self-defense training because it is very practical. Finally, we teach jumping kicks and one-on-one sparring, but no-contact sparring at this level. After the first year, I teach more advanced methods of kicking and punching. It's organized with the same routine, but has more advanced techniques. At the black belt level, I teach boxing. All of my black belts know how to box, which is combined with our kicks. But kickboxing can be sloppy. In taekwondo, punching and kicking is more focused, with many different varieties of punches and kicks. We combine everything together. After black belt, we teach weapons like the *nunchaku, bo* and *sai.*

Q: So you teach a balanced system of old and new methods?
A: People continually want to learn. I am always learning. My students are the same way. So I teach what I know and I teach what I learn. This is what it means to be a master: to keep learning and stay ahead of your students, bringing new things for them to learn! Many people limit themselves. I feel no one martial art is best. I've become an American taekwondo martial arts school. Although I teach one traditional style, I have brought in many other things. We teach meditation. We also teach the meaning of techniques. Like when you throw a kick, you must understand why. Perhaps we show a defensive position. There is a different spiritual involvement when you think about what you are doing. Besides teaching many techniques, the most important point is that I am disciplined. I know many great instructors, but they are not disciplined enough. I workout every day and discipline is the most important principle of all. The instructor must be more strongly disciplined than the students. Then everybody will follow the instructor.

"The right attitude starts by treating students warmly to bring them into our school. I require my instructors to teach gently or go elsewhere. The military approach is important, but not for martial arts schools. A beginning student is much like a baby."

Q: What is your personal training routine and diet like?
A: On an average day I work out around five hours—but it could be more depending on the number of lessons. My exercise routine includes a lot of stretching for every part of the body. Some of them are yoga postures, which have an overall benefit. For high kicks and speed I use the *barre*, similar to those in ballet. I also borrowed a few punching techniques from boxing that I include in my punching bag routine. As far as my diet, I don't follow a particular one but I try to eat healthy and clean which it means to stay away from starches and sweets. Of course, I complement my nutrition with vitamins and minerals, which sometimes are lacking due to my busy schedule.

"Hapkido also emphasizes kicking, but in a different way. Kicking develops your legs, which in turn makes you a better fighter."

Q: Would you describe your martial arts system and philosophy?

A: We begin by teaching the right attitude. The right attitude starts by treating students warmly to bring them into our school. I require my instructors to teach gently or go elsewhere. The military approach is important, but not for martial arts schools. A beginning student is much like a baby. They cannot walk, they cannot focus or punch correctly, so we have to teach them like a baby. Then slowly, after the first year, we help them develop tight discipline and tight attitude—tight and strong. By the time they reach black belt level they have developed the right attitude. Taekwondo mainly uses kicks, and I have dedicated most of my life to Korean styles—they are what I know best. Personally, I love kicking and the art of taekwondo offers me a great variety of techniques in this particular aspect of combat. Hapkido is a great self-defense method and unintentionally I began to blend one system with the other in a natural way. Hapkido also emphasizes kicking, but in a different way. Kicking develops your legs, which in turn makes you a better fighter. If the legs are weak, it will be easy for your opponent to throw you off-balance. On the other hand, training the legs to kick makes them stronger—providing a good, solid stance.

As far as my philosophy goes, I would say that I believe in change—but change for the good and for a reason. The art of self-defense is not only for royal families or warriors. I teach a modern style, not because I made it that way but because that is the way taekwondo has evolved. As I said before, unintentionally and over a long period of time, I have blended hapkido and taekwondo techniques to create a number of self-defense combinations. These combinations happened naturally and I have been using and teaching them for years. By integrating elements from Japanese hand-techniques, I have made our punching more varied and complete. Also, traditional taekwondo never makes use of throws. Nevertheless I consider them very important for self-defense situations outside the ring. That's when hapkido comes in. A timely reverse punch, like those practiced in Japanese hard styles, are excellent for counterattacks or in combination with other techniques. As far as kicking, there is nothing like taekwondo. All I can say is that this system has proved very successful for tournament competition, and for the overall black belt quality of my students.

Q: How long does it take to earn a black belt under you?
A: Three to five years. I like to say three but it usually takes five. I like to teach the entire system, but I also like to teach mind power and the spiritual way, too. We have many obstacle courses such as sparring, breaking, and jumping kicks. In the black belt test we do knife defenses, two-man defenses, two-man attacks, and jumping kicks—both single kick and double kick. Many women find it difficult to do jumping kicks. My wife has had knee operations which make jumping kicks difficult. She has studied for 23 years and finally got her black belt this year. We also teach women. We have half kids, half adults, and 30 percent of them are women. I am very proud of our women. They are very interested in learning martial arts, sometimes even more than the men. They look good and they kick fast. Women train hard. They use a very different approach from men as far as training is concerned.

Q: Do women need a different approach to train in the martial arts?
A: Just in the beginning. They need a little bit gentler training in the beginning, but after the first year, around blue belt, they are treated the same as the men. I like to teach women to have strong minds. I think nowadays, women have minds as strong as men. When it comes to dangerous moments, women have a stronger mind. I can appreciate women becoming black belts and not just honorary black belts. They must fight two against one, flip men around, perform jumping kicks, and break wood. I respect the more artistic way women do it. Men have more of a physical way behind their taekwondo. I like to encourage women in martial arts. They do very well. Sometimes when a women scores on a man, the man does not know what to do! He gets angry and loses his composure. This is stupid. When we become black belts, we choose to not let our feelings get out of control. Black belts learn to control their anger. If you are in a fight, never lose your mind. If you do that you can kill people or you can get killed. That is not the focus of martial arts.

Q: How do you teach mind power?

A: There are many ways. *Kiai,* the yelling, is one. Also through breathing and sparring. Every one—women, men and children—must learn these things. If you've been sparring for four or five years, you become confident. After many years you have no fear at all of sparring. The same is true with jumping kicks. First the front-kick, then the side-kick followed by the back-kick, then double-kicks. Each time they master one method they get more confident and their mind becomes stronger. Step by step, they go through many obstacles. After a long and hard course, they become a black belt. Unfortunately, only one or two percent of the students get the black belt. I've been teaching for many years, but we only have over 200 black belts.

Q: Is sparring important in your schools?

A: Of course, but the art of sparring does not compare to street fighting—they are two different things. Sparring is a game—even if there is contact the superior fighter doesn't need to hurt his opponent. He knows how much power must be released on impact with undeniable target accuracy. He does not draw blood. Of course, accidents occur; they come with the territory. But in sparring there is no need to hurt someone to prove who is better. Street fighting is different, very different.

Q: How often should a student train?

A: Three times a week is enough at first because the body needs time to recover—especially from a hard taekwondo class. They cannot walk the next day after all the kicking. But once they are black belts they should train every day and stay with their martial arts. Many instructors become involved in movies, too. Once they get good, they take off and do movies. I've done many movies, but teaching always comes first and movies second. The school is always here. People come to my school for how I teach—because I teach sincerely. They might be drawn in because I've done movies, but that isn't right. They should come because of how we teach.

Q: What is the essence of self-defense?

A: To me, self-defense is confidence and confidence comes from sparring. Taekwondo is a sparring art, and hapkido enables you to control your opponent. Thus, my students get a blend of the elements they need. If you spar a lot, a street fight should be very easy. If you don't spar, a street attack could be difficult because you won't even know how to relax your mind. Relaxation is the key element. In professional boxing, the first thing you learn is how to be calm so you can seize your chance. It's the same thing with the martial arts. You have to be calm so you can look for an opportunity to attack. It's the same thing in the street. You have to be calm. Wait for your chance. You don't want to panic. If you panic, you lose.

"I'd like to stay away from too much fantasy. I'd prefer pure martial arts fighting scenes. I think realism is important."

Q: How important is discipline in your student's behavior?
A: I think it is the key to martial arts training. Without it, I don't think you'll find happiness. Discipline makes you better. When you are better, you are happy. If you are not happy with what you are doing, you will enjoy it less, train less, and be disappointed.

Q: What does the future hold for you?
A: It's hard to tell. I would like to make more good martial arts movies. I'd like to stay away from too much fantasy. I'd prefer pure martial arts fighting scenes. I think realism is important. The movies with fantasy will come and go. After all these years, people still enjoy *Enter the Dragon* because it's more realistic than fantasy.

Q: What would you like to say to all martial artists?
A: My advice is to stay interested and make martial arts a way of life. The martial arts way is a good one—it contains discipline and confidence—all of this can help you in your life. Many people start to train and then quit after a short time. Instead, make a long-term commitment. You must make a commitment or you will never be successful. Find what you like—a good system and a good school—and do long-term martial arts training. The rewards are there for you.

Master Chong is facing his opponent (1). The attacker throws a roundhouse kick that Master Chong avoids by sidestepping (2) to counterattack with a roundhouse kick (4) to his opponent's ribcage (5).

1

2

3

4

Master Chong squares off with his opponent (1). He blocks his attacker's kick (2) and delivers from the inside angle (3), an inside crescent kick to the head of his aggressor (4).

1

2

3

4

Master Chong faces his opponent on an unmatched lead (1). As soon his opponent starts to move, Master Chong intercepts using a straight punch to the chest (2), followed by a left outside crescent kick to the opponent's head (3).

Master Chong faces his opponent (1). As soon as the attacker initiates his movement, Master Chong moves in (2) and connects with a roundhouse kick to the face (3).

Master Chong faces his opponent (1). As soon as the aggressor moves in, Master Chong anticipates with a lead hand punch (2), which makes the aggressor move back and set himself up by creating enough range for a roundhouse kick (3) to the face (4).

1

2

3

4

Master Chong squares off with his opponent (1). The opponent takes a step to close the distance and Master Chong stops him with a punch (2), which aborts the attack (3) to follow with inside ax kick to the head (4-5).

1

2

3

4

5

Master Chong faces an assailant armed with a knife (1). As the aggressor attacks, Master Chong blocks the attack (2) and controlling the arm, passes under (3) his opponent's right arm, hitting with an elbow strike to the ribcage (4) to finalize with an attack to the neck with the aggressor's weapon.

Master Chong squares off with his opponent who is armed with a knife (1). The aggressor attacks and Master Chong controls the arm and moves toward his left side (2) to deliver a punch to the face (3) and moving his body in a counterclockwise motion, applies a wristlock (4) that sends the opponent to the ground (5)...

1

2

3

4

5

...where he starts (6) to control the arm (7) to apply an armlock (8) which helps to disarm the aggressor (9).

6

7

8

9

Kensho Furuya

The Complex Simplicity of Aikido and Life

Born in California, Reverend Furuya is a master in aikido who is recognized as a worldwide authority on Asian culture. In 1969, Sensei Furuya was invited to study aikido in Japan by O Sensei. Unfortunately Morihei Ueshiba passed away shortly after issuing the invitation. His dojo in Los Angeles, California, is truly a traditional Japanese dojo. There, Reverend Furuya not only teaches the art of aikido but shares the culture that nurtured the art. The dojo resounds with the quietness of the old tradition. He was ordained as a Zen priest in 1989 under the Most Reverend Bishop Kenko Yamashita. Reverend Furuya is very involved in the Little Tokyo community where his school is located. For him, the dojo is a labor of love. It is a small payment on his debt he owes to the Doshu Ueshiba for teaching him. He resides in his dojo and teaches every day, living a monastic life as a Zen priest and martial arts instructor.

Q: Reverend Furuya, when did you start training in aikido?
A: I began training in aikido when I was 12 years old. It was under Sensei Mitsunari Kanai, around 1968. One year later I began my training at the honbu in Tokyo, under Doshu Kisshomaru Ueshiba. I haven't stopped since.

Q: What was your learning process?
A: Well, all my teachers taught the art in the traditional way. You never asked any questions. You watched and watched, and then you trained and trained. To watch a real master is to be inspired and I found it easy to learn. When I returned to United States after some training in Japan, I needed another way to ensure I could continue training correctly. You see, I knew the techniques, I knew what to do, but I couldn't see one line going through all the techniques. Finally, I took a piece of paper and a pencil, and I sketched out a basic technique. Then I asked myself, "Why does it work? What are the dynamics of the technique which make it effective?" I stared at that paper for three frustrating days, and finally I realized that my research had to follow a new direction. I set out on a course of intense personal

"Rather than teach Aikido from an esoteric point of view, I always wanted to teach it in the language of science. Science is a universal language, and by teaching the art in those terms, there will be no barriers to learning the art."

study on anatomy, physiology, kinesiology, and psychology—as well as religion and philosophy—relating everything I had learned to aikido. I took a very Zen-like approach. Which I thought correct, being a Zen priest.

Q: Who is your teacher in Zen?
A: Reverend Bishop Kenko Yamashita of the North American Soto Zen Buddhism. He gave me the name *Kensho*.

Q: Why did you decide to go to Japan for aikido training?
A: I was invited by O Sensei Morihei Ueshiba to go there and study, but he died shortly after send that invitation. Therefore, I studied under the guidance of his son, Doshu Kisshomaru Ueshiba, who was the Headmaster of the International Aikido Federation.

Q: Many people are attracted to aikido because of the philosophy—were you?
A: Aikido philosophy is very important and very difficult to understand. It's true that some people might feel attracted to that philosophy but the problem is that they are not aware of the physical nature of the training. And that's a mistake. Both things go hand in hand.

Q: Do you perceive many misconceptions about the art that you share?
A: I like the term "share." Anyway, yes I do. Some visitors look at the classes and they think aikido techniques are very easy to do since they look effortless. Then they sign up. Pretty soon they realize that aikido is not as easy as they believed. They end up exhausted after one hour class! Rather than teach Aikido from an esoteric point of view, I always wanted to teach it in the language of science. Since the human body is subject to natural laws, all its movements can be explained in terms of kinesiology, physiology, and physics. Science is a universal language, and by teaching the art in those

terms, there will be no barriers to learning the art.

For instance, in kinesiology an effective movement is one in which the body acts as an integrated unit, and does the maximum amount of work with the minimum amount of effort. By clarifying the basic principles behind the techniques, the students can see what makes the technique effective. In training, your teacher may correct your mistakes by saying, "Put your right foot here, straighten your posture, raise you right arm, lower your elbow." But these just correct the *symptoms* of the problems, not the *causes* of them. It's like a doctor learning the symptoms for a disease, and its source.

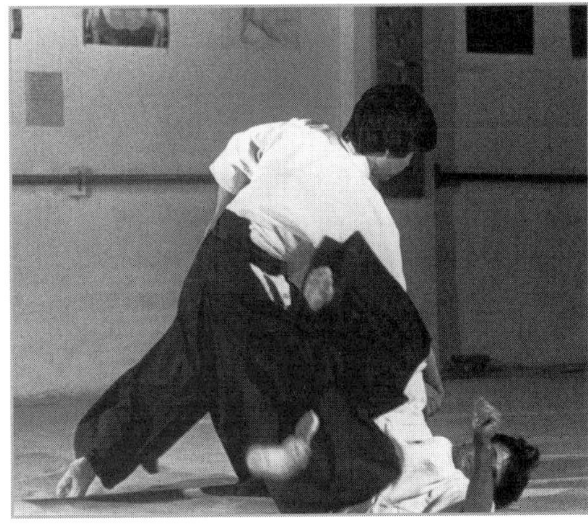

"Some people think that by breaking down the aikido movements, we become too analytical and lose the flavor of the art—but I don't think that's true."

Q: So what's your methodology to correct your student's mistakes?

A: In the process of teaching, I tested and revised my methods. I went very slowly, very painstakingly, making sure that things made sense both to myself and my students. A teacher may see that a student's hip is weak, and say, "Put strength in your hip." The student can't do it, not because the hip is weak, but because the hip is not supported by the back leg. If he understands the basic principles of body movement, the teacher can say, "Straighten your back leg to support the hip." Or a teacher might say, "Your shoulder is too weak. Strengthen the shoulder." Well, the shoulder may be too weak because the body's center of mass is too high, and this draws the heel of the rear foot up. The teacher should say, "Bring the back heel down." This will center the student's balance in his hips, which strengthens the position of the shoulder.

Q: Because of these highly innovative methods, have you ever been criticized?

A: Yes. Some people think that by breaking down the aikido movements, we become too analytical and lose the flavor of the art—but I don't think that's true. I believe that it enhances the student's understanding of aikido and brings the art to a higher level of experience. Also, since the student begins to understand the basic principles of each technique, they can see

"People in the West rule their lives according to the belief that a certain amount of effort will bring a certain amount of reward. In martial arts this idea doesn't exist."

the relationship between all techniques. Understanding principles instead of memorizing isolated circumstances helps the student's growth and gives him a clearer understanding.

Q: Why is aikido perceived as a soft art?

A: I don't know the real reason, but all I can say is that I don't train my students at a slow and static rate, but at a very fast pace which requires more energy and effort. The attack has to be realistic, direct, and strong—the student must be on his toes and make every movement count. Some people believe that aikido is easy for old men, children, and women. That is not true. Aikido is rigorous. Aikido hurts.

Q: How many years does it take to be proficient in aikido?

A: This kind of question has no relation to the art of aikido. Training and practice is the point, not achievement. The same applies to Zen training. Meditation is enlightenment and enlightenment is meditation. We must learn to focus our minds in the now. People in the West rule their lives according to the belief that a certain amount of effort will bring a certain amount of reward. In martial arts this idea doesn't exist. In Budo training the principle is that maximum effort will bring minimum return. The idea that one trains or meditates to achieve something is an illusion. The very moment—the here and now of doing something—is the goal.

Q: It said that the final goal of martial arts is to bring the body and mind together— is this also true of aikido?

A: Yes. Aikido looks for unity mind and body. The whole idea is for the students to overcomes certain limitations, both physical and mental, through the daily training. It is only when the disciple has passed this limitation—when he reaches a state where mind and body act like one—can they begin to understand the essence of the art. Of course, you need a lot of discipline and dedication to achieve that level.

Q: You have a small dojo, but there is a very special atmosphere, what's your secret?
A: There's no secret. This special atmosphere you're talking about is a sense of peace. This dojo is not for money. It's a fulfillment of my teacher's request, and it is a gift to my students. I don't keep the dojo open because I want to make money. I hope it serves as a cultural property that helps to expand the oriental philosophy that shaped aikido and the Japanese culture.

"We are out of touch with our bodies and our minds. Aikido can help to correct that if it is practiced it the right way, with the right mind. The goal of aikido is to return to the spiritual wholeness."

Q: What has your personal philosophy made you really want?
A: To be honest with you, I like farming. Yes, I see myself practicing aikido, farming, and following my Zen studies. I really see myself trying my hand at farming. That's all. But not using new technologies. No, there are many other approaches to farming that don't use questionable technology for instant growth. Did you know that a farmer's day has to be properly distributed so he has time for relaxation?

Q: No, I didn't know. But I can see that you're not a very materialistic person.
A: Not at all, and I'll tell you why. The increased technological nature of modern society has caused a deep erosion of the human spirit—both in the East and the West. It has changed the human needs, the human spirit, and the human mind. All this spiritual materialism leads to an ego-centered mentality consumed with possessing objects. We are out of touch with our bodies and our minds. Aikido can help to correct that if it is practiced it the right way, with the right mind. The goal of aikido is to return to the spiritual wholeness—the one we are losing these days due to society's technological nature of spiritual materialism.

Q: Why did you become involved with Zen?
A: Both Zen and Buddhism have a great influence on the martial arts. The Budo arts not only draw from these two, but from Shinto and Confucian doctrine as well.

"When you're facing the possibility of dying in combat, your mental state has to be clean and focused on that moment. Nothing can disturb your mind."

Q: In Budo philosophy, the idea of life and death plays a very significant role. How does this apply to aikido?
A: This is very Zen-like! The old warriors trained for death matches, not sport. They adopted Zen to prepare their minds for death. They trained in how to use killing techniques, not how to score a point in a tournament. When you're facing the possibility of dying in combat, your mental state has to be clean and focused on that moment. Nothing can disturb your mind.

Q: They had to think only in that particular moment?
A: The idea of *mushin no kokoro* goes beyond that. But living completely in the moment, and the body and mind being one, was a basic necessity for a warrior. They used Zen to develop a state of mind to deal with life-or-death situations. We say in Japan that your mind should be like a bright mirror or calm water, which reflects exactly what's there. This is the goal of Zen and the martial arts.

Q: Describe the concept of *ki*.
A: When the people talk about universal ki, and give it mystic power, they're exaggerating it to the point of distortion. There's nothing mystical about ki. I like to explain it to my students to take out the mystery. Ki is the essence of aikido and a vital part of a person's life. Scientific training is for understanding the world with clarity. Spiritual training, or developing ki, is the same thing—just another way of understanding the real world with clarity. In order to see things as they are, the individual must learn to discard his fears, hopes, and images of the past and future. One of the pathways to attaining this clarity is to become more open and sensitive to the world. If you like something you have affinity with it, and you become more aware of it. As you become more intimate with something, you remove all your barriers. Your compassion and affinity give you great awareness and clarity. In aikido, you face your opponent with compassion so that you will be open to the reality of the situation, and see him and his movements with absolute clarity. It is from that

moment of absolute clarity that aikido technique evolved.

"The attempt to objectify ki into a force which can be sent here or there detracts from understanding its true nature."

Q: So ki isn't a cosmic force like in *Star Wars*?
A: No. It's very simple and common. The attempt to objectify ki into a force which can be sent here or there detracts from understanding its true nature. It's like water flowing out of a hose. You can't concentrate and force more water to come out of the hose, but you can take out the kinks and knots. In the same way, by attempting to achieve clarity, you put yourself in a condition where more ki will flow out of you.

Q: You mentioned before that your dojo was a fulfillment of Doshu Kisshomaru Ueshiba's request. How so?
A: When I returned to the United States from Japan, Doshu Kisshomaru Ueshiba requested that I teach aikido in Los Angeles. He wanted me to build a real Japanese dojo.

Q: What was the path of aikido evolution after the World War II?
A: Every art evolves, and aikido is a living art, so we can't prevent it from changing with the times. I really think that Doshu Kisshomaru Ueshiba was responsible for the growth and shape of the art after the war. I say this because by the time O Sensei Ueshiba passed away, the art was starting to assume its present form and O Sensei was in a very deep spiritual quest. For O Sensei, physical technique was not such a big deal anymore. Unfortunately, and this is my personal opinion, Doshu Ueshiba is not receiving the credit he deserves. I believe he did and still does a great labor in structuring and formalizing aspects of the art and that not very many people appreciate it as they should.

Q: What should proper aikido training be?
A: Severe and disciplined. If we follow the true aikido precepts and Zen teachings, the training must have a big intensity—it must be all or nothing, an all-out attitude, life or death. Without the courage to enter with the

"If you can put your whole body and mind together properly just to make a cup of tea, you can do it to face an opponent. Your practice should bring meaning into your life so it shows you your true self."

whole mind and body into the training, the student will never understand anything about aikido and the arts of Budo. I'd dare to say that attitude is everything.

Q: Why is aikido sometimes accused of having an elitist intellectual attitude?
A: It is possible that there is some truth in those accusations. Aikido tries to bring the mind and body together. Some say it is an art for intellectuals—but that's a very big problem for the student. It doesn't matter how intellectual students may be, or how much mechanical or theoretical understanding of the technique they may have, they have to experience the physical action by themselves. That's the only truth. Not the words, but the action. The free expression of the student through aikido technique, must be experienced through severe physical discipline. Man has wrongly convinced himself that intellect is the most powerful weapon—and that's wrong. In Zen there is a saying: "Take off your head, put it by your side, and sit!"

Q: Do you think the reason people feel attracted to martial arts has changed over the years?
A: Of course! People's mentality has changed, their goals in life are very different compared to those of forty years ago. This is the reason I said that the martial arts evolve. Sometimes those changes are a matter of personal convenience and have nothing to do with the natural change of things. But every change is not positive. Sometimes we should to throw out the new and bring in the old. I know it sounds confusing but I'm sure a few people understand what I really mean.

Q: In traditional martial arts, why is frustration part of the teaching process?
A: If an student can't survive a injured ego, how is he going to survive the grueling training to come? Frustration is good if both the teacher and the student know how to use it. But frustration is just part of the training. The important thing is to understand it properly and keep training just as before. In fact, the idea of not being discouraged and disappointed are preconceived

ideas that we have before getting into the dojo—and fortunately all of them are shattered to pieces on the mat.

Q: Why is it said that the Tea Ceremony is very similar to both Zen and martial arts?
A: If you can put your whole body and mind together properly just to make a cup of tea, you can do it to face an opponent. Your practice should bring meaning into your life so it shows you your true self. Otherwise, what's the use of training? Just for fighting?

Q: Why was Shintoism so important in O Sensei's philosophy?
A: Life's process, the love of nature, are very Shinto principles, and a very Japanese attitude. O Sensei believed that aikido was the natural expression of our existence, and was a way toward harmony with nature. During his later years he retired to the countryside to find a greater deal of peace. You can find many pictures of him touching the trees in a state of wonder or watering plants. Aikido philosophy, and the physical techniques of the art, were highly influenced by this concept.

Q: What would be your final advise to your students?
A: I would like them to remember that if you are following a road you have never been on before, and you are confident you know the directions, you can walk without hesitation. If you are not confident of the way, you must go slowly. In olden times, a student who entered a martial arts school would have the rest of his life to devote to the art. Now everything is high-tech and instant ramen, and we have to find a way to make the art as clear as possible to the student in the limited time available for instruction. The student must always remember that a rational analysis of aikido is only a way to enhance training, and must never be thought of as an alternative to training. If there is training without analysis, the art becomes coarse—if there is analysis without training, the art becomes ineffective.

Q: Do you consider yourself a successful person?
A: These days people put too much emphasis of being successful. They don't really understand what being successful means. By my standards I'm a successful human being. I enjoy my life, I enjoy my teaching, and I enjoy my existence. Is that not enough?

From a ready stance (1), Rev. Kensho Furuya deflects (2) with the left hand, then pushes with the right hand (3). He switches hands to hit the aggressor in the face (4-5). He then steps in deep (5-6) and throws his opponent (7).

1

2

3

4

5

6

7

1

From a ready stance (1), Rev. Furuya brings the hands to the empty space in the armpits (2). He then rotates his arms forward (3). The right hand pull the attacker's elbow down as the left hand pushes his arm up (4). As he is completing the twist, he escapes the bearhug (5). He then steps in behind to break his opponent's balance. A strike to the throat (5) is followed by a throw (6-7).

2

3

4

5

6

7

Leo M. Giron

The Last of the Bladed Warriors

Grand Master Emeritus Leo Giron was born in Bayambang, Philippines, in the province of Pangasinan. He is a World War II veteran who was awarded the Bronze Star, among many other citations for heroism. As the head advisor and founder of the Bahala Na Martial Arts Association, he is world renowned as the Father of Larga Mano in America. There have only been 79 graduates from the Bahala Na Martial Arts Association over the past 32 years. Some of Giron's most noted disciples are Dan Inosanto, Richard Bustillo, Ted Lucaylucay, Jerry Poteet, and Dentoy Rivellar. Giron is still active and teaching, along with Grandmaster Antonio E. Somera, at their current home school in Stockton, California. At the tender age of 90 he still attends class on a regular bases. His knowledge of jungle warfare is an invaluable asset to those that train with him and seek knowledge of "real" combat. His appearance is that of a humble man, and he carries himself with the demeanor of a distinguished college professor. However, there is a unmistakable seriousness about him and a hint of the fist that lies within the velvet glove—perhaps something you only get when you fight against men who would take your life away.

Q: When were you inducted into the Army?

A: I was inducted on October 9, 1942, in Los Angeles, California. Prior to that I was farming in Imperial Valley, California. I was first stationed at Camp San Luis Obispo and then in the winter of the same year I was transferred to Fort Ord.

Q: How were you selected to be in the 978th Signal Service company?

A: Well, everyone was brought into the base recreation room and given an aptitude test. Many did not pass and were sent back to their regiments. Others made it and were given additional education in Morse code. The Army was looking for specific types of men. They were looking for men with schooling who could communicate well in English. I was one of the few that made it.

"I was fortunate to learn escrima as a child and later on, after coming to America, from one of my most influential teachers, Flaviano Vergara."

Q: What was your training like in the Army?

A: During boot camp we also went to school. We were learning communications like Morse code, wig-wag (flag signals), cyma four, cryptography and paraphrasing. I was trained to communicate. At the time I did not know what the Army was planning for me. We were never told why we were training; we just did what the Army told us to do.

Q: What type of self-defense training did you receive from the Army?

A: We learned all the basic training needed for soldiering. Nothing special—just how to shoot a carbine, how to use a .45 and some basic hand-to-hand combat. I was fortunate to learn escrima as a child and later on, after coming to America, from one of my most influential teachers, Flaviano Vergara. Flaviano is the man who taught me the most about escrima and how to defend myself. In fact I met Flaviano a second time in Fort Ord during which time we would play on weekdays after dinner, and on the weekends while everyone else went to town. Flaviano and I would do nothing but drill and drill using *estilo de fondo* and *larga mano.* Sometimes a soldier would come by and ask what were we doing? Some would tell us that they would never come close to a samurai sword. They claimed they would give the samurai a load of their M-1.

Q: What were you first experiences with the art of escrima?

A: As a kid, every time my friends and I heard the "click, click, click" of knives, we would be playing under the mango trees and the trail would be guarded. So I would sneak away to watch. Later, we paid so many bundles of straw and rice for our lessons. My family didn't know. I was carrying a bundle or rice when my father asked me about it and I told him I was going to take it to my uncle; we were going to make cakes!

"I learned a lot about how to use the environment for survival purposes. This is a very important aspect, especially when you're fighting in the jungle. You need to know how to maximize every tree and every bush."

In one of my first training sessions my instructor told me, "Take your bolo and let's do some training. Don't worry about hurting me because I've been fighting for a long time. Cut me anytime you can. If you touch me you'll get a month's pay." That was the way you learned in those days. I learned a lot about how to use the environment for survival purposes. This is a very important aspect, especially when you're fighting in the jungle. You need to know how to maximize every tree and every bush—the smallest advantage may be what you need to save your life.

Q: Who were your instructors and what systems did they teach you?
A: I had five teachers and I will give them to you in order and what style they passed onto me.

1. Benito Junio from the barrio of Inerangan town of Bayombang province of Pangasinan, Luzon Philippines. In 1920 I started my education in arnis escrima. Benito Junio was famous for his *larga mano* (long-hand stick) and *fondo fuerte* (fighting in a solid position) styles.

"I'm well-known around the world for my larga mano *style of escrima. But this is just a small piece of the entire Giron arnis escrima system."*

2. Fructuso Junio from the barrio of Telbang town of Bayombang province of Pangasinan, Luzon Philippines. From 1921-1926 I continued my training with Fructuso uncle to Bentio. Fructuso Junio was well-known for his *macabebe* or two-stick fighting. Fructuso was the first to share the importance of distinguishing between the old (*cada-anan*) and new (*cabaroan*) styles of Luzon.

3. Flavian Vergara from Santa Curz in Llocos Sur Luzon, Philippines. Vergara was the top student of Dalmacio Bergonia who defeated the great champion Santiago Toledo. Vergara and I started our training in the prune orchards of Meridian, California from 1929-1932. Vergara and Giron would meet again directly after the outbreak of World War II. Our lives would cross for the last time in October 1942, when I was shipped out to Fort Ord, Calif. Every spare minute Vergara and I would train until I was shipped out in January, 1943. Vergara was a master in the Bergonia style and very proficient in the *estilo elastico* (rubber band style). I always thought that Vergara had superhuman abilities. Vergara influenced me a lot and his understanding of the relationships between the *cada-anan* and *cabaroan* styles of arnis escrima.

4. Beningo Ramos from Kongkong Bayongbang. During World War II Ramos was a sergeant in the Filipino army assigned to me. Prior to the outbreak of World War II Ramos was an improbable arnis escrima teacher and was respected as one of the best *estilo matador* (killer-style) teachers in Luzon. Ramos was an expert in *larga mano, miscla contras, tero pisada, tero grave* and *elastico* styles. Ramos was so confident of his skills that he and I

would play with live bolos. Ramos bet me that if I could hit him he would give me one month's pay. I never collected a cent from Ramos.

5. Julian Bundoc from the barrio of Carangay town of Bayombang province of Pangasianan, Luzon Philippines. Julian was cousin to Benito Junio. Julian Bundoc and I would play more of the combative *larga mano* and work on conditioning the body. Julian Bundoc was also a master of *hilot* or massage. We trained in Stockton from 1956-1961. One of my teachers named Flaviano Vergara had the most influence on me and helped me greatly in developing my system.

"During combat you do not want to move your feet about, as this may cause you to lose your footing and balance."

Q: How many systems or methods comprise your own personal method?

A: I'm well-known around the world for my *larga mano* style of escrima. But this is just a small piece of the entire Giron arnis escrima system. The Giron system has 20 styles and techniques that are just as effective and just as complete. Here are the names and a brief overview of each of the 20 styles (*estilo*) that encompass my method:

1. *Estilo de Fondo*—This is a style of planting yourself firmly on the ground. During combat you do not want to move your feet about, as this may cause you to lose your footing and balance. This style counters off the 12 angles of attack using a 24-inch stick which simulates the bolo. There are approximately 160 counter movements in this style.

2. *Estilo de Abanico*—This is a fanning style encompassing the use of the side of the weapon (stick or blade) to block oncoming attacks. Counterstriking is included, with the emphasis on the tip of your weapon to get the maximum amount of power in short and powerful striking ranges.

"In Estilo Abierta *the student will calculate the opponent's strikes and will open his body position and counterstrike within the same motion, leaving the opponent with little or no counter."*

3. *Estilo Abierta*—This style refers to an open body style of fighting. This style is used by the most advanced students to calculate the distance between themselves and their opponent. The student will calculate the opponent's strikes and will open his body position and counterstrike within the same motion, leaving the opponent with little or no counter.

4. *Estilo de Salon*—This is a dance-like style. This style uses fast and solid footwork that also involves the use of stick work.

5. *Estilo Sonkete*—This is the style of poking and thrusting. As your opponent attacks you can use the components of parrying, blocking, evading, and deflection while applying the counterthrust or poke into the opponent's guard.

6. *Estilo Retirada*—This is a style of retreating used to draw your opponent in or to create an opening in the opponent's defense. Once this has taken place you can use counterstriking to render your opponent helpless. Retreating footwork, evading, and counterstriking is the key.

7. *Estilo Elastico*—An elastic or rubber-band style. It makes use of one's stretching ability to reach a given target. This style is a necessity that is woven into the *larga mano* (long hand) style. Many feel that the person who plays *estilo elastico* possesses superhuman ability and is difficult to defeat.

8. *Fondo Fuerte*—The escrimador's last stand. You must plant yourself effectively into a reliable spot where you can revolve to meet an opponent's attacks without losing ground.

9. *Contra Compas*—These Spanish words mean "against time." In terms of Giron arnis escrima this is a style of striking with off-beat timing or broken rhythm.

10. *Estlio Redonda*—This is a round or circular style of fighting. To be effective in this style you must be able to maneuver your strikes in circular movements horizontally, vertically, and diagonally, from both high and low positions.

"You must plant yourself effectively into a reliable spot where you can revolve to meet an opponent's attacks without losing ground."

11. *Combate Adentro*—This style is used to ward off opponents using paired weapons, such as the sword and dagger. With this style, you defend yourself inside the opponent's circle using solid footwork and slicing counterstrikes.

12. *Tero Grave*—This style implies the use of serious or deadly strikes to critical areas of the body.

13. *Estilo Macabebe*—Macabebe is the name of a town in the province of Pampanga, Philippines. These fierce warriors are famous for the use of two weapons or two sticks. This style is characterized by the interweaving motions of the weapons and is also known as *sinawali*.

14. *Tero Pisada*—This style incorporates the use of double or two-handed striking and blocking. The blocking is so intense that it will paralyze the opponent's hands and will create an opening for your two-handed counterstrike.

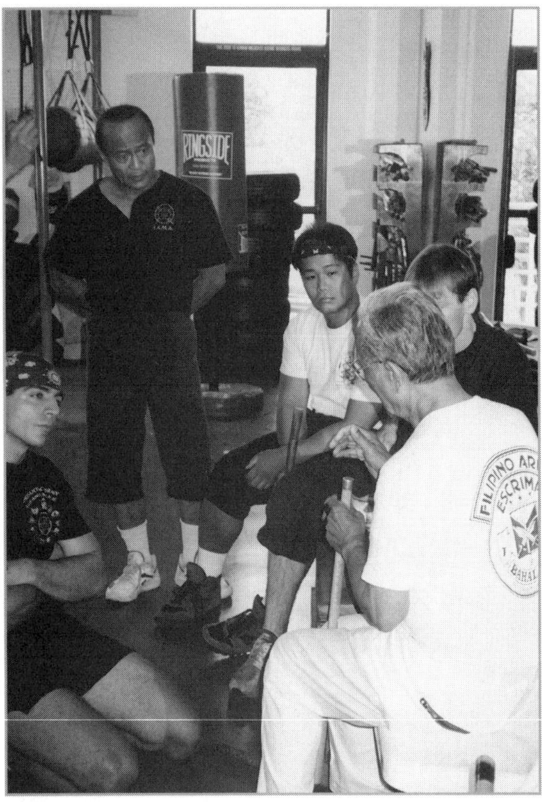

"Cadena de Mano *is a hand-to-hand combat method which uses parrying, grabbing, twisting, locking, and chocking in succession."*

15. *Media Media*—The term "*media media*" implies "half of half." In terms of fighting, the concept refers to fighting at half-range and striking on half-timing.

16. *Cadena de Mano*—This is a hand-to-hand combat method which uses parrying, grabbing, twisting, locking, and chocking in succession. In other words, you chain the hand movements together from close quarters.

17. *Escape*—This style stresses evasion and methods of warding off the opponent's attacks.

18. *Estilo Bolante*—This style is named after a person named Braulio Bolante from Dagupan, Pagasinan, Philippines. This style uses vertical striking patterns and is an excellent method of fighting in doorways and narrow passages.

19. *Miscla (Mezcla) Contras*—This style favors defending yourself against multiple opponents and multiple attacks. It stresses placing oneself in the proper place and position in relation to the opponent.

20. *Largo Mano*—This style maintains long-distance fighting without jeopardizing safety. The counter concept is centered on attacking the closest target of your opponent, and terminating the contest with the first counterstrike.

Q: When did you go overseas for the Army?

A: On December 10, 1943, two of us were shipped to New Guinea but this was a mistake by the Army as we were suppose to go to Australia. So on January 10, 1944, I was sent to Australia to a place called Camp X. It was close to the little town of Beau Desert about 60 miles from the seaport of Brisbane in Queensland. It was there that I furthered my training in Morse code, cryptography, visual communications, et cetera. I also embarked on my final training in jungle warfare in a place called Canungra. Thirteen weeks of hard training contributed to my ability to climb the high mountains of the Philippines and surviving in it's jungles jungles. At one time, for a week's period, we were given only three days of sea rations and the other four days we had to survive on our own. At this point I was a staff sergeant.

"We were loaded and armed with carbines, submachine guns, side arms, bolo knives, trench knives, brass knuckles, ammunition and a few other special packages."

Q: Did you ever meet General Douglas MacArthur?

A: Yes, several times. But on August 10, 1944 I was ordered to a briefing at the General's headquarters. General MacArthur crossed his arms and said to us, "Boys, I selected you to do a job that a general can't do. You have the training to do a job that no one else can. You are going home to our country, the Philippines—yours and my homeland. You'll serve as my eyes, my ears, and my fingers, and you'll keep me informed of what the enemy is doing. You will tell me how to win the war by furnishing me with this information, which I could not obtain in any other way. Good luck, and there will be shinning bars waiting for you in Manila."

Q: How did you land in the Philippines?

A: On August 12, 1944, we boarded one of the smallest submarines in the United States Navy armada—the U.S. Sting Ray. We were loaded and armed with carbines, submachine guns, side arms, bolo knives, trench knives, brass knuckles, ammunition and a few other special packages. While on our way to the Philippines we slept on our own cargo boxes. Myself and one other soldier slept under the torpedo racks. There was one time when we were

"After the encounter I wiped my face with my left hand to clear my eyes from the rain and found bloodstains on my face. The blood had come from my hand. I had felt the twitch on the meaty part of my left palm when I parried the bayonet, but I didn't know that I had been cut."

fired upon and had to out-maneuver several torpedoes at full speed. This occurred near the Halmahera Island on the Celebes Sea. One other time when we were attack was in Caonayan Bay just before disembarking the submarine. The attack occurred when a Japanese warplane dropped depth charges on us. They came close enough to rattle the sub and burst some pipes but luckily this was the extent of the damage. We landed on the beach on August 28, 1944.

Q: What was the most memorable encounter you had with the enemy?

A: Well, it is hard to try to choose one particular encounter because they were all very horrifying. One *banzai* attack particularly comes to mind. In early June, 1945, on a rainy day, an enemy platoon detected us and charged our position. We formed in a wedge or triangle formation, two on the side and one point man in front—me. Just like any *banzai* charge the enemy was very noisy. Yelling and shouting, they were not afraid to die. The Filipino guerrillas, on the other hand, would chew their tobacco, grit their teeth, and swing their bolos in deadly and eerie silence. They would chop here and jab there with long bolos, short daggers, and pointed bamboo. They pulverized chili peppers with sand and deposited the mixture in bamboo tubes to spray the enemies' eyes, so they couldn't see. As the enemy closed, my adrenaline shot up and a bayonet and a samurai sword came at me simultaneously. The samurai sword was in front of me while the bayonet was a little to the left. With my left hand I parried the bayonet and with my stick I blocked the sword coming down on me. The bayonet man went by and his body came in line with my bolo, so I slashed down and cut his left hip. The samurai came back with a backhand blow and I met his tricep with the bolo, chopping it to the ground.

After the encounter I wiped my face with my left hand to clear my eyes from the rain and found bloodstains on my face. The blood had come from my hand. I had felt the twitch on the meaty part of my left palm when I parried the bayonet, but I didn't know that I had been cut. There were many more encounters but we were not there to fight. Our job was to not be detected by the enemy and to send back vital information about troop movements and strength to headquarters.

"What the student should be interested in, is to learn how to defend themselves and their family against aggression. The correct attitude is to say, 'I am going to survive and not get hurt.'"

Q: When did you start teaching the art of arnis escrima?
A: In October, 1968 I decided to open a club in Tracy, California, where I was residing at the time. I was motivated after I heard on the news that a man in Chicago killed eight nursing students and some of the nurses were Filipinas. I wanted to teach people to defend themselves against senseless violence.

Q: Why did you name your martial art association "Bahala Na?"
A: It was the slogan of my outfit during World War II. I am proud of the men I fought with during World War II and of the spirit of my fallen comrades; I hold the memories of all of those I fought with in very high regard and close to my heart. I also can associate the combative spirit we had during the time of World War II with our training. Because of this I feel I have the right to use the slogan of "Bahala Na." It means "Come What May."

Q: What makes a good student?
A: A person with good passive resistance. You must have patience and not be to eager to win and be the champion. What the student should be interested in, is to learn how to defend themselves and their family against aggression. The end result will be that you will survive, and this makes you victorious. You do not need to say, "I am going to win and defeat my opponent." The

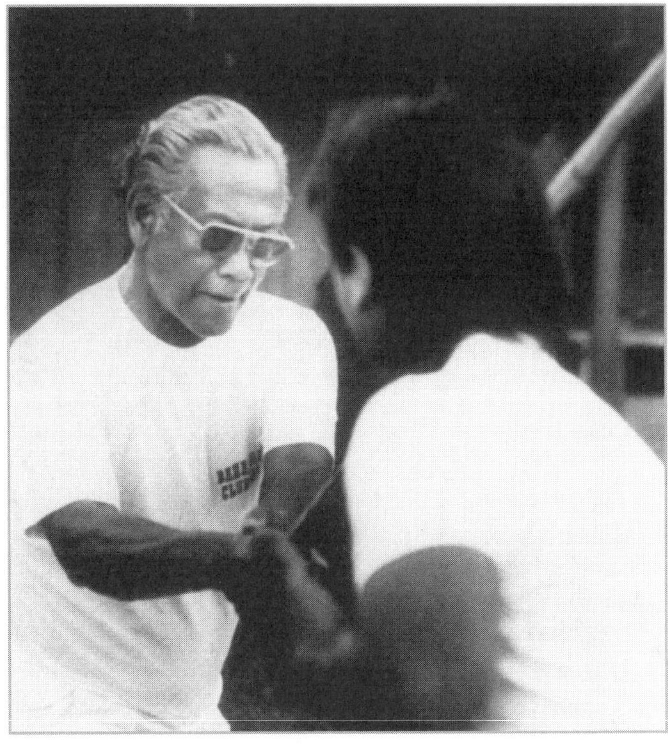

"It's different teaching during peacetime—you must have structure and good communication with your students. I like to teach more about the application and fundamentals."

correct attitude is to say, "I am going to survive and not get hurt." That's what counts. If you hold your discipline and your style during the battle, the other man will eventually make a mistake, fall into a loophole, and give you an opening—he will defeat himself.

Q: Did your experience during World War II help you to become a better teacher?
A: I know the respect of the bolo knife. Wartime is different. There is no regard for life. It's different teaching during peacetime—you must have structure and good communication with your students. I like to teach more about the application and fundamentals. It's not about how hard you hit or who is faster, its about sharing the art of our forefathers. Because if you analyze it, we are only the caretakers of the art for future generations.

Q: Why do you still teach escrima?
A: Well, first of all, it's my hobby. I have the chance to stretch my legs, work my arms, and exercise my body. I feel it is a gift to be able to learn a combative art like escrima, and being that it falls in the field of sports it is good to have and know something that not many people know. I feel proud that I have something to share with the children of my friends and with those who want to learn an art that is different than other martial arts. I feel that the Filipino art is a superior art in comparison to other arts, so I stand firm in saying that I am proud that I have learned and know the art of escrima.

Q: There have been reports of many escrima masters who have fought in death matches. Have you ever fought in a death match?

A: No, I have never fought in a death match. From what I understand, in order to participate in a death match you need to have a referee and a second—or a person in your corner similar to a boxing match. The only type of death match I had was during World War II. That was were I fought in the jungles for over a year, not knowing if I would survive from one day to the next. Our weapons of choice were the bolo knife or *talonason*—a long knife over was 36 inches long. There was no referee and no rules—the only rule was to survive.

"Practitioners should focus on the general benefits of martial arts, from self-defense to using it as a way to achieve a better life, instead of trying to be a deadly fighting machine. We should strive to be better human beings."

Q: What's your advice to martial arts practitioners today?

A: There seems to be an unstoppable, growing mentality of a need to fight and engage in combat in the current martial arts community. I fought for my life in a real war, and it is not glamorous or pleasant. Practitioners should focus on the general benefits of martial arts, from self-defense to using it as a way to achieve a better life, instead of trying to be a deadly fighting machine. We should strive to be better human beings—that should be the final goal of any martial art. Our goal should be to avoid fighting and to preserve life, not take enjoyment in hurting others and destroying life.

Master Giron faces his armed aggressor (1). As the aggressor tries to cut, Master Giron avoids and catches the opponent's arm (2) applying a wristlock to control the situation (3).

1

2

3

The aggressor begins his attack (1) to the stomach but Master Giron blocks with his left hand and strikes with the right hand to the face (2) followed by a knee strike to the stomach (3).

1

2

3

Master Giron faces his opponent (1). As the aggressor attacks, Master Giron covers from the inside (2) and checking with his left hand, applies a finishing strike to the stomach (3).

Master Giron waits for the attack (1). He blocks the incoming circular attack with an inside block and a check of his left hand (2) and delivers a finishing blow to the opponent's head (3).

Master Giron receives the incoming attack with shield block (1) that passes over to the outside with a twist of his wrist (2) which allows him to place himself on the other side of the attack (3) to control the aggression with applying any fatal blow (4).

Master Giron faces his opponent (1) who attacks him to the right side of the solar plexus. Master Giron reacts blocking to the outside (2) and pushing the arm away (3) to apply a final blow to the aggressor's arm (4).

Joseph Halbuna

The Hard Way

He is one of kajukenbo's old guard. His techniques and words are direct and to the point, with no beating around the bush. Joe Halbuna kept alive the tradition started by Professor Adriano D. Emperado many years ago, when he founded the kajukenbo system.

Respectful of other arts, Professor Halbuna doesn't hesitate to clarify some of the main aspects of the art. He advocates the "hard way" of doing things. He began his kajukenbo training with Joe Emperado at the YMCA in Honolulu. His teachings come from the bottom of his heart and his words leave no room for misunderstanding. He is a successful tournament promoter and is responsible for tournaments such as The Battle of the Bay, The Golden Bear, and The Hawaiian Open Karate Championships, held in the Hawaiian islands.

His dedication and love for the art of kajukenbo is evident in his every sentence. After all his years of training and teaching, Professor Joe Halbuna is still one of the few old masters who can show the new generations the right way.

Q: When did you begin your martial arts training?
A: It was in 1955 under Joe Emperado. Joe Emperado was Professor Adriano D. Emperado's brother. In 1962, I moved to San Francisco and opened my first school. A little bit later, in 1964, I opened a new school in Pacifica, California.

Q: Who were the main kajukenbo instructors at that time?
A: The Emperado family, obviously, but in the Bay Area the main instructors were Al Dacascos, Professor Charles Gaylord, Professor Tony Ramos, Al Reyes, and myself. We were close to each other and there was great communication among us. Those five instructors spread kajukenbo all over California.

"When a kajukenbo instructor decided to open a school, he couldn't charge a lot of money for the classes. The training was very rugged and a lot of people used to leave the school complaining. The instructor couldn't make a living and he to do something else to survive."

Q: Was it difficult to move kajukenbo from Hawaii to the Mainland?

A: In 1962, 80 percent of the California instructors were from Hawaii and only 20 percent were from Japan, China, and Korea. Ten years later, a lot of Korean instructors began to land in the state and teach taekwondo and tang soo do. At that time, the art of kajukenbo was not as popular as the other arts. It wasn't very commercial and the way it was taught didn't help to bring new students. When a kajukenbo instructor decided to open a school, he couldn't charge a lot of money for the classes. The training was very rugged and a lot of people used to leave the school complaining. The instructor couldn't make a living and he to do something else to survive.

Q: What was the main reason for creating the kajukenbo system?

A: James Mitose's system and William Chow's method weren't good enough for Professor Adriano Emperado. He began to research other martial arts systems such as kung-fu, jiu-jitsu, judo, et cetera. Five different people got together in order to combine the very best of their research. They created a system that would be useful to protect them on the street. That's why the kajukenbo art is so strong, because it is based on the reality of the street. Sijo Emperado was a revolutionary pioneer and had a very open mind, so he didn't limit the approach to his system. When you have an open mind you can incorporate a lot of good things into your style. If you close your mind, your appreciation of the fighting systems will be very narrow.

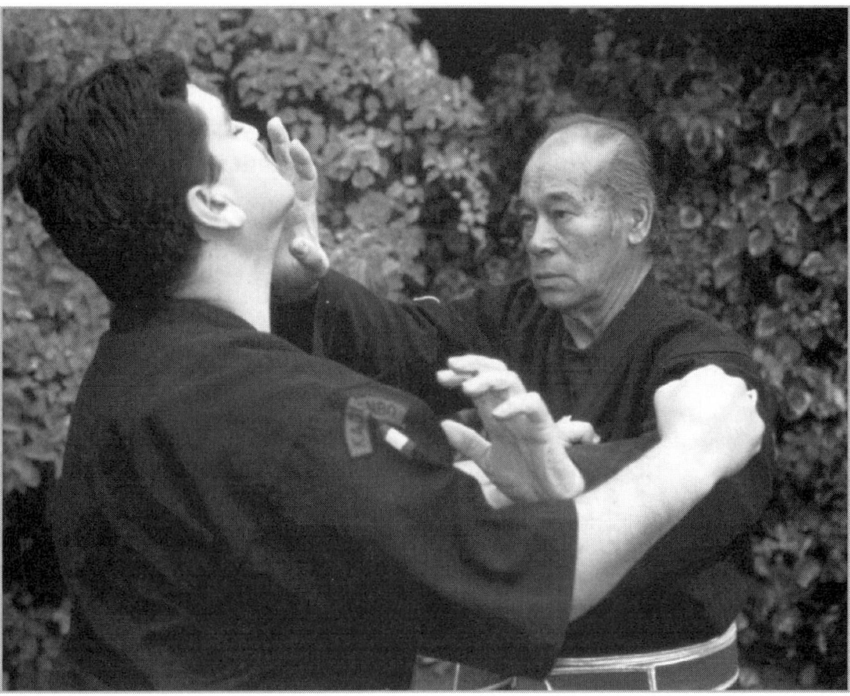

"When you have an open mind you can incorporate a lot of good things into your style. If you close your mind, your appreciation of the fighting systems will be very narrow."

Q: What was the main difference between kajukenbo instructors and teachers from other styles?
A: The kajukenbo instructors were teaching from the heart, they weren't looking for money. They were advocating traditional teaching. If we had decided to commercialize kajukenbo, the teachers would be millionaires by now. In 1962 and 1963 there were no karate schools, only judo schools. Our idea was not making money but teaching the art of kajukenbo the right way. We didn't have any contracts nor charged a lot of money. Teachers from other styles did.

Q: Is it still the same today?
A: Yes. If you visit a kajukenbo school these days, you'll find that only a 20 percent is business and the other 80 percent is teaching from the heart. Unfortunately, in other schools, it is 80 percent business and 20 percent

"In a commercial school you can't teach and train very hard because the people will drop out. If students leave the school or get injured because of the physical contact, you're not gonna be making money."

sharing the art from the heart. Some instructors don't realize that if it is money you are looking for, you'll miss the great opportunity to correctly share the art. In a commercial school you can't teach and train very hard because the people will drop out. If students leave the school or get injured because of the physical contact, you're not gonna be making money. If you teach the hard way, you won't have a lot of students. Hit slow and soft and you'll make a lot of money. That's what is happening these days.

Q: Which kajukenbo instructors were personally trained by you?
A: Fortunately, we have a lot of great teachers all over the world. Some of them have received the kajukenbo knowledge from my hands. This includes Max Togisala, Lucky Luciano, Frank Bianchi, Frank Conway, Bob Maschmeier, Angel García, and our European representative. I have a lot of students who are 4th and 5th degree black belts. I never believed in the easy way. Therefore, I haven't promoted a whole lot of students. If I had done it the "easy way," I would have hundreds of high ranking disciples now.

Q: It is true that Thomas Barro Mitose was your student?
A: Yes, he was. He was a student at my San Francisco school in 1963. He used to train very hard and was very dedicated. He earned a black belt in kajukenbo, but he was James Mitose's son and had to continue the kosho shorei-ryu tradition. When he went to his father's art I told him that he had my blessing. I understood what he had to do. His martial arts roots are in kajukenbo system but his blood was Mitose's. I feel very proud of him.

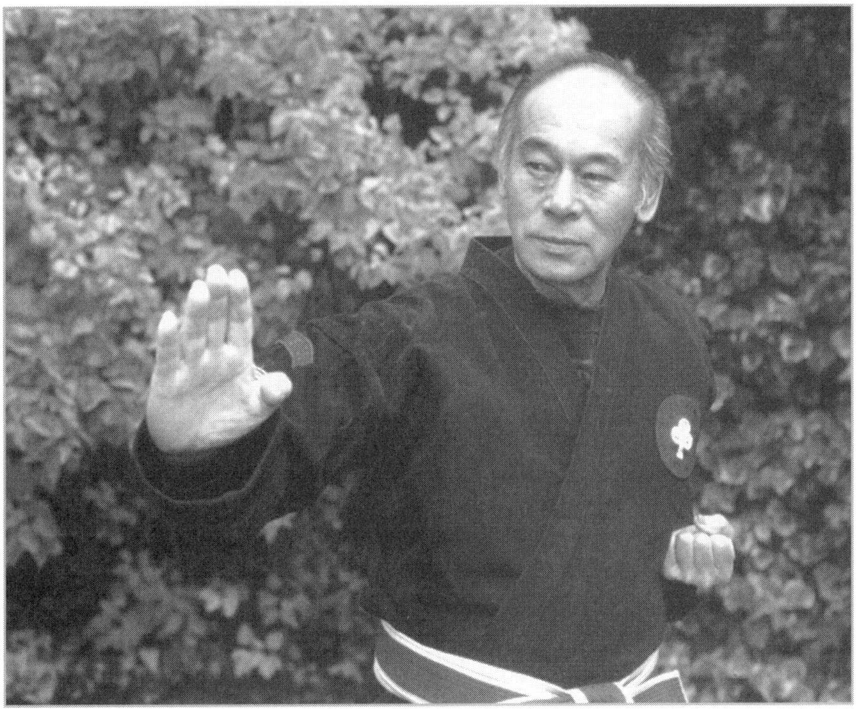

"The technical aspects are just one of the many requirements for a black belt. But I have to be sure that the attitude is correct and they are very respectful of their elders and the practitioner of other styles."

Q: What are your requirements for a black belt in kajukenbo?
A: The technical aspects are just one of the many requirements for a black belt. Of course, the student needs to have the technical knowledge and extensive understanding of the kajukenbo art. But I have to be sure that the attitude is correct and they are very respectful of their elders and the practitioner of other styles.

Q: Why have you only trained in kajukenbo?
A: I love kajukenbo, but I also know how to appreciate other martial arts. I firmly believe that all the styles are the same—they teach you to protect yourself. So I don't see the point in creating jealousy between different systems. I think all martial artists should be working together. Teaching respect is something very important, and unfortunately I don't see this aspect being taught in many schools now.

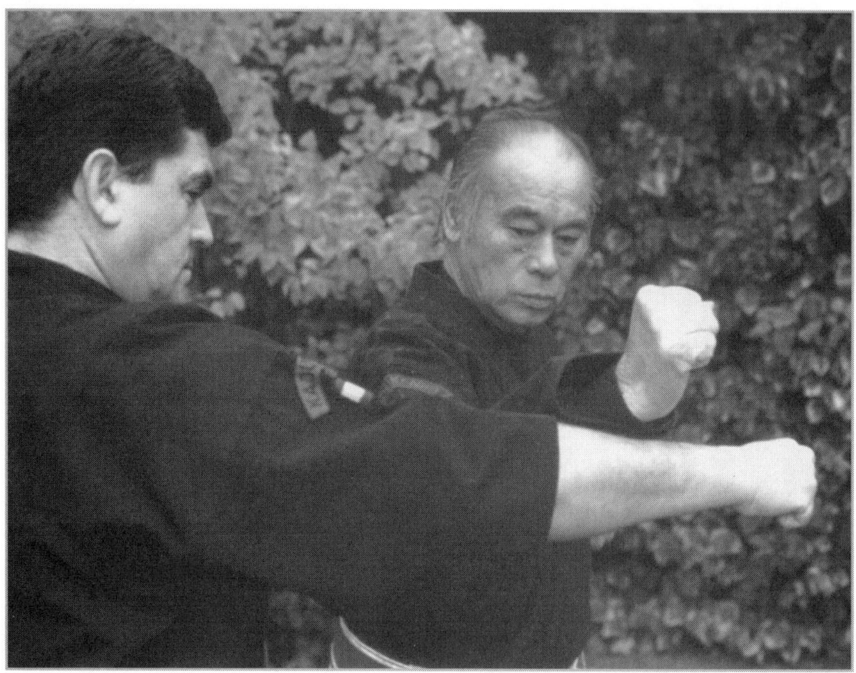

"I think all martial artists should be working together. Teaching respect is something very important, and unfortunately I don't see this aspect being taught in many schools now."

Q: Which aspect of kajukenbo do you enjoy the most?
A: I believe that kajukenbo has everything. It has karate, kenpo, judo, jiu-jitsu, kung-fu and escrima. It doesn't matter what you do within the system, it will still be kajukenbo. Even if you learn the other side of one of these systems, it's still kajukenbo. That's why we teach our students to have a wide technical spectrum. Sijo Emperado told me once: "Joe, it doesn't matter what you do or what you add to the system. It will be kajukenbo anyway."

Q: Do you use a common thread when you add something new?
A: There are certain basic principles used in kajukenbo, but the system evolves according to the practitioner's level of understanding. When you get old, you might exchange the strength element of karate for the soft aspects of kung-fu. On other hand, some kajukenbo practitioners lean more towards the

hard side, as I've been doing all these years. Conversely, other instructors like Al Dacascos prefer to use the soft aspects in his personal expression of the art.

Q: What's your opinion about combat sports such as kickboxing and the UFC?

A: Well, all these sports are OK. They teach you how to react under a certain kind of pressure in a ring and that's perfectly fine. But the way I was raised in kajukenbo was not to look at a fight as a sport, but as survival. When you are involved in a real fight, it is very different than any kind of combat sport. I think this type of competition may help the student, but the real and final test is on the street and in the street there are no rules. None.

Q: What do you think of people who only look for the "flowering" techniques in martial arts?

A: It is probably good for impressing your friends at a party, but I think it is a stupid idea to practice martial arts just to learn pretty moves that will be useless in a real fight. You have to learn to defend yourself on the street. You have to feel sure about what you're learning. If the material you're learning is not practical for the street, then you're living in fantasyland. I teach the practical techniques to my students. Other instructors can teach what they want.

The opponent seizes Joseph Halbuna's lapels with both hands (1). Halbuna blocks both arms to the outside (2) and steps-in applying a upward elbow to the chin (3) and follows up with a neck control and an upward knee (4) and a groin kick to finish him off (5).

Master Halbuna and his opponent square off (1). As his opponent punches, Master Halbuna sidesteps blocking with his right hand (2) and follows up with a hammer fist to the groin (3) a backfist to the temple (4) and a heel hook kick to the opponent's groin (5).

1

2

3

4

5

Facing an opponent, Master Halbuna waits to defend himself (1). As his aggressor attacks with a front hand punch, Halbuna blocks it with a left inward forearm motion (2) and turns around to apply a rear elbow strike (3) followed by a hammer fist to the groin (4) and a knife hand chop to the back of the neck (5).

Halbuna squares off with his opponent (1). As his opponent launches a front punch, Halbuna covers himself with a outside block and (2), delivers a lateral elbow attack to the aggressor's midsection (3), and stepping back to adapt his striking distance (4), applies an upward knee (5).

STEPHEN K. HAYES
TO-SHIN DO

Stephen Hayes

Out of the Shadows and into the Spotlight

After dreaming of finding a martial arts teacher as a child, he began his training as a teenager in the mid-1960s in Korean karate, earning a 3rd degree black belt. In his quest for "anything goes" pragmatism he also experimented with aikido and other fighting methods. Looking for the ultimate art, he decided to give up everything and move to Japan to train in ninjutsu, the legendary art of the "invisible warriors." In 1975, he became the first American to be accepted as a personal student of Togakure Ryu Ninjustu Grandmaster Masaaki Hatsumi. After many years of training in the home of Master Hatsumi, he returned to United States as a shidohi, *a common ninjutsu term used to describe those capable students who "left master's personal instruction to found training organizations on their own." He founded the Shadows of Iga Ninja society, and was the first to invite Grandmaster Hatsumi to visit the U.S.A. in 1982. That same year, he was awarded the grandmaster's Kokusai Yukosho medallion in recognition of his efforts in bringing ninjutsu to the Western world.*

Q: When did you start training and why?

A: When I was a kid I lived in Ohio, and there were no martial arts instructors around. So with a couple of wrestling lessons and some judo books I tried to teach myself. My first "official" martial art was taekwondo in 1962, but it wasn't until 1975 that I decided to go to Japan to find a teacher of ninjutsu. My first introduction to the art of ninjutsu was from a James Bond novel which I read in high school. I was really fascinated with the whole idea. The reason why I started to train is because, as a child, there was something inside of me that wanted to be prepared to handle any situation—intellectual, physical, or emotional—that might occur in life. My family always encouraged me to be a gentleman, to be considerate of other people, et cetera, and I was never beaten up or attacked as a child. But like I said, there was something intrinsic in my nature about wanting to be prepared to handle any situation. Everybody was crazy about Bruce Lee and kung-fu, but I went to Japan to study an art nobody had ever heard of! I

"When I met Master Hatsumi I knew that he was the warrior-sage I dreamed of as a child."

firmly held the belief that the Oriental martial arts were combative ways of enlightenment that could make your life better. When I met Master Hatsumi I knew that he was the warrior-sage I dreamed of as a child.

Q: Ninjutsu is a very old art. Do you consider yourself a traditionalist?
A: Well, if you think about how old that art is—over 34 generations and eight centuries of history—I guess I'm very traditional. But some people think I'm not because of the clothes I wear and some of the modern weapons I use.

Q: What was it like in Japan, when you decided to move there and receive martial arts instruction?
A: Well, I had to sell everything I had in United States in order to get over there. I didn't have much money so my life there was very, very humble. The physical training was very hard and brutal. Don't forget they weren't teaching the art in those days. They were training and we were their dummies. They practiced the techniques on us and we had to try our best to steal the art from them. Just by watching and being on the receiving end, we

were able to learn the art. Of course things changed after a few years, when they realized that I was serious about the art and I was going to stay there. Only then did they took good care of me and make sure I received all the training.

"I remember that I was very happy about being accepted for the training but later on I found out that the reason they accepted me was because I was big and they thought it would be fun to train with me."

Q: How did you feel emotionally?
A: Like I said, the physical training was hard. But because I was doing what I wanted to do and everything was a new adventure I was very happy. It was a wonderful experience to be there fulfilling my dreams. I remember that I was very happy about being accepted for the training but later on I found out that the reason they accepted me was because I was big and they thought it would be fun to train with me.

Q: You studied under Master Hatsumi for many years. Why did you strike out on your own?
A: Well, it is not that I'm suddenly on my own now—you're always on your own. Going out on your own is something inevitable. Eventually, any warrior has to go out and take risks without the comfort of having his teacher behind him. Also—and this is not a good reason—some people have a big ego and they need to be seen as a world authority in whatever they are doing.

Q: In the '80s, ninjutsu was a big success. Did you see the art as business?
A: To me, ninjutsu has always been a very personal thing. This is the way I live my life. Since I was a kid I wanted to learn the art of the warrior. To be honest, I was never fascinated with the image of Stephen Hayes the martial art. I was doing this for myself, not for anybody else. I felt I had gone as far as I could with what I had learned in Japan. I ran a little workout group here and there but resisted having my own school. The reason for this is that I was more interested in my own personal growth that in my students' progress. I felt I needed more proof of what I was exploring as a martial artist. If you are trying to teach too soon, you are teaching from a pretty shallow reservoir of experience.

"Unfortunately, there is a tendency in some people to reduce everything to a simple answer—and that's not possible—nothing is really that simple. A part of the science of martial arts is looking at the emotions."

Q: What are the strong points of the art?

A: It looks for total warrior pragmatism. The student is not taught to think about any limitations at all. Whatever technique does the job effectively is what it should be used—especially in life and death combat. Of course we place a lot of emphasis on the development of spiritual power through meditation and energy channeling drills. Unfortunately, there is a tendency in some people to reduce everything to a simple answer—and that's not possible—nothing is really that simple. A part of the science of martial arts is looking at the emotions—in the mind anyplace where weakness can dwell. As a teacher I would be very negligent if I did not address those areas of the mind when I'm teaching my students.

Q: When you came back from Japan and started to popularized the art of ninjutsu, you had several critics.

A: Some, but they never bothered me personally. I knew from day one that was going to happen. My teacher, Master Hatsumi told me that any person with a small spotlight on him will have people resent him and antagonize with him. I don't like to argue so I could deal with that fairly well. The problem was that a lot of people came to me because I was the only American who had ever trained in Japan, so it was very hard for me to tell who the fans were and who wanted learn the art. Even when I was in Japan there were people who didn't like my being there, and there are a few of the Japanese today who I don't think regard me very highly. But I think it is more of a human characteristic than a racial thing.

Q: Some people have speculated that you might be Master Hatsumi's successor in the ninjutsu style of togakure-ryu. Is that true?
A: No, I never wanted that. It was never my personal goal so it is not true. Some people made that thing up probably just to create controversy.

Q: What is your personal goal?
A: I don't look for fame or popularity. I like to see myself as someone who helped to bring something important into people's life, more like a bridge for the ninjutsu art. I'm sure that Master Hatsumi's successor will be someone closer to the real essence of the style. I'm trying to make some timeless principles in my daily life. That's all.

"The arts that I studied in Japan are ageless. I never changed the principles and the time-tested foundations, but I incorporated other insights from my personal background."

Q: Have you made any innovations in ninjutsu?
A: You have to adapt things, but that's part of the arts philosophy, so it is hard to say that I changed anything. The systems are based on innovation since it was founded in the late 1100s. So innovation is part of the tradition. But I understand your question. Yes, I adapted the ninjustu principles to modern Western situations that are unlikely in the Japanese culture where I was trained. In fact, Master Hatsumi used to get after me if I failed to keep up the innovations. The arts that I studied in Japan are ageless. I never changed the principles and the time-tested foundations, but I incorporated other insights from my personal background. I would say that I arranged and interpreted the principles of Master Hatsumi so it will better serve our students. Our training provides direct instruction in the skills needed to succeed in life. Of course, that self-protection is an important issue but we are more likely to feel attacked by other factors such as lack of confident will, lack of focus, et cetera. The full program of authentic ninjut-

"You need total creativity in using you body, mind and the environment for surviving a real fight. A real fight is a potential death or maiming, so there no time for half-committed actions."

su covers every possible thing that we could consider an area of improvement in life. Unfortunately, some individuals want only a certificate with the word "ninja" on it. Perhaps they don't feel that they want to go through all they would have to in order to authentically earn the word. They don't want to change, and they really don't want to grow and go through anything is painful or awkward.

Q: Do you regret anything?

A: No. I know that in the early '80s I was in the spotlight and I wasn't all that seasoned. I was in a position to have done big things in the entertainment industry but I felt that would have compromised my whole message so I declined. Maybe I was wrong, maybe I could reach even a higher number of people and do more for the world. I don't know. At that time I was really amazed that without any kind of promotion, I was receiving thousands of inquiries from people around the world interested in becoming my students.

Q: Why did you turn them down?

A: I'm a very private person—very conservative. But I remember that my father used to tell me that people like to be entertained rather than educated, so maybe I should have accepted some movie deals and entertained people in order to educate them. I realize, now, that entertainment industry is the key to get any message across to people.

Q: What's your philosophy of fighting?

A: You need total creativity in using you body, mind and the environment for surviving a real fight. A real fight is a potential death or maiming, so there no time for half-committed actions. In ninjutsu there no such thing as blocking. Even the defensive moves carry the capability to control or damage the opponent's body or limbs. The seriousness of a real fight can't be underplayed. You know, that these days nobody can tell how far an aggressor will go.

Q: Have you studied other arts?
A: For anyone who call himself a serious practitioner, it is very important to look at what other great teachers are doing. I have worked with karate people, aikido people, Filipino escrima teachers, Thai boxers, et cetera, since I believe it is my responsibility as a teacher to get as much scope as I possibly can. It is not that I've incorporated their systems or anything like that, but what I have done is to add some types of attacks and types of movements that our students would have to deal with. Of course, I keep training with other teachers of my own martial arts system. I'm always studying to advance my knowledge.

"I have worked with karate people, aikido people, Filipino escrima teachers, Thai boxers, et cetera, since I believe it is my responsibility as a teacher to get as much scope as I possibly can. Of course, I keep training with other teachers of my own martial arts system."

Q: Have you tried to go away from the negative aspects of the ninjas, such as their image as assassins?
A: It is true that the word ninja had some negative reaction in a lot of people, but I really look forward to the day when ninjutsu will be taught as karate or kung-fu—as a martial art. I think some day the art of ninjutsu will get rid of that image and will be a legitimate martial art being taught with training methods and correct philosophy.

Q: Is it true you worked for the Dalai Lama?
A: Yes, I did and it was a great pleasure. One of my personal goals was to go to Tibet, which I did, and we developed a relationship after that. I was granted an audience with him in 1986. He asked me about my personal feeling and impressions of the Tibetan people. After another three personal meetings, he asked me to become his personal security escort. It is one thing to train with your friends and another to protect somebody from a possible harm that can come from anywhere. I must say that being in that position was a great way to test and season my studies of the martial arts. You

"I like to be in positions where I'm not the boss. I went to different places to learn different things where I was not the so-called authority."

learn a lot about how to deal with the possibility of danger.

Q: How is Stephen Hayes' life these days?
A: Very quiet. I have some dojos that I visit regularly. Then I have my training center in Ohio and I usually go to Japan once or twice a year.

Q: You mentioned that you like to put yourself in difficult positions. Why?
A: What I meant is that I like to be in positions where I'm not the boss. I went to different places to learn different things where I was not the so-called authority. Once I went to a Zen archery temple just because the teachings were so different from my approach to the arts.

Q: Do you follow any particular diet?
A: I really like the rural Japanese diet—unpolished rice, miso soup, sea plants, uncooked vegetables, et cetera—but I also eat Western food, of course.

Q: Grappling has been the latest craze in the martial arts community, does ninjutsu use this combative aspect?
A: Of course, ninjutsu teaches grappling skills, but it does not use them in the sportive sense. Grappling skills are important to real street survival. When I traveled to Japan for the first time I had no grappling skill whatsoever, and they realized that right away, so the ninja teachers used to wrestle with me until I got choked. I had to develop the skills very fast!

Q: How important is breathing in your art?
A: Breathing is very important—not only in ninjutsu also but in life! I think this aspect is often overlooked in martial arts teaching and too much emphasis is placed on the raw combative motions alone. To understand and control breathing is the key to directing our won energy. This is the only

way to real power. If a martial artist relies only on his muscles will lose his strength as he advances in years.

"The way you deal with a gloved fist or in a ring is far different from the one needed to prevail in a vicious barehanded life or death struggle."

Q: What do you think of full-contact kickboxing matches and no-holds-barred fights?

A: It is a great way to test the courage, stamina, and skill of individual fighters. But many people think that these events are the ultimate application of the martial arts and do not correctly see it as just one small piece of the total training one needs for street survival. The way you deal with a gloved fist or in a ring is far different from the one needed to prevail in a vicious barehanded life or death struggle. On the other hand we all know that in the no-holds-barred fights, there are actually many rules. In the street there are none. Neither the requirements needed to survive in the street nor the tactics and strategies of street defense are the same needed to win a championship. Environment dictates.

Q: What do you mean?

A: In ninjutsu I learned to adapt certain principles to the environment or the way a person is dressed. It is very different living in Philippines, where you are wearing a T-shirt all the time, than living in Quebec in wintertime wearing a big, thick coat. The fighting techniques have to adapt and change.

On other hand, people look for self-defense, but not everybody is a physical specimen and has the fighting instincts of a Joe Lewis—so they have to learn how to be tricky. That's what I try to do, teach some tricks so they can find what works.

Q: How do you think other martial artists could benefit from ninjutsu training?

A: First of all, I'm talking about the view of the art. Other people took the principles and developed it in a very different way. I believe that all martial artists can benefit from ninjutsu because the art emphasizes the practical

"What I've found is that in many cases people are afraid of facing their own fears and so are quick to criticize or attack others who are being honest."

concepts that make martial arts training more realistic and therefore more geared towards real life benefits. Any practitioner can begin by realistically reassessing all that is involved in actual street fighting and allow their training system to reflect that reality. What I've found is that in many cases people are afraid of facing their own fears and so are quick to criticize or attack others who are being honest.

Q: You talk about ninjutsu as being a lifestyle.
A: Yes, that's what the art is for me, a way of life—a philosophy used to look at daily life. I'd like to return to the idea of martial arts being a lifestyle more than simply a method of punching and kicking. To do this, you have to analyze what's going on in your mind and where the conflict and the fear is coming from. We have to face many fights every day at the job, the office, the freeway, et cetera. We have thousands of these fights but, comparatively speaking, we might have a couple of real fights in our lifetime—perhaps none. That's the reason we have to look for the parallels in daily life, so that the physical way of handling a situation can provide models for understanding how we could win out in psychological conflicts, too. The techniques and strategies of ninjutsu have been adapted as lessons for taking control of life in a way that leads to happiness and safety.

Q: You have ended up creating your own style called To-Shin Do. Don't you think some people may think that you are disloyal to your origins?
A: To be honest, I think this the highest form of compliment that a student can give to a teacher, in my case master Masaaki Hatsumi. I learned a lot from him, I went through all the necessary phases in his program and now I am into the phase where I can create something new based on all the knowledge he passed on to me.

What I'm trying to do is provide the students with useful modern training in self-defense. I emphasize the real approach to our modern society and, of course, contemporary weapons are taught in order to be able to deal with certain kind of situations. "To" means sword. It represents the technology of the mechanical knowledge and conditioning of our martial art. "Shin" means "heart and mind" as one word. "Shin" also represents the greater lesson to be learned in the arts—lessons that go beyond the physical phase … for example, how to win in a verbal intimidation scenario.

"My real message remains to recognize what our dreams are as individuals, to be true to our hearts, and follow those things that will fulfill us as human beings."

Q: Are you sad to see how the art of ninjutsu has been treated?
A: Yes, definitely. I saw a lot of people "playing games" and calling it ninjutsu. This kind of attitude brought a lot of bad attention which, in the end, made a laughing stock of authentic ninja arts. Then, of course, there were the movies and other media stuff that brought a lot of misunderstanding about what the real ninjutsu art is all about.

Q: Do you study Zen?
A: Yes. After training I spent most of my time working at home in the woods or garden ripping out trees and clawing up rock, et cetera. It is a very good way to build up devastating combat strength. Authentic martial arts training is not a toy. Every martial artist should examine themselves thoroughly as human beings. My real message remains to recognize what our dreams are as individuals, to be true to our hearts, and follow those things that will fulfill us as human beings. ↄ

The attacker grabs Stephen Hayes' arm and fires off a hit to the face to which Hayes reacts by shifting sideways and grabbing his opponent's hand to pull him off balance (1). This forcer the punch to miss wildly (3). Using lateral stepping footwork, Hayes moves so far past his opponent's center that the attacker cannot hit with his original grabbing hand (4). Hayes then turns into and elbow-breaking arm bar (5) and steps back to lock into the elbow bar.

1

2

3

4

The aggressor grabs Hayes' arm and threatens him (1). An instant later, he fires off a sudden blunt punch to the face (2). Hayes drops his right shoulder toward his aggressor's centerline, allowing the punch to fly off target (3). Hayes rocks back and away, pulling his opponent's punching arm out where it cannot reset for an effective second hit (4). Then he lifts his wrist and rolls them over while stepping back to straighten his adversary's arm (5). Hayes sets up a wristlock with his aggressor's momentum (6). While his adversary works at escaping (7), Hayes throws a kick to the groin (8).

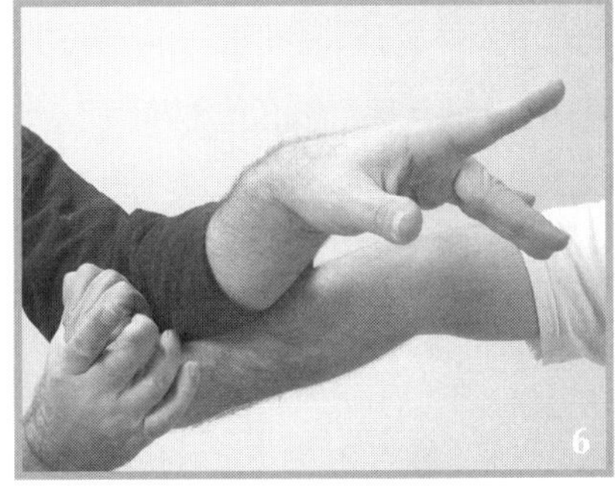

Heo In Hwan

Master of the New Millennium

He is the world leader of the hapkido system known as "hankido." Its conceptual structure resembles the Japanese art of aikido, and the techniques are based on the "circular motion" principle. Based on tradition, but open to new forms and training ideas, this icon of Korean martial arts has evolved to the highest levels of skill and understanding. The way he explains the philosophy and technical foundation of his art, using common sense and keen logic, is refreshing and soothing in these days when martial arts in general are leading us to more combative and violent approaches. Master Heo In Hwan is a living example of how the past and the future can work together.

Q: Can you explain your martial arts system?
A: Of course. The art of hankido is a very complete system. I practiced other systems such as taekwondo, boxing, et cetera, before being introduced to hankido. This method teaches different approaches for using the body as a self-defense tool. Its final goal is to develop the practitioner both physically and spiritually.

Q: Is there any kind of competition in the hankido system?
A: No, there's no competition in hankido because we decided to preserve the martial roots of the art. The sportive aspects of the martial arts might be OK if addressed in the proper way. Unfortunately, too much sport is not positive if what you're looking for is a true martial art. Hankido is a traditional martial art without competition. We don't trade popularity for a watered-down combat system. I understand that sport competition helps a lot as far as the promotional aspects are concern, but our goal is self-defense and inner-energy development.

Q: How long does it take to master the basics?
A: I would say that in three or four months the very basics can be learned. If your mind thinks it is easy then it will be so. Your state of mind is very

"In Korea there is not a big difference in the hapkido art. Although there are several schools and branches they respect to each other and got together for big demonstrations. All schools have the same goal—to promote the real hapkido."

important because it dictates your will to train and progress in the art. Technique wise, the system is divided into 12 basic forms that can be applied with a partner when the student advances to the next level of proficiency. The techniques are varied and include punches, kicks, locks, throws, et cetera. This is the basic program in the hankido art and its understanding will open new avenues for the higher stages of the system.

Q: Is the art of hankido similar to hapkido?
A: All the hapkido systems have the same base. According to the teacher's preferences, each style focuses on different aspects of martial arts. This is OK and happens in every martial arts style. There are many schools or branches in the hapkido art in America, but the foundations are the same. In Korea there is not a big difference in the hapkido art. Although there are several schools and branches they respect to each other and got together for big demonstrations. All schools have the same goal—to promote the real hapkido.

Q: Watching you perform the hankido techniques, it's very easy to tell some differences to other hapkido styles.
A: Yes, we use circular motion very much. Our system is not only about applying locks but mainly about using the opponent's energy to control the situation. The big difference can be found in the application of the inner energy and the overall mentality. The hardest part in the hankido training is to control our own body, not the opponent's.

Q: What it is the technique known as *hwan won chon ki bup?*
A: It is the complete set of the twelve basic techniques in the art of hankido. In this set, the student finds the complete foundation comprised of stances,

"From the technical point of view, the student should pay attention to the development of the basics. This is paramount. Then he needs the right mentality and attitude for the training. Strive to develop yourself as a whole, not only as a fighter but as a complete human being."

hand and leg techniques, et cetera. If you pay attention to a hankido practitioner performing this set, you'll see many similarities with the Japanese art of aikido because the principles of circular motion are the essence and the main concept of the style.

Q: What's your advice to those who wish to practice your method?
A: From the technical point of view, the student should pay attention to the development of the basics. This is paramount. Then he needs the right mentality and attitude for the training. The four basic elements in the hankido system are courtesy, respect, right attitude and the understanding of one's own center. Strive to develop yourself as a whole, not only as a fighter but as a complete human being.

"Everything evolves and the environment and circumstances change as well. Therefore, the techniques have to adapt the new environment. There is nothing wrong with this. The problem is that some people want to stick to those things that are not useful anymore."

Q: Your approach to the arts seems to be very different and open minded compared to other masters.

A: I consider myself a traditionalist because I maintain the ethical and moral principles of the art as they were passed to me. From the technical point of view I tried to evolve with the times and make the art useful for modern times. This is a concept that many teachers misunderstand. The styles of martial arts are based on what was useful at a certain period of time. The physical techniques were suitable for that particular moment in history. Everything evolves and the environment and circumstances change as well. Therefore, the techniques have to adapt the new environment. There is nothing wrong with this. Look at the car racing technology. The cars are not the same as 15 or 20 years ago. The driving skills are changed because the cars have changed. The cars are faster and new skills and knowledge of physics and aerodynamics are necessary to bring out the most of both cars and drivers. The physical training for the drivers has changed as well. Do

"If you want to learn to fight you don't have to spend five years in a martial arts school polishing your punches and kicks. It takes less time to buy a gun. This is one of the reasons why people criticize other arts."

you see how improvement and evolution affects the whole car racing world? Well, it is the same with the martial arts. The problem is that some people want to stick to those things that are not useful anymore.

Q: Do you agree with mixing martial arts styles?
A: To a certain extent yes, but you can end up doing many styles and being a master at none. The way I like to think about mixing is more like adapting. For instance, my style has arm locks. I'm not going to study judo or jiu-jitsu and mix their techniques with my system, but I may research and study the principles they use and I'm sure I'll find one or two points that I can adapt every time I apply a lock. The idea is to absorb useful material and information to improve what you are already doing and not to jump to other styles and accumulate more techniques just for the sake of adding.

Q: Why do you think people are attracted to martial arts?
A: I believe everybody has a different reason, but mostly self-defense and health. Today if you want to learn to fight you don't have to spend five years in a martial arts school polishing your punches and kicks. It takes less time to buy a gun. This is one of the reasons why people criticize other arts. Let's say I am not interested in fighting but I truly enjoy the physical demands of the training. Then I may enjoy aikido or kyudo or any other less violent

"The future of the style lies on a few talented men who are willing to work, research and develop the basics to a higher level. Of course, the media has a lot of responsibility in deciding which style is the most popular."

styles than Thai boxing for instance. The art you choose and that makes you happy and the makes you enjoy your training are highly effective in your life, and if you become a better human being, then those are good for you.

Q: How important is diet in a martial artist's regimen?

A: Well, you have to think that the food is for your body like gasoline is for your car. You don't fill the tank of a F1 prototype with unleaded, right? The same goes for your body. I don't agree with the idea of being a slave to your body not allowing yourself to enjoy certain things, but I believe you must have a balance in your diet and try to eat clean food so your body remains healthy. This holds true not only for the practice of martial arts but for you daily life as well. It's important that you look for the proper nutrients and supplements to fully achieve this nutritional balance.

Q: What makes a martial art style special?

A: The talent and skill of the practitioners. It's that simple. A good teacher shares his knowledge and experience with the students. Some of them are capable of becoming masters in the future, others are not. Either they don't have the talent or they don't have the motivation. They won't be those who will make the style grow. The future of the style lies on a few talented men who are willing to work, research and develop the basics to a higher level. Of course, the media has a lot of responsibility in deciding which style is the most popular. Movies have their weight, too, in deciding the most popular style. Remember the ninja craze? Movies made that happen and then the magazines supported it. It has nothing to do with the techniques or approach of the martial art style, it has to do with several external factors impossible for the average martial arts instructor and student to control.

"In reality, only constant, diligent practice and dedication is what allows the students to progress, learn, and understand what he is doing. Fortunately there is always more to learn and the knowledge is endless."

Q: What advice would you give to students of the martial arts?
A: There are no secrets in these arts—it's all there to learn and the only secret is practice. There is a new generation of instructors who hold knowledge back. These people, for one reason or another, feel threatened by their students and therefore keep back certain teachings. This is not good. I understand that there are students out there who want to be instant masters—not an uncommon expectation, unfortunately. But in reality, only constant, diligent practice and dedication is what allows the students to progress, learn, and understand what he is doing. Fortunately there is always more to learn and the knowledge is endless.

Q: How would you like to be remembered?
A: As a teacher who shared his knowledge with his students; as someone who did it with love and dedication; and as someone who strove everyday of his life to help others and become a better human being.

Dan Inosanto

The Eternal Master and the Forever Student

One of the three men chosen by Bruce Lee to carry on the art of Jeet Kune Do, Dan Inosanto was originally a kenpo karate student and Ed Parker's assistant instructor and top black belt. Inosanto met Bruce Lee in 1964 and he became his student and personal training partner after a long conversation where Lee explained art and philosophy to Dan. Appointed by Bruce Lee as the instructor at his Los Angeles, Chinatown kwoon, Inosanto also did extensive research into the Filipino martial arts, becoming one of the most outstanding FMA scholars and instructors in the world. Inosanto's many activities have also included writing a variety of books on Jeet Kune Do and the Filipino martial arts.

Inosanto's ever-growing learning desire led him to study under the most important teachers in the American martial arts scene including Ed Parker, Bruce Lee, Ark Wong, Leo Giron, Ben Largusa, Paul de Thouars, Herman Suwanda, Edgar Sulite, Wally Jay, Gene LeBell, and many more. He searched out and studied under the most famous martial artist of all time.

His philosophy of using the instructor's wisdom to achieve further heights in the martial arts is what makes Dan Inosanto one of a kind, and his academy the meeting point for practitioners of all styles from over the world. Simply said, Daniel A. Inosanto is the master every student wants to be, and the student that every master would like to have.

Q: Do you consider martial arts violent?
A: Many people look at the martial arts as a sign of violence. The goal of a good martial artist is to preserve life, not to destroy it. All the training in the world can't make you secure from every form of violence so the objective is to train the body to be able to preserve your life and the lives of your loved ones. Martial arts can bring people together and it is a very interesting way to educate ourselves about different cultures. Of course, the reason why you practice martial arts at 50 are different from what motivated you to begin training when you were 20.

"You have to find out if the style really fits your body type, which is very important. Some systems require a great deal of practice before you can effectively use them."

Q: Do you think there is a single "best" style?

A: I don't think so and I'll explain why. Some styles are efficient at a certain range of combat. Some look very impressive and you think right away they are devastating. Others don't look that impressive but they are very practical but you won't realize it until you're in the receiving end of one of their techniques. You have to find out if the style really fits your body type, which is very important. Some systems require a great deal of practice before you can effectively use them. Other styles can make you a very strong fighter in six months. In short, there isn't anything close to a "best style." You have to find what is best for you.

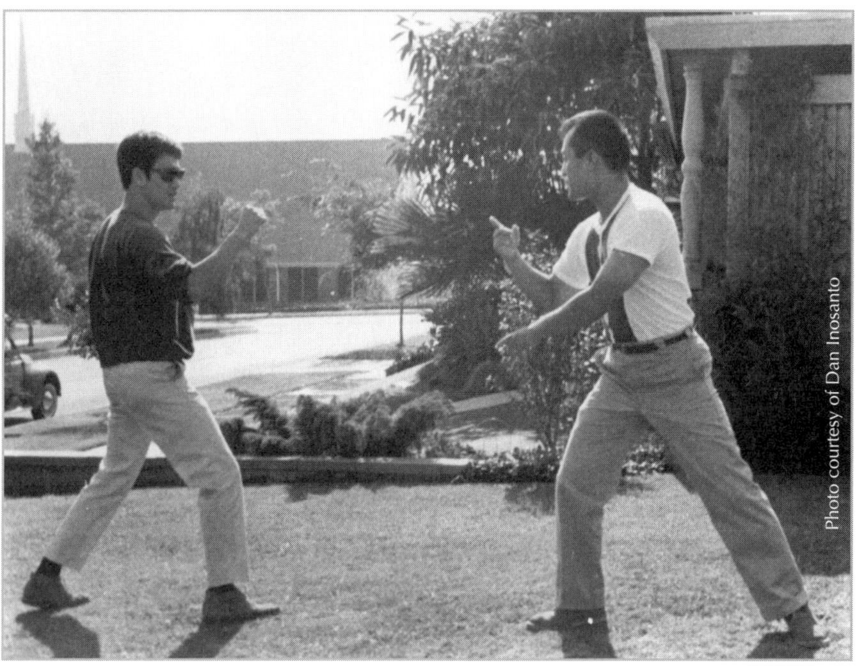

Photo courtesy of Dan Inosanto

"I would recommend that if they have the time and the money, try and cross-train in as many styles as possible so you can get a deep understanding of different fighting forms and cultures."

Q: What kind of advice would you give to students?
A: I would recommend that if they have the time and the money, try and cross-train in as many styles as possible so you can get a deep understanding of different fighting forms and cultures.

Q: Don't you think this can be very confusing for the student?
A: Don't misunderstand me. I don't mean the student has to jump from one system to another. First he needs what I call the "base" system. He needs years of training and understanding in this base system because it is from there that he will evolve. So he needs a strong foundation. This foundation is going to provide his building blocks.

"If the student doesn't want to learn, there's nothing the teacher can do. No matter how well the instructor can impart the knowledge, it's up to the student to have the desire to learn."

Q: You mentioned once that you like to be a student every chance you get. Why?
A: I believe that in order to be a good teacher you have to be open to new learning. I don't have any ego problems in becoming a student. Everybody feels awkward or clumsy the first time. You can get the best kickboxer in the world, and put him on the ground against a wrestler, and he's going to be like a kid—or vice versa. I realized that only when you put yourself in what I call an "insecurity position" can you really learn something. And when you learn something you get better. I don't mind being a student in savate, or Thai boxing, or wrestling. In fact I really like to be in that position. It probably has something to do with my personality. You need experiences to grow, and it's important for an instructor to remain a student in order to constantly seek better ways of training and teaching.

Q: Do you think experience is the best teacher?
A: If not *the* best, then definitely *one* of the best. But having experiences without the understanding to evaluate and learn from them is not good. You have be able to understand your experiences—this is where knowledge takes place.

Q: Is that why you like to give experiences to your students?
A: Right. If the student really wants to learn he will, despite the method or the system that the teacher is using. If the student doesn't want to learn, there's nothing the teacher can do. No matter how well the instructor can impart the knowledge, it's up to the student to have the desire to learn. This

is the reason why every instructor has very good and very bad students. Some students only need to hear "Hands up!" one time, and they won't drop them again. For others, you have to correct that point class after class, for years and years, and they will still drop the hands!

Q: You advocate change. What kind of change do you mean?

A: I think that a better word would be "adaptation" or "evolution." I don't think the term "change" is totally understood in martial arts because it gives the notion that you're changing styles all the time, when you're not. Let's say that I'm a boxer and I know nothing about kicking. If I have to face a kicker, some of the boxing aspects have to be slightly modified to deal with those kicks. The head can't lean forward, the block has to be adjusted to protect my face, et cetera. I'm not 'changing' styles, but rather adapting my system.

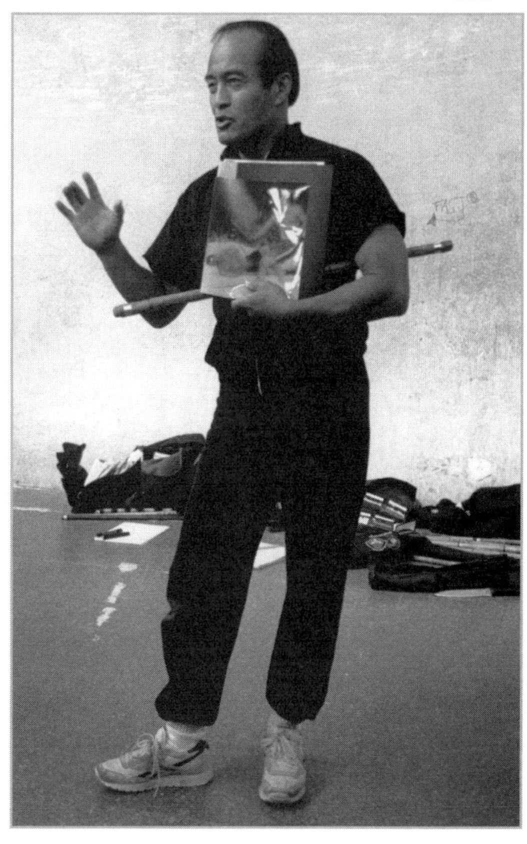

"I've always believed that learning was a process of accumulating knowledge. Sometimes the knowledge is not just a physical technique, but rather the understanding you get from the experience of training in other systems by learning their techniques and tactical approaches."

If I face a fighter that likes to kick to the legs, like a Thai boxer or a savate man, I need to learn the technical knowledge for blocking those kicks. Otherwise, I'm going to get in trouble. So my defensive structure starts to be a little bit different because my weight distribution has to be different than the on-guard position that I was using in boxing—which would make my front leg very vulnerable. Of course, knowing how to kick will raise my offensive level and my attacking possibilities. I may still prefer my boxing hands to finish the fights, but I still need to adapt according to the opponent. We can introduce wrestling and groundwork into this, making the complete equation even more complex. But the whole idea is that the more you know, the better prepared you are.

"If you know how to use the tactics and the rhythm and timing with only two techniques, you can be very unpredictable in combat."

"To understand yourself is the very beginning of the self-discovery process. If you lack of understanding about yourself, you become an ignorant, second-hand martial artist because you are the one in charge of expressing yourself and making the art work."

I've always believed that learning was a process of accumulating knowledge. Sometimes the knowledge is not just a physical technique, but rather the understanding you get from the experience of training in other systems by learning their techniques and tactical approaches. As a fighter you can learn ten different ways of blocking a kick to your legs, and after many hours of sparring and trial-and-error, you might decide to use only two for your fights. The opponent may know your two techniques, and some people may think that this makes you predictable—but that's wrong. If you know how to use the tactics and the rhythm and timing with only two techniques, you can be very unpredictable in combat. But if you're an instructor you have to be very careful to never discard any knowledge because what may be useful for you (the two ways of blocking the low kicks) may not be useful for your students. So you have the responsibility to giving to the students the ten techniques for blocking the low kick and let them, through experiences in sparring, decide which are the best for them. Knowledge is relative to the user and the practitioner. To understand certain experiences you need to have previously accumulated knowledge.

Q: So trial and error is the key to learning?

A: For me it is. I introduced Bruce to the foam football shield and kicking shield around 1964. He rejected its usage because at that time he preferred to train solely on the heavy bag. I told him to experiment and work with it for a while, and after two weeks he fell in love with it. He even developed drills that he modified or changed as he got more familiar and learned more about it's usage. Let's take football. The difference between a rookie and a veteran is experience. A veteran is more knowledgeable than a rookie. His knowledge come from previously accumulated learning experiences. It is true that every moment is different, but one can better cope with a situation if he has the knowledge to flow from moment to moment. Only after you had many experiences can you "chisel away" the many nonessentials.

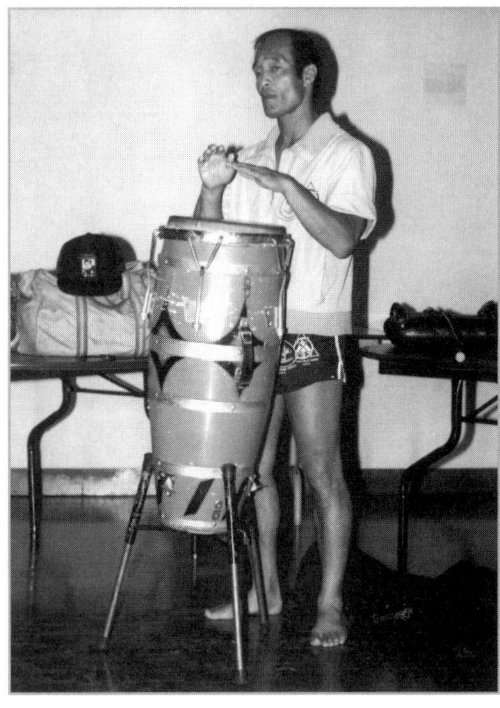

"The goal of a good martial artist is to preserve life, not to destroy it. Martial arts can bring people together and it is a very interesting way to educate ourselves about different cultures."

Q: Do we have to accumulate knowledge then?
A: We have to be inspired by the previously accumulated knowledge and not to be bound by that previous knowledge—which is very different. That's why I encourage my students to study and look into other systems and instructors. No art, person or system is better than any other. It's important to understand not what is right in general, but what is right for the moment.

Q: How important is it to know yourself, in your martial arts philosophy?
A: I think it is paramount. Only you can answer certain questions—not your instructor, or your sifu—but only you. To understand yourself is the very beginning of the self-discovery process. If you lack of understanding about yourself, you become an ignorant, second-hand martial artist because you are the one in charge of expressing yourself and making the art work. And the only way you can do this is by being an expert on yourself.

"The teacher has to understand that the student will find his own way when he's ready. In fact, that's what the very essence of the JKD philosophy is all about."

Q: You mentioned that teaching martial arts is a two-way street. Why?
A: Because good instructors produce good students and good students help the instructors to be better. Instructors should realize that everyone has his own path—that's why I would rather be a pointer to the truth than a giver of the truth. The teacher has to understand that the student will find his own way when he's ready. In fact, that's what the very essence of the JKD philosophy is all about.

Q: What do you think about forms?
A: I have to say that Bruce was not anti-form and neither am I. Forms or katas are a way to learning proper body mechanics. Forms can be a part of your training, but your entire training shouldn't be based on them. They can be useful to structure certain knowledge so you can preserve it, but once you understand it you should freelance. You don't have to follow any particular sequence—you can flow. But as far as teaching is concerned, the instructor needs to have a format, a structure, and a technical progression in order to pass-on knowledge—even if later he discards that structure and mixes the material. The key is not to be bound by the form, but to learn from the form.

Q: Some people might ask why Dan Inosanto is still seeking knowledge for other instructors if he personally trained with Bruce Lee? Wasn't Bruce Lee enough?
A: Bruce was a very knowledgeable and talented teacher—especially on one-on-one—but no one man has it all. Bruce himself went to study and research under different people because he realized that principle a long time ago. It is true that I do it more openly, perhaps due to my own person-

ality. But make no mistake, Bruce wanted to liberate his students. He wanted no one to take his advice as gospel.

Q: What are your personal goals as a martial artist and as a teacher?

A: I'd like to see my students develop themselves. They will take the arts in many different directions and that's fine as long as they don't insist that their way is the only way. A good martial arts instructor can be a combination of many things—from a guide and father figure, to a close friend and counselor. A truly good instructor may well be worth more that he could ever be paid, because there is not enough money to pay those who are so relevant to the development of your character, education, and confidence. My goal is to create a standard of excellence for all the martial art, regardless of origin, and to perpetuate the art and philosophy of Bruce Lee's Jeet Kune Do. Ↄ

"A good martial arts instructor can be a combination of many things—from a guide and father figure, to a close friend and counselor. A truly good instructor may well be worth more that he could ever be paid, because there is not enough money to pay those who are so relevant to the development of your character, education, and confidence."

Long Range Outside (Largo Mano)
Armed Application

1. *Guro Inosanto faces his opponent.*
2. *When the opponent attacks, Inosanto's body is outside the reach of his opponent's weapon.*
3. *Yet, the opponent's hand and forearm are within reach of Inosanto's weapon.*

1

2

3

Unarmed Application

1. *Inosanto faces his opponent.*
2. *When the opponent sidekicks, Inosanto's body is outside the reach of his opponet's foot ...*
3. *Yet, the opponent's limb ...*
4. *is within reach of Inosanto's counterkick.*

1

2

3

4

Long Range Inside (Fraile)
Armed Application

1. *Inosanto is ready facing his opponent.*
2. *Although countered, the opponent's attack is within reach of Inosanto's body.*
3. *And Inosanto's counterattack is within reach of the opponent's limbs and body.*

Unarmed Application

1. *Ready position.*
2. *Opponent's roundhouse kick is within Inosanto's body.*
3. *But his counterkick is...*
4. *within reach of the opponent's limb.*

Close Range Outside (Tabon)

Armed Application

1. *In the course of combat, Inosanto crosses weapons with his opponent.*
2. *He uses his free hand to trap the opponent's weapon hand.*
3. *Then, immediately counterattacks.*

1

2

3

Unarmed Application

1. *Inosanto slips inside his opponent's jab, striking a nerve in the opponent's biceps.*
2. *Then turns his attack into a trap and thrusts his rear hand at his opponent's eyes.*
3. *Then, Inosanto's eye poke converts into an elbow attack.*

1

2

3

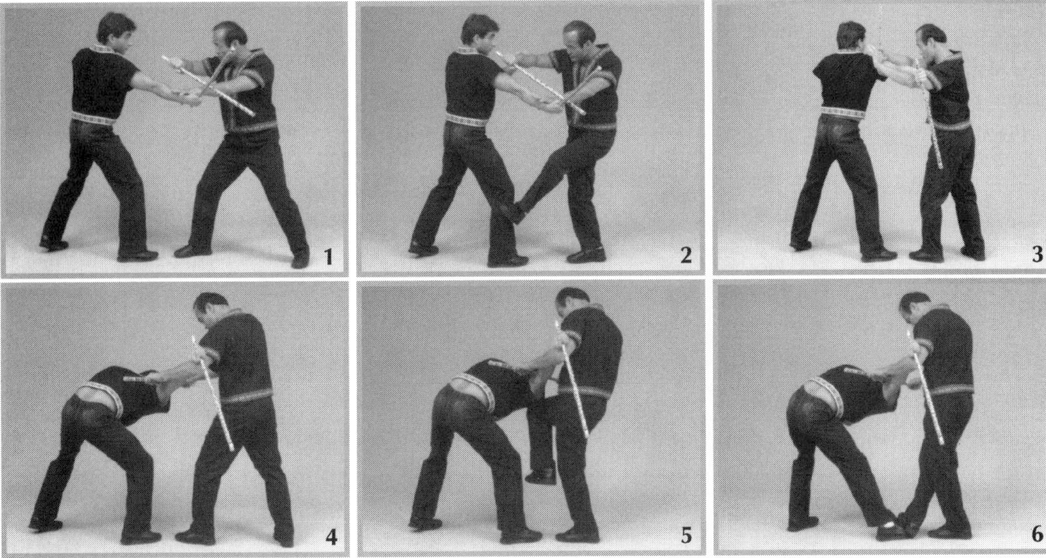

Close Range Inside (Punyo)
Armed Application

1. *Inosanto traps his opponent's weapon*
2. *and counterattacks with the butt end of his stick,*
3. *maintaining control over his opponent.*
4. *Inosanto applies a joint-lock using the stick,*
5. *completing his attack with a knee to the solar plexus*
6. *and a final stomp on the opponet's lead instep.*

Unarmed Application

1. *Inosanto parries and strike a nerve on his opponent's attacking limb...*
2. *and follows by trapping opponent's rear hand for control.*
3. *The trap is converted into an arm-lock with an upward knee attack*
4. *followed by a*
5. *stomp on the opponent's lead instep.*

Lateral In-Fighting Range (Tabi-Tabi)
Armed Application

1. *Inosanto defends the opponent's attack*
2. *and counterattacks with a strike to the knee...*
3. *a strike to the head...*
4. *finishing with a leverage technique.*

1

2

3

4

Unarmed Application

1. *Inosanto parries the opponent's jab and strikes the bicep's nerve.*
2. *He continues his attack with a trap and eye-poke...*
3. *and another trap and 'ordabis' (backfist)...*
4. *to finish his action with a leverage technique.*

1

2

3

4

1

2

3

4

5

Rear In-Fighting Range (Lacud)
Armed Application

1. *After defending his opponent's attack with an 'inside deflection'*
2. *Inosanto moves to his opponent's side striking at his head...*
3. *and simultaneous attacking in the low line with his left knee.*
4. *Then, maintaining control of his opponent's weapon arm...*
5. *applies a rear choke hold.*

1

2

3

4

Unarmed Application

1. *Inosanto deflects his opponent's punch and strikes his bicep's nerve*
2. *Then moves to his opponent's side with a trap/eye-poke/knee-kick combination.*
3. *Maintaining control over his opponent's lead arm, Inosanto finds the rear position*
4. *and applies a rear choke hold.*

TWINS
TWINS

Rob Kaman

The Dutch Duke

Rob Kaman started his martial arts training in the Indonesian art of pencak silat during his early teens. Like so many others, he began his training primarily so he could learn self-defense. He moved into a more contact-oriented method and felt in love with the sport of kickboxing and became one of the top fighters in the world. His career as one of the best kickboxers who ever lived is guaranteed to inspire any serious martial artist. And although it was never Kaman's style to thump his chest and compose limericks about the devastating power of his low kicks—he admits to being flattered by all the attention he still receives. After retirement, Kaman began a film career, appearing in several actions films where he was able to display his martial arts skill. A true Muay Thai celebrity where ever he goes—including Thailand—Rob Kaman continues to teach around the world, sharing his knowledge and expertise as one of the best fighters in history.

Q: When did you first start martial arts?

A: In 1975. Before that I used to play soccer, not professionally though. I was only 14 or 15 years old and I played for Ajax, a famous Dutch squad and one of the best in Europe. But I never really liked team sports, where you depend too much on other people's performance and decisions. I used to watch martial arts, and I found that I liked it and so I got into it. I started with pencak silat, an Indonesian martial art. Roy Matida was my first teacher. He was a pencak silat teacher. After two years I competed in pencak silat free-fighting. Then I saw Thai boxing and I also liked it very much. Finally, in May 1978, I started kickboxing. I began training in kickboxing with Jean Claude and Kabil. And then I joined the Mejiro Gym—the school of champions.

Q: When did you start competing?

A: After four months of training I had my first fight in Paris. But I fought as if it were a street fight—not much technique. The fight was three rounds of two minutes each. I lost to a European champion. In kickboxing, you are

"There aren't many practitioners who make the switch from no-contact martial arts competition to kickboxing or muay Thai. The main change is your mental approach to what you're doing."

forced to do the things for real. You don't score a point—you either hurt the opponent or you don't. It's that simple. This concept changes the whole game plan—not only your techniques and the way you deliver them, but your personal training as well. You have to train to endure, to last in the ring giving and receiving punishment—to really fight with contact. There aren't many practitioners who make the switch from no-contact martial arts competition to kickboxing or muay Thai. The main change is your mental approach to what you're doing.

Q: When you started martial arts, did you have anybody to look up to?
A: Everything started out with Bruce Lee, I think. I liked to watch his movies and he was my idol. But when I started kickboxing I looked up to my own trainer, Kabil. Later a Japanese fighter, Shima, who was a great champion in Japan, inspired me. Then I went to Thailand and had a few Thai fighters as idols.

Q: What attracted you to martial arts?
A: I came from a big family. When I was young and small I was very fragile, and felt easily intimidated. I saw martial arts as something that could give me another identity. Martial arts brought me personality and gave me the charisma and self-confidence I didn't have. It gave me power. It made me a better person, a stronger person. In the sport, and in everyday life as well, I can easily take difficult periods and handle them better. Mentally I grew a great deal.

Q: You went on to become very famous. What was your big break?
A: I think my turning point was when I fought Blinky Rodriguez, the cousin of Benny Rodriguez. I was already a European champion, but I did not know what my level was worldwide. Then I fought him and beat him in the second round. I knocked him out with a low kick to the leg. After that things began

to change for me. My international breakthrough came. I became world champion in 1983. I beat Albuquerque in Amsterdam. Everyone said it was just luck. Then I had a rematch in Miami where I knocked him out with a punch. That was my international debut. From then on I started to fight in Thailand and overseas. I gained the confidence to compete internationally at a much higher level.

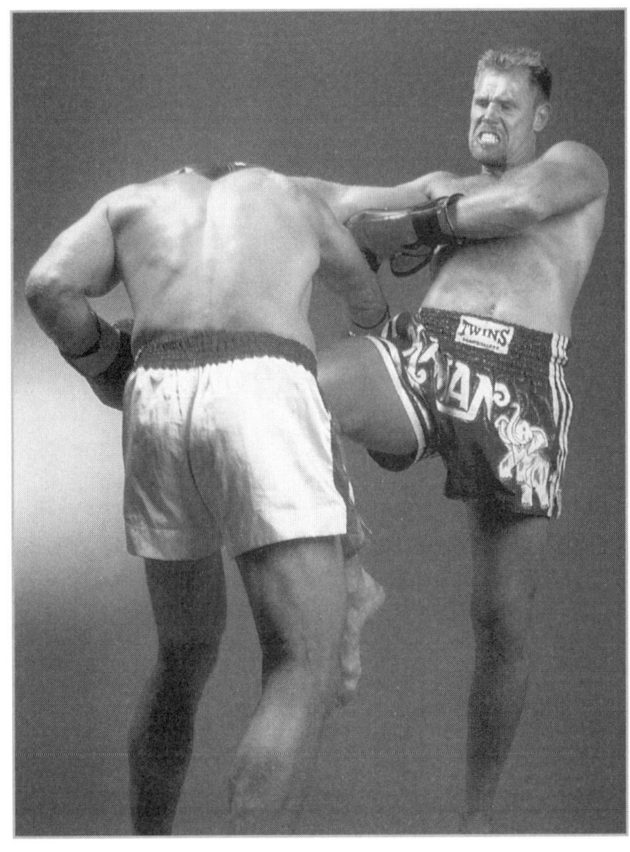

"I guess there is a time for everything and no-holds-barred events are today what kickboxing was in the '80s. Every time a new sport comes up it seizes the moment."

Q: How popular is kickboxing in Europe?

A: I think it has its ups and downs. Right now, no-holds-barred fighting is more popular than kickboxing all over the world. I guess there is a time for everything and no-holds-barred events are today what kickboxing was in the '80s. Every time a new sport comes up it seizes the moment. But very few survive the way karate, judo, and boxing have. On the other hand I have seen kickboxing's popularity growing all over Europe. It has been doing very well in Italy, Holland, and France for a long time. It is now spreading and catching on in Russia and other countries in East Europe. Holland has been always the place where top kickboxers came from. I guess our mentality and the way the trainers structure the training methods and techniques is very good.

"The United States did not have many good fighters in the past but there are some very good coming up. I guess the United Sates is a very big country so it takes longer for any kind of activity to catch people's attention and interest."

Q: What is the difference between martial arts in Europe and the United States?

A: I think martial arts is, except for no-holds-barred, much harder and tougher in Europe than in the U.S. In general, I think Europeans are more motivated and have more discipline and more courage. That's why a lot of the best kickboxers come from Holland, France, and Spain. The United States did not have many good fighters in the past but there are some very good coming up. I am not sure why that is; I guess the United Sates is a very big country so it takes longer for any kind of activity to catch people's attention and interest. In boxing the Americans have a lot of good people. There's not so much money in kickboxing, so maybe that's the reason.

Q: When you trained for competition what did you do? How did you keep in shape?

A: I've been retired from fighting since December '97. But what I used to do to prepare for a fight was six-to-eight weeks before the event, I started long distance running for conditioning. The closer I got to the fight, the training sessions got shorter but more intense. I did a lot of sparring, a lot of pad work—kicking pads and striking pads. We do a lot of Thai training. Thai fighters kick the pads in many combinations. In addition I did technical training with pads, focusing on repetitions: counters, block, counter, et cetera.

"Motivation is a very strange factor in a fighter's mental approach. Nobody feel the same kind of motivation every day to go to the gym and have a tough workout. Now that I'm retired I need to approach the reason to go to the gym a little differently."

Motivation is a very strange factor in a fighter's mental approach. Nobody feel the same kind of motivation every day to go to the gym and have a tough workout. It's good to have several training partners that help you to keep going when your motivation and spirit are not as high as they should be. As a professional fighter, money was a major motivating factor. Now that I'm retired I need to approach the reason to go to the gym a little differently. I tend to use the principle of cycling more and more. I cycle my workouts, emphasizing different aspects of total conditioning so I don't get mentally tired.

Q: Why did you decide to retire?
A: I had a lot of injuries to my shin. It was hard to get motivated. I was in kickboxing for 19 years. I was a champion from 1983 until I retired, with 107 fights. Also, I have been doing movies. I did two movies last year and I also have a real estate business in Holland. I could hardly concentrate on fighting; my motivation was not there. I put all my concentration on movies.

Q: What movies did you work on?
A: The first one was *Maximum Risk* and the second one was *Double Team,* both with Jean Claude Van Damme. Also I appeared in some others, one of them starring Dennis Rodman and Mickey Rourke. Movies are fun to do and they pay well.

"I always felt that I should fight as many good opponents as I could, so I went up and down in weight. I realized that every time you change your body weight substantially, it affects the way you fight because you can't do everything the same."

Q: How tall are you and what is your competition weight?

A: For my last fight I was 202 pounds. I'm six feet, one inch tall. For my first fight I was 160 pounds. So I moved up through the weight divisions. I always felt that I should fight as many good opponents as I could, so I went up and down in weight. I realized that every time you change your body weight substantially, it affects the way you fight because you can't do everything the same.

Q: Who do you like, right now?

A: At a certain moment the best fighters come from Holland but now there are good fighters coming from all places. The Dutch were winning it all at the K-1 Tournament in Japan. Ernesto Hoost was one. I fought him twice. He's from Amsterdam. Then there was Ramon Decker. He's smaller, a lightweight, but a very tough fighter. Now it's different. I also think Mike Bernardo, a heavyweight, is a very good fighter. Japan has some young fighters coming up, but not yet anybody who is a real good. The Thai fighters, in the lightweight division, are always very good. I don't think anyone can compete with the Thai fighters in the light division, maybe only one or two. Then there was some good fighters in France; Dida, for example, but he retired. There are some good Australian fighters coming up, too. The kickboxing sport is catching on in the United States with the K-1 event and I'm sure this will help to increase the popularity and the interest in the sport.

Q: What are your views on no-holds-barred fighters?

A: I don't see it as a regular sport such as kickboxing. I see it more like the gladiators—spectacles from the time of the Romans and the Greeks. I think the only thing that they show is who is stronger. It doesn't matter what kind of rules and what kind of format. I think it has nothing to do with martial arts. It is natural that the grapplers will always win because all the kickers and the punchers have too little time to put their techniques in combination in the fight. After one punch or kick it's grappling all the way to the floor. So the fight ends on the floor. Usually the grapplers win. In the ring and in the mat you have to outsmart your opponent. Just like playing chess. And that's what I like about the Gracie Family—all of them. They are smart fighters. Not because of their strength, since they are not really big guys, but because they have flexibility and above all the technique. That's what I like about martial artists: the technique. Everybody can jump into a ring and fight but fighting and winning with technique, using tactics and strategies, doing it in a clean way, with class—that's a whole different story and that's what I always wanted to do.

"Everybody can jump into a ring and fight but fighting and winning with technique, using tactics and strategies, doing it in a clean way, with class—that's a whole different story and that's what I always wanted to do."

Q: Was there any particular strategy that you enjoyed using in the ring?

A: I always tried to adapt to the opponent I had in front of me. When you get into the ring you need to have an idea, a plan of what you're going to do. But this plan has to be based on your opponent's ability and game. A low kick is a low kick but there are many variations of how you can use it offensively or defensively. Any technique, in the end, is the same but the way you use it to adapt to your opponent's game is the important aspect. I fought a lot of fights taking the initiative and attacking, and I also fought many fights waiting for the opponent to move and basing my game on counterattacking. It depends on your opponent. Fighting is like a chess game—you have to use your head and not receive blows. Every fighter knows that a fight is some-

"When you find yourself in the line of fire, confidence is your main tool. It will trigger everything else you have inside. The only way to be successful both in the ring and in life is to believe 100 percent in yourself."

thing unpredictable, you never know what's going to happen. All you can do is prepare yourself the best you can and have all your tools ready to use at the right time. This will bring self-confidence and confidence opens every door. When you find yourself in the line of fire, confidence is your main tool. It will trigger everything else you have inside. For me, confidence has been a huge factor in my success as a fighter. The only way to be successful both in the ring and in life is to believe 100 percent in yourself.

Q: How important are the mental aspects in fight preparation?
A: Very important and extremely relevant. You have to understand that there are two kinds of competitors: those who are natural fighters and those who are competitors. The mental approach is different. A natural fighter is already there, but the competitor needs to get himself into that particular mood. Regardless of your nature, once you step into the ring you have to think and move as a fighter, otherwise everything you do will be out of place and off target.

Q: Can a fighter become overconfident?
A: It is a definite danger. I never was overconfident. I liked to keep a healthy doubt about my abilities so I was never overconfident. I guess that's a line every fighter needs to draw. Unfortunately, I have seen some fighter's lose as result of overconfidence. Losing is not a big thing if you look at your career as a long term project. Everybody loses at least once—even the greatest like Muhammad Ali. Losing can be a good thing if you know how to use that defeat to come back stronger than ever. Winning? Well, winning definitely

boosts your confidence and helps you to get a better paycheck!

Q: What are your plans for the future?
A: I believe I'll keep working in movies. I believe in personal growth, not only as a martial artist, but as an actor or a director as well. At this point, it is still too early to say whether I have the ability to be a good actor in addition to a good martial artist. So that's what I want to find out in the near future. I plan, in the next couple of years, to invest in myself and work on my acting career and see if I like it.

Q: Do you still feel connected to kickboxing?
A: Yes, very much so. I am glad to see that kickboxing is getting more popular, especially here in the U.S. That way we'll be able to see more, high-level kickboxing matches. I hope to see some good American fighters emerge who can compete with the rest of the world, so pay-per-view and promoters will be interested in bringing the sport to a higher level.

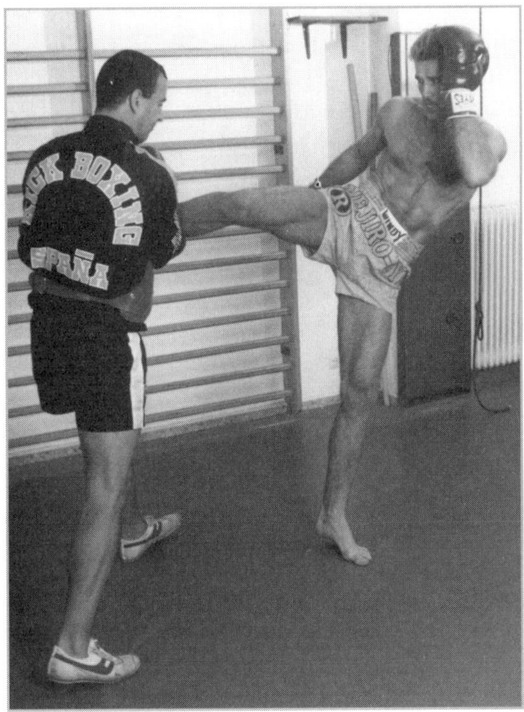

"It's important for all practitioners to study and have an understanding of the close range strategies and grappling moves in order to be more effective in a real situation. If you combine muay Thai with some other grappling methods such as wrestling, Brazilian jiu jitsu, sambo, judo et cetera, you'll have an unbeatable foundation to become a complete fighter."

Q: What do you think about the interest in grappling arts?
A: As a fighter I would say that it's great to see that the grapplers get the recognition they deserve. In Europe we had great judo men since the early '60s. Grappling is a very common aspect of the martial arts in the Old Continent. In fact some of the greatest karate-do and aikido men in Europe are black belts in judo, since judo was the first Japanese art allowed in Europe.

It's important for all practitioners to study and have an understanding of the close range strategies and grappling moves in order to be more effective in a real situation. If you combine muay Thai with some other grappling methods such as wrestling, Brazilian jiu jitsu, sambo, judo et cetera, you'll

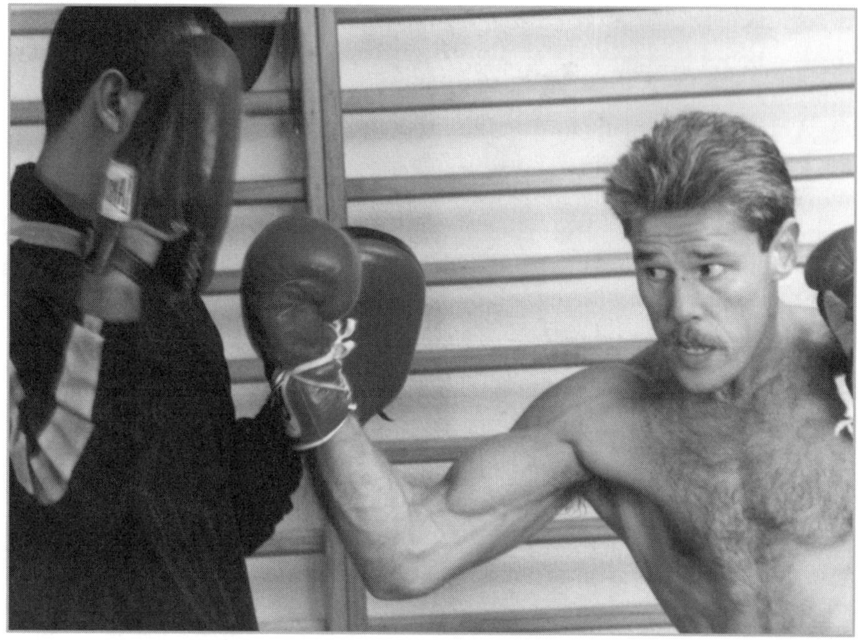

"A good fighter is a combination of several factors and all the main elements should be part of your routine. Professionals should work out every day. It's important to gear your training for the distance you're going to fight."

have an unbeatable foundation to become a complete fighter. And there is where the martial arts are going these days—the complete approach.

Q: Would you give an example of one of your workouts?

A: A good fighter is a combination of several factors and all the main elements should be part of your routine, from cardio and proper nutrition to all the specifics of your chosen sport. I recommend working out three times per week if you're an amateur fighter. Professionals should work out every day. It's important to gear your training for the distance you're going to fight. With this in mind, begin your routine with aerobics in synergetic order—working the muscle groups in sequence in order to achieve maximum efficiency. You should begin by jumping rope for 5 minutes to start, then working up to 20 minutes or more.

Next, do some basic roadwork, generally starting with a walk and working up to a jog of three or four miles. After running, start working the muscle groups from the feet up to your neck. Hop on both feet for two minutes, then hop on one foot for one minutes before alternating and working on the other leg. After that, go into two minutes of jump squats, followed by running in place for two minutes.

From there, you should begin your stretching routine. After a few minutes of this, do several stretches to both front and side. Add some shoulder shrugs, forward and back, in order to give the muscles in the upper torso a workout. I used to add some push-palm exercises at this point to work my arms, hands and shoulders.

"Keep in mind that your brain is literally floating in fluid within the cranium and when you take a hard shot to the head, it's that snapping reaction that jars the brain and sends it to the surrounding skull, bruising it. Good neck muscles development helps to reduce snapping action."

Afterwards, do some neck-strengthening exercises such as head rotations, side-to-side and chin-to-chest up-and-down movements. In addition, you should add some neck-strengthening exercises similar to those used by a football players. Have a training partner place a hand next to your head while you push against it, When that's completed do the other side, along with forward and backward resistance. It's the muscles in the neck that really help you from getting knocked out. Keep in mind that your brain is literally floating in fluid within the cranium and when you take a hard shot to the head, it's that snapping reaction that jars the brain and sends it to the surrounding skull, bruising it. Good neck muscles development helps to reduce snapping action.

After neck conditioning, begin your workout on the heavy bag, fighting it for five three minutes rounds with a minute rest in-between. From the heavy bag go to the shadow boxing, using the combinations and techniques that you use in the ring while sparring with an imaginary opponent. Then, practice those same combinations against a partner who is holding Thai pads and focus gloves to help hone your coordination and movement. As

"The name of the game is finesse and style: sparring should be approached as a solid preparation for a fight and not as the fight itself."

your partner moves, you should concentrate on tagging the focus gloves and pads with consistency.

From the focus gloves and Thai pads move on to actual sparring with a partner. I can't stress enough the importance of always sparring with proper equipment, including safety pads for the feet, full-length shin pads, a good protective cup, mouthpiece, and 12 to 16 ounce gloves. Occasionally, you can put headgear on.

When sparring, the techniques you work on are intended to hurt your opponent in the ring and it's absolutely critical to be able to work on your technique, form, and movement without hurting your sparring partner or getting hurt yourself. It really doesn't take much to ring somebody's bell and the aim of a good fighter is not to get hit. The name of the game is finesse and style: sparring should be approached as a solid preparation for a fight and not as the fight itself.

After your sparring session, do some sit-ups in order to tighten and toughen your stomach area that inevitably takes its share of punishment during a bout. Add some push-ups in sets of 25 repetitions. Cool down and relax while stretching slowly before taking a shower. I never trained with weights during my fighting days because I was really focused of the technical aspect of the sport but I understand that weight training can be beneficial for some fighters. If you feel like doing it and it helps your performance, go ahead and pump iron. Just remember don't get to bulky since this will slow your punches and kicks.

This used to be the bulk of my training but I certainly changed it many times in order to adapt to the circumstances. I recommend that young fighters do quick bursts of hand speed on the bag. Somebody called it the 10/20 drill. This means 10 second bursts where you punch and kick the bag as hard and as fast as is humanly possible. Then follow with 20 seconds of stick and move, using a lot of footwork. This technique will help you to build endurance and speed for fighting. Strength and conditioning are the cornerstones to becoming a top fighter. In short, find a good gym and train hardly but safely.

Q: You're a hero to kickboxing fans around the world. What do you think of yourself?

A: I'm a quiet guy. I don't look at myself as a hero but as someone who made mistakes in life, learned from them, and did his very best to be the best in what he loved the most. And I'm extremely happy if I set an example for the next generation to follow.

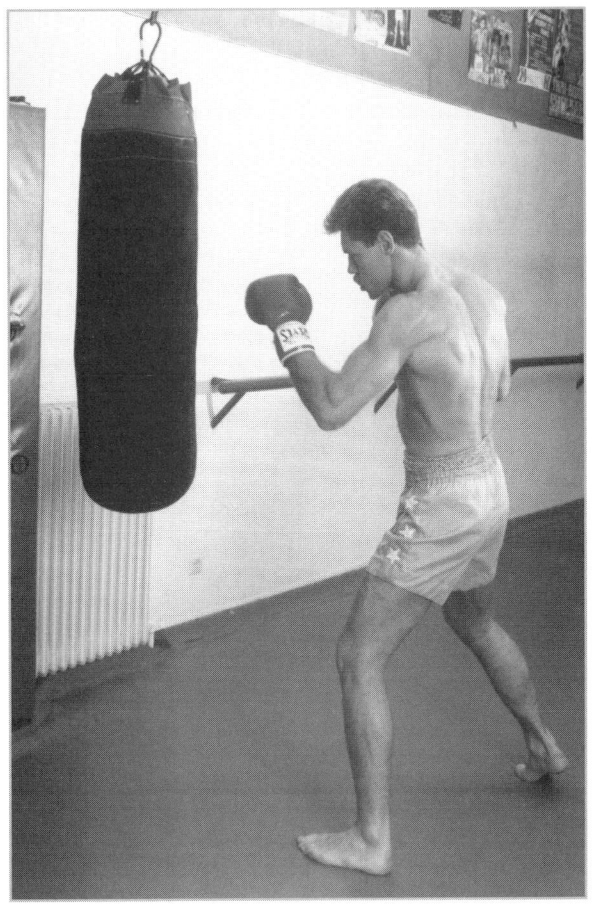

"I never trained with weights during my fighting days because I was really focused of the technical aspect of the sport but I understand that weight training can be beneficial for some fighters."

Kaman faces his opponent (1). He closes the distance with a left, low, inside thigh kick (2) followed by a left jab (3) right cross (4), left hook (5) and finishes with a right low kick (6).

1

2

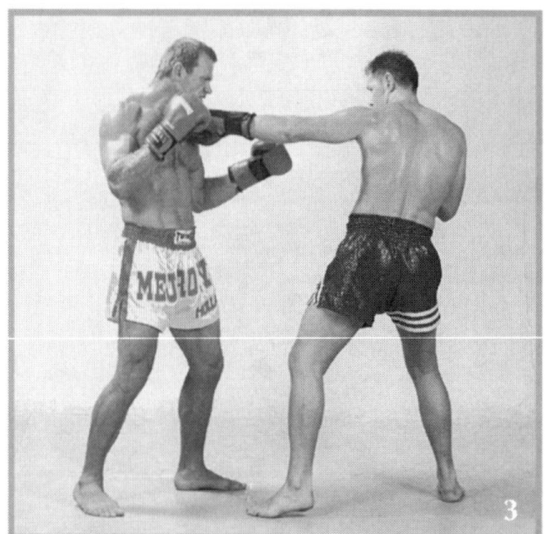
3

4

5

6

Kaman squares off with his opponent (1) who throws a right cross that Kaman counters with a right low kick to the lead leg, making his opponent step back (2) and follows with a right hook to the face (3) a left cross (4) and finishes with a right low kick (5).

Photos by Todd Hester

Ben Largusa

A Simple Man of Kali

Ben Largusa, one of the highest ranking Filipino martial artists in the world, simply describes himself a man of kali—a system so effective in combat that some southern Philippine island tribes successfully resisted the armored steel might of the Spanish Empire for nearly four centuries. Kali is the source of all escrima styles and Largusa is widely regarded as the final word on this devastating and effective weapon. As the only student of Grandmaster Floro Villabrille, the Philippine's most revered fighter and victor of numerous stick-fighting "death matches," Largusa learned a unique blend of methods, strategies, and techniques unknown to any other man in the world.

As his years of training passed, Largusa realized that his training under Grandmaster Villabrille was primarily comprised of fighting techniques and theory. Because the only sparring experience he had was with Grandmaster Villabrille himself, Largusa realized that he could not teach the system the way it was taught to him. The genius of Ben Largusa soon became apparent when he broke down, step by step and move by move, Grandmaster Villabrille's complete system of kali. In recognition of this accomplishment, Floro Villabrille gave Ben Largusa a signed legal document designating him the sole heir to the Villabrille method.

On March 8, 1992 Grandmaster Floro Villabrille passed away, and Tuhan Ben T. Largusa automatically became the second grandmaster of the Villabrille-Largusa Kali System. Currently living in Kauai, Hawaii, Grandmaster Largusa continues to perpetuate the warrior art of kali and the Filipino culture as part of the legacy handed down to him by one of the most legendary fighters of modern times, Floro Villabrille.

Q: What was the legendary Floro Villabrille like?

A: First of all I would like to mention that Grandmaster Floro Villabrille was a man of great integrity. He had sound moral principles, and was very honest and sincere. He firmly believed that giving was more important than taking, and he proved that not only as a martial artist but also as a civilian by

"Grandmaster Floro Villabrille was a man of great integrity. He had sound moral principles, and was very honest and sincere. He firmly believed that giving was more important than taking."

making numerous charitable contributions for athletic scholarships and equipment.

His first martial arts instructor was his uncle, Master Villagano, and after many years he decided to search for another instructor. Moving from island to island and village to village, he finally met the blind princess Josefina of the Pulahane tribe in Gandari, Samar. Honestly, it would take a book to describe this extraordinary man's traits, feats, and achievements. He came to Hawaii during his late teens and settled in Honolulu. He later married Trinidad Pontis and became a well-respected U.S. citizen because of his involvement in community affairs. He loved singing and dancing and was a natural performer on stage. He loved Frank Sinatra—whom he met while employed by MGM Studios in Hollywood. To maintain sharpness and harmony through the philosophy of "Individual Oneness" and "Universal Oneness," he would sometimes work out with karate, kung-fu, aikido, and judo men. Grandmaster Villabrille was also a proficient fisherman, Two of his specialties were throw-net and spear-fishing. Through kali training he developed powerful lungs that allowed him to stay underwater much longer than normal. The practice of kali and his self-development through the *tulong pisage*, or "triangle theory" enabled him to achieve high physical and metaphysical peaks. He contributed annual scholarships to a high school and provided the varsity football team with complete new uniforms. His advice was sought by political officials and candidates alike.

Q: How did he decide to train under Princess Josefina?

A: Well, he didn't plan to do it—it just happened that way! After years of training under his uncle, Master Villagano, he decided to travel and find other teachers. As I said before, he went to the tribe of Pulahane, in

Gandari. This tribe had the reputation of being very wild, and Grandmaster Villabrille was warned by many people to not make the trip. But he was sure nothing bad would happen to him because he had a positive reason to go there, wanted to learn, and also knew how to talk to people. He recited his *oraciones* or "prayers" so he could calm other people's anger by speaking nicely to them. He considered himself well-protected by the *oraciones* and by his *pangkubal* or "talisman."

"From his training under the blind princess, Grandmaster Villabrille developed a deep understanding of new principles and concepts such as offensive zoning, defensive zoning, minor and major movements, options and extensions, et cetera."

So when he got there, and that was an adventure in itself, he approached the leader of the tribe and asked to meet the best kali teacher they had. The leader introduced him to a woman, blind from birth, named Josefina. After talking to her for a while, Grandmaster Villabrille told the leader that she was nice enough, but that he wanted to learn from their top master. The leader replied, "If you want to learn from the best, then you must study with her." Grandmaster Villabrille was surprised and could scarcely believe what the man was saying. Finally, with many misgivings, he agreed to try out the blind princess but to take it easy on her so as not to hurt her. Josefina approached and asked him to attack her any way he chose. The grandmaster was very skeptical and also afraid of hurting her, so he attacked very soft and slow. The princess easily blocked the attack and then told him to attack harder. This time grandmaster held back his power but not his speed, and was surprised how the princess could avoid the blows without being able to see. Finally, upon the princess's insistence, he started to hit fast *and* hard. Easily avoiding the blows, Josefina began to move in a way grandmaster never had seen before. What shocked him the most was that she was able to read the first blow with no previous contact or positioning information of any kind. He realized that the princess knew a method of fighting different from any he had seen before.

From his training under the blind princess, Grandmaster Villabrille developed a deep understanding of new principles and concepts such as

"Occasionally, he used to spar with me to check my progress in fluidity, angling, pivot points, de cadena, *and my ability to react to an unexpected attack or counter."*

offensive zoning, defensive zoning, minor and major movements, options and extensions, fluidity and sensitivity, large angle and small angle fighting, and the running attack. These principles made him look at kali from a very new and different perspective. A more sophisticated method of fighting was in front of him, independent of strength, power, and speed. The theories, principles, and laws of physics that he observed from Josefina allowed him to discover new and effective ways of training and fighting. He realized that everything Josefina did had an underlying principle and that understanding these concepts and principles was the key to his own personal development.

Q: When did he decide to create his own method?

A: After training with Josefina, his kali no longer looked like the taught by his uncle, Master Villagano, so he decided to develop his own method. It's not that he *invented* or *created* a new style; he integrated the teachings of his uncle and the blind princess and formulated a cohesive structure and method once he went back to his home in Cebu.

Q: What method did he use to train you in kali?

A: At the time I started training under Grandmaster Villabrille, the training was somewhat clandestine and I didn't have any sparring partners at all. For my training he used something he called the "four corners system," where I had to visualize imaginary opponents and react to different kind of attacks. Occasionally, he used to spar with me to check my progress in fluidity, angling, pivot points, *de cadena,* and my ability to react to an unexpected attack or counter. In his method of kali, we used different principles illustrated by geometrical designs like the "figure 8," "360-degree circle," and "Four leaf clover." Once you understand how these geometrical patterns work and how to look for them when you face your opponent, you'll be amazed by the number of techniques and possibilities you have. All of these pattern are incorporated in the logo used in the Villabrille-Largusa method, but it takes a qualified instructor to take you to the highest levels of application.

"Many fighters did not walk over to their fallen opponent and deliver the death blow. Don't forget that the majority of the old escrimadors who fought in these death matches were honorable men, who, if they had the chance to spare the life of their opponent, did so."

Q: Were death matches truly to the death?

A: Let me clarify a misconception about death matches. I remember a top escrima instructor telling me that Felicisimo Dizon never competed in real death matches, because he lost one but was still alive. Well, it is true that he did compete, did lose, and is still alive. Death matches did not always finish with one man dead. It was up to the winner to decide to kill the opponent or not. Of course, the defeated fighter would be maimed and crippled with broken bones and serious injuries—but if the winner decided to let him live it was well within his rights. Grandmaster Villabrille allowed many of his opponents to live, especially those who showed him respect before the fight. There were some other that were very cocky and disrespectful so Grandmaster Villabrille had no mercy with them. It all depended on the attitude of the opponent. He would mirror their intentions back to them. Unfortunately, and I need to really address this point here, a couple of books have been written in which Floro Villabrille was mentioned. One of these books stepped over the line of good journalism by saying he exaggerated some of his matches. He never had any reason to lie or exaggerate, nor did he ever have to ride on anyone's coattails to gain fame or notoriety. Many fighters did not walk over to their fallen opponent and deliver the death blow. Don't forget that the majority of the old escrimadors who fought in these death matches were honorable men, who, if they had the chance to spare the life of their opponent, did so. Not

"Stick fighting doesn't mean to fight only with the stick. The complete use of the body was necessary. The stick opened a lot of possibilities but in short range many times a kick, knee, elbow or punch was used with success."

all of Grandmaster Villabrille's death matches ended in death.

Q: In these death matches, how often was the rest of the body used such as fists, elbows, knees, and feet, for kicks and punches?
A: Very often! Stick fighting doesn't mean to fight only with the stick. The complete use of the body was necessary. The stick opened a lot of possibilities but in short range many times a kick, knee, elbow or punch was used with success.

Q: How many death matches did Grandmaster Villabrille have during his lifetime?
A: Forty-four total—which it doesn't mean he only fought 44 times. That is the official record but he fought many other times that were never counted in his official record. He was never defeated. At that time, fighting and challenges were a common way of testing your skills. Through a challenge, you could find out whether a particular person was able to teaching you something or not.

Q: What can you tell us about Grandmaster Villabrille's famous fight with the prince?
A: That's a very interesting story! Felicisimo Dizon was defeated by a tribal prince from Mindanao who was a Moro fighter. Dizon sent a telegram to Grandmaster Villabrille and told him about this fighter. Grandmaster Villabrille was 18 years old and was working on a ship at that time. The prince was really good and people said that he was like a kangaroo because his footwork was so good that when you tried to hit him in once place, he would bound to another almost before you struck. Grandmaster Villabrille decided to fight this man after learning of Dizon's defeat. Not wanted Floro to

"Training in nature allows you to interact with the forces of the Earth. The energy of the universe is there for you to grasp and your mind focuses with more power—with more energy."

get hurt or perhaps even killed, his uncle Villagano tried to change his mind, but with no success. Grandmaster Villabrille isolated himself in the countryside and started his training for the fight. Training in nature allows you to interact with the forces of the Earth. The energy of the universe is there for you to grasp and your mind focuses with more power—with more energy. Being aware of this, Grandmaster Villabrille always trained in the open air, feeling the energy of the universe surrounding him. He realized that if his opponent was so fast with his footwork, he should be able of lure him in and then move back at the same time he delivered a powerful blow. This tactic of hitting while retreating allowing him to develop a very particular style of footwork. After practicing and perfecting this strategy, he became very proficient in moving back and delivering a finishing blow. Needless to say that during all this time he always recite his oraciones in order to receive the supernatural powers he needed to win. The oracion is a very important part of the art of kali and Grandmaster Villabrille always recited those even when he was not training for a fight.

Q: What happened?

A: He came back and finally fought the Moro prince. In the beginning the prince was successful in moving in and out, but Grandmaster Villabrille had developed the strategy of allowing him to get close enough to hit—and that's what happened. The prince kept trying to strike, but the grandmaster moved out of range and returned powerful blows. Very soon, his uncle Villagano, who was in his corner, realized that Grandmaster Villabrille could handle himself and encouraged him to "fight his fight." Finally, grandmaster hit the prince with a blow to the neck that finished the match.

It's very interesting that Grandmaster Villabrille developed a certain type of footwork very similar to that used by Cassius Clay (Muhammad Ali) years later. Years later, Ali became the greatest boxer in history and you can see how he used to lure his opponents in and then counter them while he was moving back.

"The actual fight can be broken down into many components such as reflexes, sensitivity, coordination, footwork, power, body angling and positioning, et cetera. If you don't have any of these it doesn't matter how many times you spar—you'll never become a good fighter."

Q: You mentioned that Grandmaster Villabrille never had a sparring partner and neither did you. How can you develop high fighting skills without any sparring?

A: This is not that simple to explain. In order to be a good fighter it is not necessary to be fighting all the time. The actual fight can be broken down into many components such as reflexes, sensitivity, coordination, footwork, power, body angling and positioning, et cetera. If you don't have any of these it doesn't matter how many times you spar—you'll never become a good fighter. This is because your foundation is weak. Through drills, we can develop all the necessary qualities for fighting. It's like football: the players drill and drills for the whole week—but they don't necessarily play actual games every day. What is very important is once you have all these qualities, you need to put the emotional aspect in there. When emotions are involved, then you're not drilling, you're fighting. Your attitude changes, like night to day. Your body is ready but you have to make sure that your mind also is.

Through the proper drills used in kali, you can get really close to actual sparring. For instance, if you understand the drill progression in *sumbrada,* you'll see that when you incorporate feints, *enganos,* half beats, et cetera and keep increasing the speed—it becomes a fight. Everything is unpredictable and happens at high speed. You are actually drilling but it is close to a real fight. You can get seriously hurt if you're not careful. The higher the level of the drill, the closer to a real fight you are. The only difference is that when you have to fight, your mental and spiritual state is different.

Q: When did you move to San Francisco?

A: When I was approximately 35 years old. Grandmaster Villabrille told me to train and spar with opponents of different styles. Once in the Bay Area I met some people from different karate and kung-fu styles. I remember being invited to a martial arts school and asked to spar with practitioners of choy lee fut, wing chun, and praying mantis. I could easily handle these fighters and the student asked the teacher how long did he thought I had trained in kung-fu. The teacher said a minimum of ten years each! It was very funny. The principles and art handed down to me by Grandmaster Villabrille allowed me to effectively deal with these other martial arts styles. At the time I was very strong and in incredible physical shape.

"Kali is the ancient form of the martial arts of Indonesia and the Philippines. The old art was always played alongside its counterparts, the other Indonesian martial arts of silat, pentjak, and kuntao. Kali was the martial art practiced by the Indonesians during the Indonesian empires."

Q: Kali, escrima and arnis are terms used generally to describe the Filipino martial arts; are they different names for the same art or different methods as well?

A: Kali is the ancient form of the martial arts of Indonesia and the Philippines. Before the Spanish colonization, the Philippines was always part of the old Indonesian empires back to the Sri Vishayan Empire in Sumatra in the 5th century with Hindu-Malayan influence by Arab missionaries. Chinese records note that in 983 AD a ship owned or commanded by an Arab and loaded with valuable merchandise arrived in Khanlu (Canton) from Ma-I or Mo-yi (the Mayid of the Arabs). Mai is an island in the Philippines. Eventually this led to Ma-I Nila on Maynila and then to Manila.

The old art of kali was always played alongside its counterparts, the other Indonesian martial arts of silat, pentjak, and kuntao. Kali was the martial art practiced by the Indonesians during the Indonesian empires. Tribal chieftains such as the sultans, datus, and rajahs and their warriors fought with this ancient art. Magellan and his men were defeated by Chief Lapu-Lapu and his warriors with kali—not escrima or arnis as is said and written in some places.

One theory says that the name came from "kalis," a bladed weapon; and the letter "s" was eventually dropped. Another theory says that "kali" came from the names "kaliradman," "kalirongan," and "pagkalikali." Still another theory says that the word comes from the first syllable of "kamut"

"Culturally, the Spanish had a lot of influence. As far as the martial arts, and kali in particular, not that much. Please note that I'm talking about kali. In other methods such as arnis and escrima they did have more influence."

(hand) and the first syllable of "Likok" (movements).

The names "escrima" and "arnis" came into existence during the Spanish colonization period. "Escrima" came from the French word "escrima" meaning "to fence." "Arnis" came from the Spanish word "arnes de mano" meaning "harness of the hands." Of course, the ancient art of kali includes fighting techniques of empty hands, feet, bladed weapons of a number of sizes and designs, hard rattan sticks, hard wooden weapons shaped like long blades, lances and staff, bow and arrows, and even explosive projectile weapons from guns to cannons. This makes an important difference. So "kali", "escrima," and "arnis" are not exactly the same.

Q: How much influence did the Spanish culture really have on the Filipino martial arts?

A: Well, I believe we have to analyze this carefully. Culturally, the Spanish had a lot of influence. As far as the martial arts, and kali in particular, not that much. Please note that I'm talking about kali. In other methods such as arnis and escrima they did have more influence. Kali was already developed when they arrived, and if you look at the different methods of fighting and training you'll see that the Spaniard were mainly using what we call the small circle. Kali is based on the simultaneous use of the small and big circle. The Spaniards had big problems dealing with the kali men. The kali fighter used to move their weapons into the big circle, which completely surprised the opponent—since the Spanish had never seen an attack or defense from there—and placed them in a vulnerable position. This gave the kali fighter more than enough time to the small circle and finish the opponent.

Q: Is the espada y daga method the basis of the Villabrille-Largusa system?

A: It is definitely a very important aspect of the art, and our system emphasizes this phase very much. The method of espada y daga opens many new possibilities to the student who has only trained in the single *olisi* (stick). It forces you to learn the use of the left hand in a more versatile way, for both defense and attack. In combat, the left hand become a very dangerous tool that can be used to finish your opponent. The very essence is that when facing an opponent with two weapons the empty, or alive, hand is in danger. It's very dangerous to block, monitor, or deflect an edged weapon with your empty hand. Using the espada y daga method, your left hand (where the dagger is in case you're right handed) can safely block the edged weapon without risk of being cut or damaged. Because of the training method, the left hand becomes more alive and reaches a new stage of combat skill. The possibility of seriously damage to the hand holding the dagger makes you aware of many other possibilities in combat. This aspect is definitely one of the most important in the Villabrille-Largusa method.

Q: What about the *sinawalli*—the double stick phase?
A: This phase offers a more aggressive approach. Both weapons are long and the reach is bigger than if you use the espada y daga. Therefore, is more commonly used for attacking, since you have the reach advantage on your side. Part of the strategy is similar—but only part. Don't think that because you have two weapons they are meant to be used the same. The sophistication in the use of the dagger is different from the use of the double sticks.

Q: Some Filipino instructors teach the art starting with the single stick, then proceed to *espada y daga, sinawalli,* dagger, et cetera. Do you teach phase by phase or you take the student through all the categories simultaneously?
A: In kali we try to make the student grow by themselves. If we teach only single stick and something happens to the teacher, or the student has to move to another place, the practitioner will be limited and it will be impossible for him to evolve. However, if I teach the basics and fundamentals of every phase or category, the student will be able of develop even if I'm not with him. The idea is give the student enough tools to grow as a practitioner and not limit his evolution. Let's say that someone is able to training under me for the short period of time of two years. Well, after two years this student, instead of having only knowledge about the single stick, will have a fundamental understanding of the single stick, double stick, espada y daga, empty-hand methods, dagger, et cetera. He'll have the basis to keep growing and evolving. This is the main reason why I introduced this change in the teaching progression and methodology. I think is more beneficial for the student and the training is more enjoyable as well.

Q: What can you tell us about the ranking system used in the Villabrille-Largusa system?
A: We have four different categories: the higher rank is called *apohang tuhan* and there is only one person in this level, which is currently myself. Then we have the *tuhan*. Only one person can have this title also. From level 7 to level 10 they are called "Professor," and from level 1 to level 6 they receive the title of "Guro." There is no limit to the number of professors and guros, but there is a limit for tuhan and apohang tuhan.

Q: Would you please explain the Blood Ritual Ceremony?
A: In February of 1972, I gave the first public demonstration of the Villabrille system of kali in the Serramonte High School gymnasium, in Daly City, California. On that day I was presented with the red sash, elevating me to the rank of tuhan. This was made through the right of the Blood Ritual Ceremony, which was presided over and performed for the first time before the general public by Grandmaster Floro Villabrille. In this ritual, blood is drawn from the person to be promoted and from the person presiding over the ceremony. Each participant writes their name from the drawn blood on a piece of paper. The paper is then burned and the ashes are mixed with red wine in a chalice. After the proper prayers are recited, each participant then drinks from the chalice. It is from this ritual that the blood of Grandmaster Floro Villabrille continues to flow from generation to generation. All certified guros of the Villabrille-Largusa system go through this ritual.

Q: You were a good friend of the late kenpo master Ed Parker—what can you tell us about him?
A: Ed Parker was a great man and a great martial artist with a very open mind. I remember he asked me about the art of kali and said, "Stickfighting, right?" I replied, "No, there is much more than just sticks." And I proceeded to show all the empty-hand movements and techniques. He was very surprised and decided we should get together more often. He loved the kali hand movements and footwork. We used to get together with another friend who was a choy lee fut practitioner. When Ed Parker decided to put his tournament together he asked me to demonstrate there. He knew that the more people there were around me the better I did! I guess I enjoyed the adrenaline rush of being on center stage! Those were great times.

Q: Is it true that you were approached by Ed Parker to be Kato in *The Green Hornet?*
A: Yes, that's correct. Ed Parker had a lot of friends in Hollywood and was teaching some of the top people in the industry. To make a long story short, I got a call from Ed saying that Hollywood needed a person for that role and he thought of two people—myself and Bruce Lee—but he decided to offer the part to me first and Bruce second. I told him that I truly appreciated his offer but that I couldn't answer right then—that I needed time to think about it. I talked with my wife and after seven days I called Ed back and declined the offer. He was disappointed I didn't accept but he understood. "I'll have to call Bruce Lee," he said. And the rest is history.

"Bruce Lee deserves all the credit he has today—because he took his opportunity and made things happen for himself and others. He helped to popularize the martial arts like nobody else before or after."

Q: Why you didn't accept?
A: I'm a family man. I had a wife and kids and I was really enjoying their company and seeing them grow up. I was never attracted to the world of Hollywood—that world has always seemed shaky to me. My wife actually told me, "Go! Do it if you want!" But I decided otherwise. The Hollywood world is not something I was dying to get into. I decided that my family was more important than fame. On the other hand, Bruce always wanted to be in Hollywood—it was his dream, he wanted it badly. He was ready to make any sacrifice to reach the top—and I wasn't. It was a matter of priorities, that was all. I met Bruce Lee several times after that—Bruce and I demonstrated together in Ed Parker's Internationals in 1964. But I never mentioned this to him and neither did Ed Parker. Bruce Lee deserves all the credit he has today—because he took his opportunity and made things happen for himself and others. He helped to popularize the martial arts like nobody else before or after.

Q: Did you ever regret not accepting Ed Parker's offer?
A: Not at all! I made a decision based on my personal principles; why I should regret anything? I had a great life, a good job I was truly enjoying,

"It's important to notice that a technique may look not effective at first sight, but after further analysis you may find out that a slight adjustment in the angle will make the difference. Sometimes a couple of inches in the body angle will give you a different view of what you're doing."

and a great family. Maybe I could have been a star, but maybe I would have lost something dear along the way. The things I could have lost were far more important to me that the glamour or stardom of Hollywood. It's true that sometimes you think, "What if had decided the other way?" But that is just human nature, right? Curiosity is human and that's all. No big deal.

Q: I won't mention any names, but it is obvious that many masters and grandmasters of other styles learned from you, copied your movements, and adding those to their systems without giving you credit. How do you feel about that?

A: Well, let me put it this way, I could say they are copycats, but I would rather look at them as people who were touched by what I had to offer—they took kali into their lives and it improved whatever they were doing. As far as giving no credit to me—I don't really care. I know who I am, and what my art is all about. That's all I can say.

Q: What to you feel about the idea of mixing different martial arts styles?

A: You have to be careful with mixing styles. Sometimes it can be beneficial and sometimes not. It's important to have an strong base and foundation. Once you have this, it is not that necessary to incorporate many other things. You may look for some specific elements that help you to improve what you have, but you don't necessarily have to add more and more just for the sake of adding. If a martial art system is used for fighting then there's not too much to be added—if you do anything I think "integrating" would be a better term. As I said I don't really believe in studying many different styles of martial arts and putting them together to create a new system. Sometimes martial artists do this because they don't think what they have is truly useful. It's important to notice that a technique may look not effective at first sight, but after further analysis you may find out that a slight adjustment in the angle will make the difference. Sometimes a couple of inches in the body angle will give you a different view of what you're doing. What *is* important is to find a system that allows you to be efficient and competitive in the different ranges and situations. Then it is more a matter of polishing and refining what you have rather than adding movements to the style.

Q: Did you modify what Grandmaster Villabrille taught you?
A: Not in the technical sense. I realized that in order to properly teach the art you needed a progression, a way of organizing the material so the students could go from A to Z and grow at the same time and at the proper pace. The way I was taught by Grandmaster Villabrille was a very intuitive one. I never had any sparring partners and all my training was one-on-one. When I started to teach I found out I couldn't apply the same method. Therefore, I decided to structure what I was taught by my teacher. It's not that I changed or altered the techniques, but I did organize them in a more cohesive and comprehensive way. I did this so the students in the class could follow a logical progression in their training, going from one step to another in an organized way. I understand that some people may think that some "original flavor" has been lost through this process. But I truly believe that nothing has been lost and a lot has been gained since this allowed me to reach many more people who were interested in learning the art of kali.

Q: How important are the spiritual aspects of kali?
A: Very important. Grandmaster Villabrille mentioned that the oracion is as important as the physical techniques. Don't forget that a fighting art without philosophy and spirituality is only brutality. Without the spiritual and mental aspects one moves mechanically, like a robot, with no feeling or meaning. The oracion is important because it makes our minds stronger and develops our fighting spirit, what we can call plain old guts or courage. Everybody has a different degree of courage, and you either born with or without it. Now with kali spiritual training one doesn't have to be born with courage—it can be developed. In the same way that our emblem, with the internal, external and rhythm triangles and circle, represents all the possible actions and teaches how to break down the angles, attacks and counter-attacks when facing an opponent. The oracion allows us to reach the higher levels of spirituality and mental conditioning for training, fighting, and even daily life.

Q: What did kali bring into your life spiritually?
A: A lot of things, but mainly peace, love, wholesomeness, and a oneness with others who love the art. Who could ask for anything more? ❍

Rene Latosa

A Higher Level of Martial Art

Rene Latosa has been studying and teaching the Filipino martial arts for more than three decades. He began his training in 1968 and has studied under such masters as Dentoy Revillar, Serrada *style, Max Sarmiento,* Cadena de Mano *style, Leo Giron,* Larga Mano *style, and Angel Cabales, Serrada style. However the most influential man in his life was his father, Juan Latosa. The training under his father's tutelage was far from easy and comfortable. The elder Latosa forged his son in the harshest and most difficult elements of the traditional Filipino arts and shaped in Rene's mind the basic structure that would one day become the Latosa escrima system.*

In 1973, Rene Latosa left Stockon, California for duty in the U.S. Air Force and taught the SWAT teams of the local law enforcement agencies. This was the first time that local police had used the Filipino arts in their training. It was an exceptional opportunity for Master Latosa to test some of the theories used in developing his system.

Now retired from the Federal Government, Master Rene Latosa is known for never hiding information from his students, but freely sharing his knowledge and experiences to make the Latosa escrima one of the most effective methods of Filipino martial arts in the world.

Q: How long have you been practicing martial arts?

A: I started at the age of 17, and I have been practicing for about 33 years. It has been a 33-year learning experience. I am confident that I will continue to learn and discover more during the next 33 years. I initially started in the *Serrada* system under Grand Master Angel Cabales in Stockton, California. At that time the school had many visitors and people who just liked to train. I also trained with Maximo Sarmiento who was proficient in a *Cinco Teros* system, and was the best *Cadena de Mano* (empty hand) and knives expert that I have ever seen. Then there was Dentoy Revilar who was Angel's protégé, and extremely talented. Another well-known master at the school was Grand Master Leo Giron, who taught us *Largo Mano* and other combat techniques. Being one of three students at the school, I was surrounded by a

"There was a variety of old men at the Filipino Center where I also practiced, who would pass by and offer up a secret technique to counter someone else's secret technique."

flood of Filipino martial arts information, and I reveled in the one-on-one attention. There was a variety of old men at the Filipino Center where I also practiced, who would pass by and offer up a secret technique to counter someone else's secret technique. My Father was my last instructor of any great length. His system didn't really have a name. In the Philippines he had trained in several different systems and at secret camps in the mountains.

Q: What were the teaching methods like?

A: Angel Cabales would train us one on one. He believed in this method of teaching. There weren't very many students so it worked to our advantage. As the school grew, many students were being ignored or forgotten so Angel had to adjust to group training. There was nothing formal or anything that resembled rank. Angel was the master, then came Max, then Dentoy—that was the pecking order. Again, your training depended on who the instructors wanted to work with during the time they wanted to teach. Much of the time was taken up with countless hours of stories about their many experiences. I would sometimes be at the school until 11:30 at night talking and training with Max. He had great stories about his early days in San Francisco's Chinatown.

The training I obtained from my father was very intense. His only method of teaching was for me to strike at him and observe how he executed his movements as he struck back. There was no time for any trial and error. I knew he cut me some slack, though, because my Uncle Pedro got the same lessons when he was younger and he ended up always getting hit.

My father would emphasize that attitude in a fight is just as important as movement. He said you must be brave or you will lose. In other word, he rarely moved back; he used forward pressure and constantly knew where his power was based.

"My father would emphasize that attitude in a fight is just as important as movement. He said you must be brave or you will lose. In other word, he rarely moved back."

Q: What was your childhood like?

A: My father was a very influential individual in the Stockton Filipino community. He often watched me perform demonstrations with Angel at various grand openings and functions, and I would always be introduced as "Johnny's son." I did so many demonstrations that I began to feel very invincible—I was fast, strong, and my timing was on. My ego really got the best of me at the age of 18. One day while practicing at home, I needed someone to feed me some hits; my father was gardening so I asked him literally if he would be "my dummy." He just looked at me and continued gardening. When I asked him again, he dropped his shovel and walked over to me. I used to be very afraid of my father because he had a big voice, was very strong, and yelled at everyone—but now that I was a skilled warrior my fear vanished. He picked up a stick and said, "Hit me." I just looked at him as if he was playing with fire. I explained with a bit of an attitude, that I needed to practice and didn't have time to fool around. He asked me again to hit him, so I gave him a real easy, soft hit so as not to hurt the old man—and I felt a stick land hard enough on my head to get my attention. I explained the dangers of using a weapon you can't control, and he ask me to hit him again, and this time I hit him slightly harder and faster, and it ended up with the same result, a stick on my head. I was getting angry because twice this accident happened. He wanted another hit and I thought I would fake him out and tap his head, and then block his strike. So I faked the hit and again his stick landed on my head and this time he was laughing. I went for him and he moved his stick hit me

"Sometimes your natural talent comes into play. If I wasn't a natural at escrima, I had to become one fast. My father taught one way—which was to hit me."

on the shoulder and I fell to the ground. He put the stick down and went back to gardening. My mother was watching and told him to stop tormenting me. As I brushed myself off, feeling bewildered, frustrated, and ready to give up, my father explained to me that he was the top fighter in his region—not a sports fighter but a real fighter. From then on I listened and learned all I could. The funny thing was that everyone in the older community knew how good he was but no one ever told me. Even when I visited his village in the Philippines, there was a look of confusion as well as amusement when I asked the old men at the square about finding a master I could train with. They kept telling me, "Go home and see your papa."

Q: How has your escrima developed over the years?

A: Sometimes your natural talent comes into play. If I wasn't a natural at escrima, I had to become one fast. My father taught one way—which was to hit me. When I tried to get him to show me a movement again, he would demonstrate five different moves—none of which looked like the one I asked about. He said he didn't know how to do a single technique for a single attack. He reacted on instinct and his movements were based on the intent of the opponent coupled with his own fears. Early on I realized I could mimic any system I saw, by looking at it conceptually and not technically. Escrima has not changed, but rather my method of teaching has. For example, pro-football coaches saw the need to enhance individual skills and in order to do this they developed certain drills to develop these attributes. A defensive lineman's job is to protect the quarterback. It takes more skills than just being big and strong. The skilled athlete needs awareness of the field, the proper use of their body weight, watching the body language of the opponent, and a quick explosion off of your stance. The elements utilized by the skilled athlete are timing, explosiveness, balance, and proper center of gravity. Each of these elements is necessary to the development of a lineman, and each of these elements is practiced separately and then put together to achieve peak performance. To me, the martial arts are exactly the same; you need to develop each skill, and transition this into the execution of the technique. In my teaching I have five basic concepts which I use in every technique. These concepts consist of power, focus, speed (timing and distance), balance, and transition.

"You need to develop each skill, and transition this into the execution of the technique. In my teaching I have five basic concepts which I use in every technique. These concepts consist of power, focus, speed (timing and distance), balance, and transition."

Many of my teachings focus on the individual concepts. For example, when I teach power I want the students to achieve the maximum amount of power their body can generate. Then the students will know and understand what is achievable. Once they understand maximum power, the trick is to understand how to balance power and use it to your advantage. Sometimes generating that much power doesn't leave you much room to recover if you miss your target. A boxer throwing a hook at full power every time, usually falls off-balance, and eventually the other boxer will read this and take advantage of the twisted balance with a straight right. In other words, I developed drills and exercises to obtain power, and also to teach how to control and balance power. In teaching the concept of focus, it goes beyond your opponent or adversary and towards other important elements such as the opponent's movement, sounds, aggressive and non-aggressive actions,

"Tournaments help to develop some of these qualities and have their place in the martial arts. I set up my tournaments to have value, not to find out who the best fighter is in the world. My concept of a tournament is training."

awareness of multiple attackers, and environmental weapons (dirt, cars, tools, etc.). In other words, a heightened awareness and the utilization of the five senses play an important roll in understanding the full spectrum of each concept.

Q: Do you think there is still a "pure" system as taught by masters such as Angel Cabales, Leo Giron, and Ben Largusa—or we are going to a more "mixed" approach?

A: I really don't think there ever was a pure style. Everyone has their own version or interpretation of what they know and what was taught to them. I am not so sure a pure system can exist because of all the influences and experiences one draws on when teaching. I am certain that every individual injects his own meaning, individual innovations, and creativity—which obviously influences any system. I think different styles help people to understand what elements tie these arts into the Filipino martial arts. Personally, I feel a person can study any system they want; the effectiveness depends on that person's ability to execute the right concepts to make it work. No style is effective unless you can hit your target. In order to hit your target, you need to understand the concept of distance, how much speed is necessary, and the coordination of these two efforts, which gives a person their timing. I actually had a person come up to me and tell me that they are one of the fastest stick practitioners in the world. So I grabbed his throat and said, "So what's your point?" Speed doesn't help you unless you know how to use it, which also means understanding the concept of balance.

Tournaments help to develop some of these qualities and have their place in the martial arts. I set up my tournaments to have value, not to find out who the best fighter is in the world. My concept of a tournament is training. Tournaments are drills to find the relationship between distance, timing, and speed. In a full-contact escrima tournament, there is an obvious safety factor, so in this instance you will not learn about power, since power becomes a moot point with safety equipment and the safety of others. In a fight, the fastest guy in the world is not the most dangerous if he doesn't hit his target. I want tournaments to help students realize that the timing of a hit depends on how fast you can close the distance or work the distance when you see the opening. The second most important aspect of tournaments is assuring that the students maintain balance. Balance is one of my main concepts—everything else revolves around it. Tournaments should be used to learn specific parts of the martial arts. Obviously, it is also fun because of the adrenaline rush and the competitive spirit. In our tournaments punches and kicks are allowed.

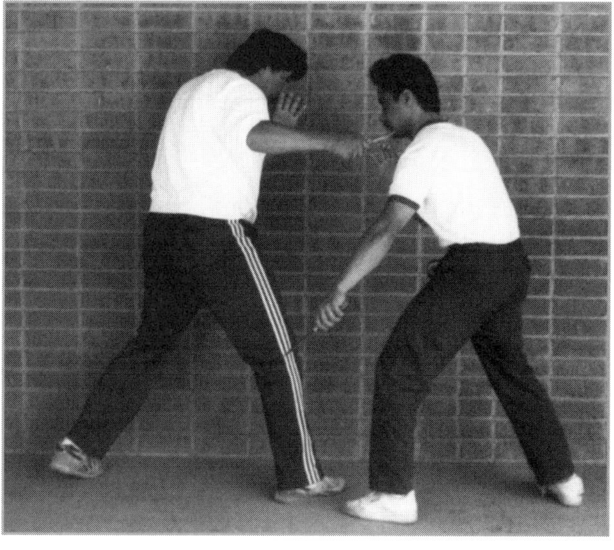

"As an instructor, you can see your influence on the students. If the student does not understand the point you are trying to make, you, as the instructor, must try to find a different route to comprehension."

Q: Do you think no-holds-barred events bring positive or negative aspects to the martial arts?

A: I don't think it is mainstream enough to bring any negative aspect to the martial arts. I personally love a good fight—or rather like to see a good fight. Besides, unless it is on TV, like the Friday night fights, I don't think the general public will find it very interesting. The new movies on the other hand like *Crouching Tiger, Hidden Dragon* and *Rush Hour* are mainstream and seem to overshadow these type of extreme fighting events.

Q: Do you think that martial arts in the West has caught up to the level of the Philipines?

A: I think so. In today's shrinking world, everyone has the opportunity to look at what athletes are doing in their training and the physical size of today's individuals. Take football for example; 10 to 15 years ago, being 6 foot tall and weighing 200 pound would have been big enough to play a

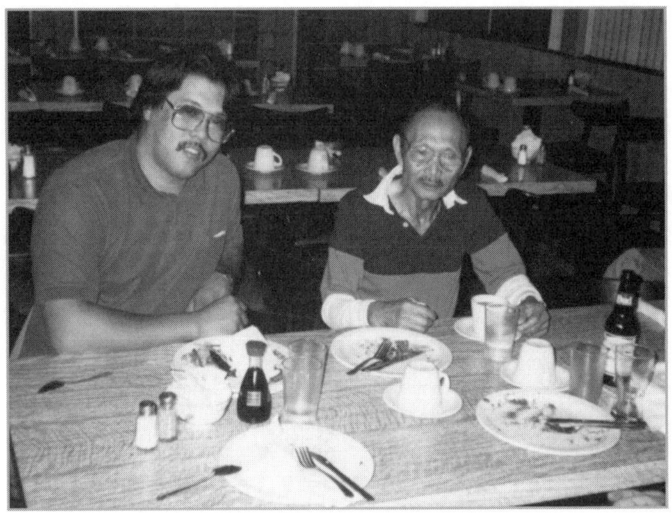

"Training with weapons also means understanding the attributes of the weapon. Because I use concepts to teach, when you learn weaponry you can automatically transfer what you learned to your empty hands. An instructor must understand the real meaning of transition from weapons to empty hands."

lineman. A person today of that size may not even make the team. The training level an athlete can achieve is very progressive, and the martial arts have to progress in the same manner. Look at boxers in the 1970's who were considered heavyweights, and then look at the size of today's heavyweights. They are two different weight classes now.

Q: Are martial arts a sport or a way of life?
A: Certain areas of the martial arts can be called a sport, but the martial arts are very complex because of the emphasis on tradition, self-defense, and reality usage. The competitive spirit in sports is the opposite of the martial arts. We were taught to be humble and not use the art in a way that shows arrogance. In a combat sport you have to have this or you will never get to the next level.

Q: Do you think it helps students to physically to train with weapons?
A: I think it is important for the student to experience the weapons essence. In other words, its weight, length, density, how balanced or out of balance it feels, and understanding when and where the weapon is the most powerful. For example, with a chain, at what point does it achieve the most power or impact? On the other hand, if you wrap the chain around your hand, the power structure of the weapon changes. So training with weapons also means understanding the attributes of the weapon. There is 100 percent teaching in empty-hand and weaponry phases. Because I use concepts to teach, when you learn weaponry you can automatically transfer what you learned to your empty hands. Logically, if the weapon is an extension of the hand, then there should be no difference other then adjusting for the length

of the weapon and the distance between you and your opponent. An instructor must understand the real meaning of transition from weapons to empty hands.

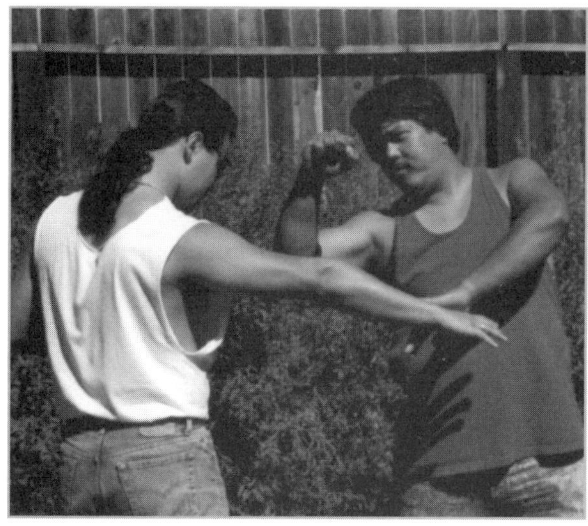

"Tournaments should be used to learn specific parts of the martial arts. Obviously, it is also fun because of the adrenaline rush and the competitive spirit. In our tournaments punches and kicks are allowed."

Q: Do you have any general advice to pass on?

A: Be truthful, logical, and question what you are taught. Make sure that everything you are taught has a purpose, a meaning, can be used, and is flexible in any situation. Secondly, practice from a natural standing position. Most people practice in a somewhat safe environment such as a school, which means practicing with a person in front of you who you know is going to attack. The point is you are practicing being reactive instead of being proactive. Why did you wait and let the person get close enough to attack? Did you not notice the aggressive behavior? As the person got close did your hands get into a position that didn't display aggressiveness yet protected yourself? Did you prepare for an attack or wait until the attack was coming? If you waited to see whether you were going to be attacked, then you have to depend on your speed and hope you are faster then your attacker. What is overlooked at times, during practices, is the fact that the person attacking may be as fast as you and as skilled. That being the case—and all things being equal—then the attacker has the edge. On the other hand, a practitioner's personal training is closely associated with how they teach their students. As an instructor, you can see your influence on the students. If the student does not understand the point you are trying to make, you, as the instructor, must try to find a different route to comprehension. Each time you do this, you learn to think outside the box.

Q: What are the major changes in the arts since you began training?

A: The two major changes are the open teaching method and reality training. I break down every aspect of a movement, especially those unique to

"I want my students to feel free to challenge what they are practicing when they feel uncomfortable. I want the students to believe in what they practice."

the Filipino martial arts, and substantiate the reason for its use. There are movements in the Filipino martial arts that people train in and are led to believe that work. I want my students to feel free to challenge what they are practicing when they feel uncomfortable. I want the students to believe in what they practice. I want students to think for themselves rather than taking my word that the movement works. On the reality side, I feel students must practice as if there is no second chance and must make what they know work the first time. From the stick twirling, locks, stabs, fakes, and to all the movements associated with the figure-eight's, the students must validate these movements within themselves. I train to become more efficient and to eliminate wasted movements while assuring the concepts I teach are still in place. I also teach with the attitude that a person must be able to read their opponent, or in other words, hit your opponent before he hits you. This training teaches to not only read an attack, but also to have the ability to instantly change a defensive posture to an offensive one.

Q: Who would you like to have trained with that you have not (dead or alive) and why?

A: One person would be Japanese swordsman Musashi—because he was straightforward, he anticipated the results and the opponent, and simplicity was his expertise. The second would be my Great Grandfather Esteban. The main reason would be to see the Filipino martial arts back in his day. I would like to see his skill level, the effectiveness of his skills, and the types of opponents he was confronted with.

"The quest for knowledge never ends. When something is at the pinnacle of perfection, it can always be improved on. Study means learning, and every time you teach you learn something new—whether it is from what you may discover or what you may have seen your students do. No one is immune from learning more, discovering more, and creating more."

Q: What keeps you motivated to train after all these years?

A: The look on my students' faces when they make an application work. The pleasure I get when they thank me for teaching them the knowledge I have given them. Lastly, I take pride in continually sharing my Filipino culture and heritage through the martial arts. Of course, there is always further to go in any form of study. The quest for knowledge never ends. When something is at the pinnacle of perfection, it can always be improved on. Study means learning, and every time you teach you learn something new—whether it is from what you may discover or what you may have seen your students do. No one is immune from learning more, discovering more, and creating more.

The marital arts is an equalizer. If you get into a situation, the martial arts gives you the ability to equalize physical size, strength, natural ability, and experience against a normal opponent. For example, if someone bigger wants to start trouble, you know you can get the advantage by kicking him in the groin. Thus you equalized his size by using skill and knowledge.

"Free fighting gives you a sense of reality without the full danger of combat. It allows you to make mistakes and live to fight another day. Fighting on the streets is without any sort of gentlemen's rules—anything goes. Don't forget, luck and awareness is a huge factor in wining a street fight."

Now if the attacker is highly skilled in the martial arts and is bigger and stronger, the outcome will depend on who is better skilled, who gets to hit first in the right spot, who impedes who's balance first, and who maintains control of the offense. So my point is, I will always be honest with my students and have them keep the martial arts in the right prospective. As in any endeavor anyone undertakes, a person must pay his dues with hard work and practice while understanding the basic concepts of the martial arts.

Q: Is it necessary to engage in free-fighting to achieve good street-fighting skills?

A: Free-fighting certainly raises the level of understanding the distance, timing and speed necessary to find an opening and respond to the opening. Much like any sport, certain training gets you in tune for the opportunity. In football, as a running back, you must see an opening between two defensive linemen and shoot for the hole. If you hesitate, someone is coming at you because you are an easy target. Free fighting gives you a sense of reality without the full danger of combat. It allows you to make mistakes and live to fight another day. Fighting on the streets is without any sort of gentlemen's rules—anything goes. So if you are free-fighting, at least your skills are somewhat practiced and your percentage of survival moves up a couple of percent. Don't forget, luck and awareness is a huge factor in wining a street fight.

Q: What's your opinion about mixing different Filipino styles?

"I decided to train my students to not concern themselves with anything but reaction and movement—to attack and win at all costs. I taught them a simple five-strike box system."

A: If you look at it like an educational institution, a student with a well-rounded education mixes math with economics, history, language and perhaps with a spot of tennis. In this society, knowledge is a key element in developing a person. Knowledge in the martial arts does not mean memorizing a technique, but learning why the technique works. Mixing martial arts' styles is just getting to the same point by choosing a different road. When a person reaches the pinnacle of a specific martial art, they should have reached the pinnacle of all martial arts. I would like to think that what I teach is usable and effective—that what I teach is the truth. In other words, when someone leaves my seminars I know that I didn't fill up the seminar time with useless movements or busy drills but useful information. Secondly, I like to raise the normal rate of retention for the students. I always want people to obtain good value when they come to seminars and to remember what was taught. It would be like going to a movie and forgetting the plot because there was so much action to distract you.

Q: Do you have a particularly memorable training experience?

A: When I opened my school in San Francisco, I decided to train my students to not concern themselves with anything but reaction and movement—to attack and win at all costs. I taught them a simple five-strike box system. Two weeks later a group of students from another school came by and wanted to work out and I said OK. I had one side throw a strike and then the other side do the same—that way we could train regardless of system or

"Our personal understanding or beliefs and our journey along that path is very individual. Discipline and practice in any art form is meditation. As you exercise, practice, and acquire discipline in the martial arts you will become aware and in touch with your inner or spiritual self."

style. The outside group was the first to throw to my new group of students who had no training in formalities or anything else other then pure fighting. The outside group kept asking my students what they wanted for a strike and my group didn't care because we never practiced that way. When it was my student's turn to throw strikes, the outsiders kept tapping their sides, and their shoulders indicating where they wanted the hits to land. Since my students had no idea what they wanted they hit them anywhere they pleased and threw them all off-balance again and again. They soon left, although a few came back to ask how long my students were training because they thought they were pretty good and would it be possible for them to train with us. I told them my students had just started two to three weeks earlier—the look on these higher-level student's faces, which was priceless.

Q: How do you think a practitioner can increase their understanding of the spiritual aspects of the arts?

A: I believe we are all spiritual beings. Our personal understanding or beliefs and our journey along that path is very individual. Discipline and practice in any art form is meditation. For example, the runners high experienced by a dedicated runner, and the loss of time an artist experiences as they paint a canvas are all forms of meditation and a glimpse into our spiritual essence. As you exercise, practice, and acquire discipline in the martial arts you will become aware and in touch with your inner or spiritual self.

Martial arts is like so many other endeavors we begin in our lives. There is the initial thrill of learning new things, being a part of something, and practicing until you get it right. I figure that after about two years, a person starts to contemplate whether they are making the right investment of money, time, and effort. At this point, you may look around and see other people who may have natural talent and can learn easier, and your confidence level goes down. This is the point where people make a decision to continue training or find a new thrill. Obviously, there are certainly more reasons than this, but this is just one scenario.

"Martial arts is like so many other endeavors we begin in our lives. There is the initial thrill of learning new things, being a part of something, and practicing until you get it right."

Q: What do you consider to be the most important qualities of a successful martial artist?

A: There are several ways of defining a successful martial artist. Are you successful because you have hundreds of students, because you turned out some very good martial artists, because you have been credited with giving inspiration, or because you are the fastest, strongest or most talented? I think the most important quality of a successful martial artist is being a thoughtful human being. Everyone should be treated fairly, and with respect and dignity. Just because you are titled as a master, grandmaster or whatever does not change your status as a human being. These titles are only reflective of your skill and knowledge. If you have worked very hard

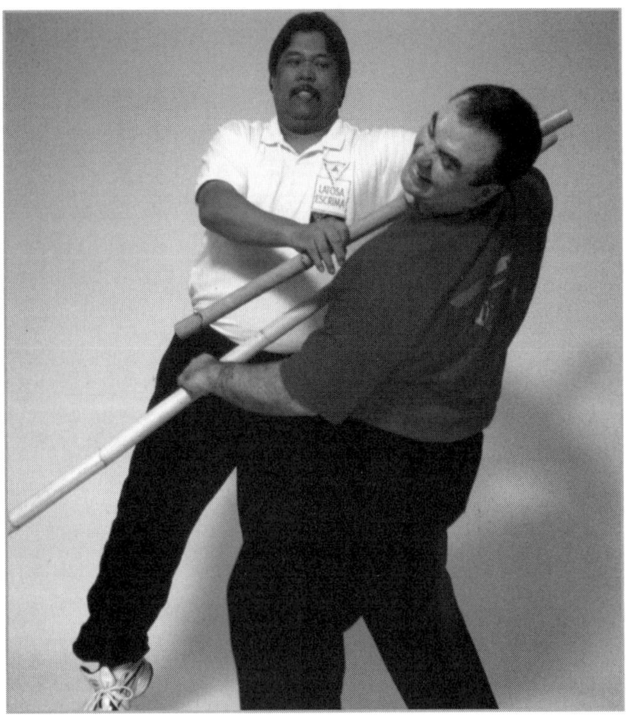

"Students sometimes forget I am there as a teacher, not trying to be the biggest baddest dude in the world. It is important to always see the truth in what you do. I know everyone says this, but they have to look deep into what they do and ask themselves whether what they do works."

and earned a title, then by all means you deserve it; but it is an honor that should not be abused. More knowledge is good, as long as it is the truth or it is something you enjoy. Sometimes I feel that people take the martial arts too seriously and collect too many titles, too many ranks, and not enough enjoyment. We must never forget the thrill of learning something new, discovering why things work, and making movements that don't work, work.

Q: Have ever felt fear in your training?

A: My fear is the fear of accidentally hitting someone I am training with, because they thought it might be fun to get in a hit when they saw an opening. There are always those students who come at you like gangbusters because they feel you won't hurt them. The essence of training is taking in knowledge—not trying to win. I hit outrageously hard and I know the damage I can inflict. Because I have trained all my life in being aware of everything, I react to sudden and unwarranted movements. When you are trained to react, my response is usually automatic—and I could easily end up hurting someone very seriously. Students sometimes forget I am there as a teacher, not trying to be the biggest baddest dude in the world—but they still must remember I have always been trained to instinctively protect myself at all times.

It is important to always see the truth in what you do. I know everyone says this, but they have to look deep into what they do and ask themselves whether what they do works. If there is any doubt, and you are only doing it because that is the way you were told, then you must explain to your stu-

dents that it is being done to preserve the art and keep it intact. For an instructor to let a student out on the streets, knowing that it only works in a school environment, is like sending someone out to battle a bear using a butter knife.

Q: What are your thoughts on the future of the martial arts?
A: The martial arts should be geared toward the next generation. Students should focus on the style and quality of instruction they are receiving, and the role models they will have to follow. Martial arts politics always hurt the students because they suffer for the wants and needs of a few. The reason we got involved and the reason we teach the martial arts seems to diminish as people start looking around and concerning themselves with what other people think, who said what about who, who is better then anyone else, and who will steal who's students. The idea of the martial arts is a way of living life. You set a goal and you accomplish it and work on making it more efficient. If you can accomplish a high level in the martial arts, then perhaps nothing is out of reach and your potential is limitless. As a teacher, your students look to you as a role model and will act similar towards the next generation. Martial artists should also understand that instructors, masters, and gurus are just people like themselves. The fact that they may have more knowledge does not make them better than anyone else. ↄ

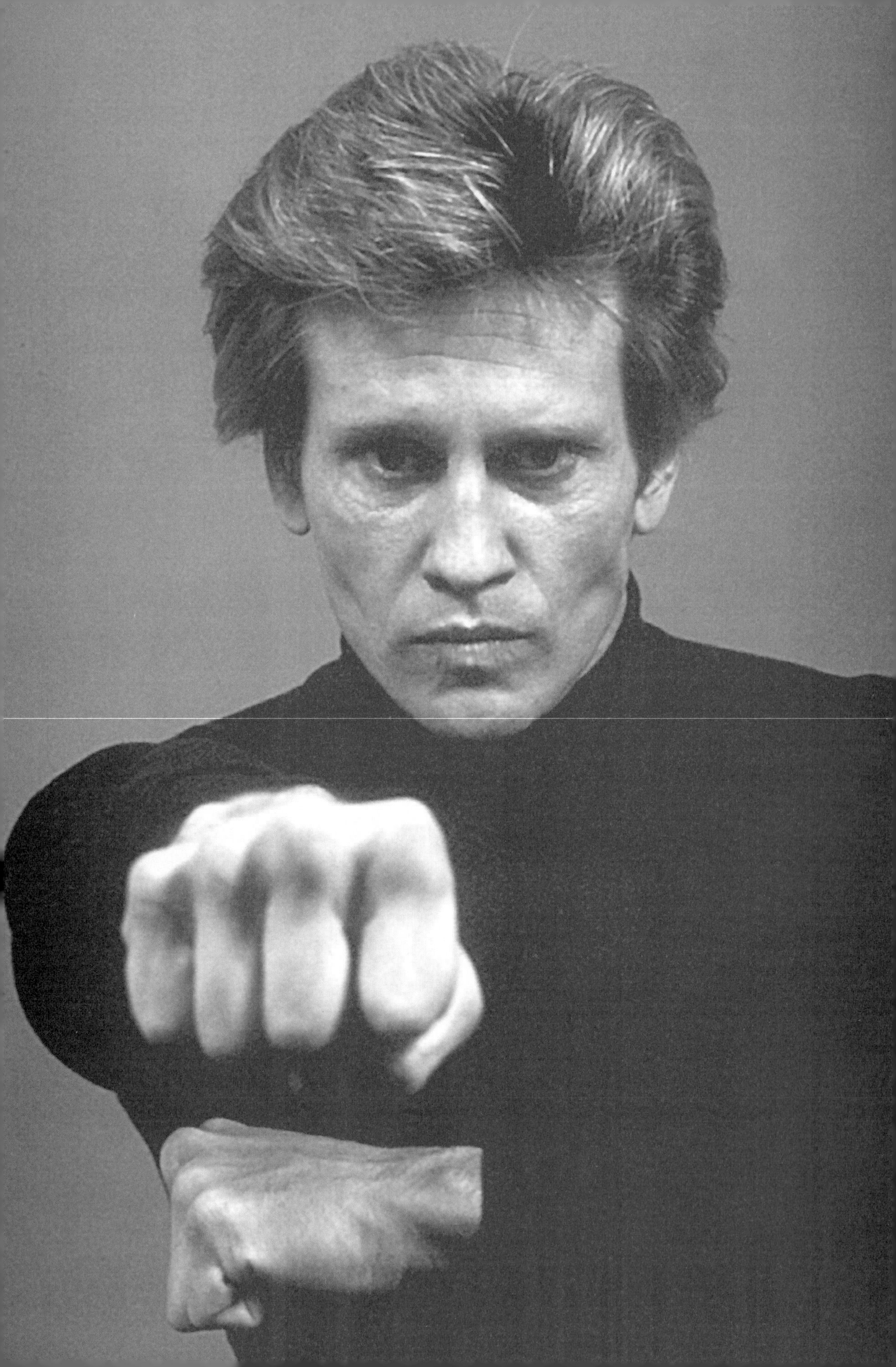

Joe Lewis

The Golden Boy of American Karate

Joe Lewis was the icon for full contact karate and the one fighter everyone looked up to. Many said that Joe Lewis was the closest thing humanly possible to Superman. Not a bad compliment, and perhaps not that far from the truth.

In 1966 Joe Lewis won the first national karate tournament in Washington D.C. after only 22 months of training in Okinawa. His back fist and side kick were the only tools he used—basically the only two he ever needed. He was one of the few karate champions who worked with Bruce Lee, and perhaps the one who spent the most time and gained the most insights from the Little Dragon. Joe Lewis was the most feared fighter of his day and he created Full Contact Kickboxing in 1970.

In September, 1974 Lewis became the first PKA Heavyweight Full Contact World Champion of the world. After retiring, he starred in two major Hollywood films but decided to move back home to North Carolina and to return his roots. His time and energy are now consumed by seminars, where he can share his superior martial arts knowledge, practical experience, and ring savvy.

Q: How did it all begin?
A: I began competing in 1966 with only 22 months of training. I won the United States National Championship. I was coming back from Okinawa and the only names I knew were Mike Stone and Ed Parker.

Q: Chuck Norris was one of your toughest opponents, wasn't he?
A: Yes, we fought four times and he won three of them. But I won the last one in 1968. Chuck and I used to be sparring partners in California. I felt that Chuck was one of the best balanced fighters back them. But I guess my toughest fight was against one of Ed Parker's top students, Scott Lorning. He was strong, fast, and technical. I beat him and he went into some kind of business afterwards.

"I was competing for almost three years. I was beating everybody and I lost all my sparring partners. The only thing I was in karate for was the sparring—I wasn't into it for competition."

Q: You mentioned once that you got bored after winning so many tournaments.

A: I was competing for almost three years. I was beating everybody and I lost all my sparring partners. The only thing I was in karate for was the sparring—I wasn't into it for competition. Then I ran out of information, out of things to learn, and yes, I got really bored.

Q: What happened then?

A: Bruce Lee came along. We met a couple of times before I really started taking him seriously. Bob Wall, Mike Stone and I had been putting together a nightclub act. You know, tell jokes, do some self-defense techniques and do a little bit of sparring. Anyway, Mike Stone started to talk about this Chinese guy named Bruce Lee and that he was phenomenal. Coming from Mike, who was a guy who didn't believe in much of anything, that it was kind a big compliment. As a matter of fact, I don't remember ever hearing Mike Stone compliment anyone. So it was really strange. So I hooked up with Bruce and began going to his house once a week.

Q: Why did you feel like training with him?

A: Well, he started to conceptualize things for me. Most of the teacher tell you to "move faster," or "hit harder." But they can't structurally tell you the progression for you to get there. They can point out your mistakes, but not how to properly correct them and improve your performance. Bruce taught me how to apply a different kind of footwork to become more mobile, and how to become more relaxed in order to increase my speed.

Q: Did you study boxing films together?
A: Boxing and fencing films. He liked to study Muhammad Ali's and Willie Pep's footwork. He showed me a lot of fighting principles and added a lot of mobility to what I was already doing. He made me more cognizant of explosive initial motion. He was great because he was able to give a label to things that I was doing intuitively.

"I wasn't focusing so much on the physical techniques per se, but on adding a new dimension to what I had. So what I did was to use the conceptual part and create my own movements for it. I tried to figured out things by going to boxing gyms and looking at myself in the mirror."

Q: Where did all his information come from?
A: I don't know and I honestly think that no one knows exactly—he was very reserved about a lot of things. Obviously, he had to get a majority of what he knew from other sources because he didn't go to tournaments and do it himself. He was very creative and analyzed a lot of things. He was taking things from one source and things from another source and putting them all together.

Q: What kind of techniques was he doing at that time?
A: He was a kung-fu guy and I didn't relate to those kind of techniques very much. In fact at that time, I didn't understand certain thing because he was presenting them in terms of kung-fu.

Q: How you did get along with his information and teachings?
A: I wasn't focusing so much on the physical techniques per se, but on adding a new dimension to what I had. So what I did was to use the conceptual part and create my own movements for it. I tried to figured out things by going to boxing gyms and looking at myself in the mirror. Kung-fu techniques are very different from kickboxing and tournament techniques.

"Some of the people who trained under him have an over-rationalized mental standpoint, which leads to a loss of spontaneity. I really think that Bruce had a lot to offer, but couldn't pass his talents on to his pupils. I was a fighter and many of the people around Bruce were not very talented fighters."

Q: Didn't Bruce use Western boxing?

A: He didn't use the orthodox Western boxing approach. He boxed using the vertical fist and with the cover hand right in front of the chin. In Western boxing you hit with the horizontal fist and place your rear hand on the side of your head. He was using more the wing chun structure. I couldn't relate to the idea of putting the strong side forward, either. He took this from the fencing use of the foil, sabre or epeé. To me, in theory, it works pretty good, but if you have the practical experience you'll began to see things differently. Basically his theories on independent motion—moving the hand before the body, and the forward and backward shuffle—came from fencing. His overall mobility was from boxing. Kung fu practitioners don't move like that. A lot of his knowledge came out of books, his own abstract thinking and, of course, controlled sparring.

Some of the people who trained under him have an over-rationalized mental standpoint, which leads to a loss of spontaneity. I really think that Bruce had a lot to offer, but couldn't pass his talents on to his pupils. I was a fighter and many of the people around Bruce were not very talented fighters. All the guys that Bruce taught, who got into competition, got their butt kicked and that's a fact. Not even once did one come close to winning a tournament. I knew that if I couldn't make it work no one could. I don't know a man that even came close to making it work. The principles were sound but the techniques didn't seem to work in competition. Now, if there is someone out there that feels he can do it, he sure hasn't come out and proven it—at least not in competition.

"There are some kung fu movements that may work well in combat but as fighting systems I think they are finger painters. I don't see anything positive in a man trying to move like a crane or crocodile."

Q: So you don't believe in traditional kung fu movements?

A: There are some kung fu movements that may work well in combat but as fighting systems I think they are finger painters. I don't see anything positive in a man trying to move like a crane or crocodile. Maybe some trapping could work, but moving like a spider has nothing to do with combat.

Q: What do you think he got from you?

A: Well, on a physical level I taught him a few things about nutrition, vitamins, protein powders, and things like that. He wanted to put some meat on his body because I told him that he had no muscle mass and he could be stronger if he knew how to eat and train with weights. He had a flat rib cage, skinny legs and skinny neck. You don't see great champions with pencil necks out there.

On a personal level I think he wanted to be recognized and get respect from the kung fu world. He was too young at the time to get any acclaim from his peers, yet he wanted to be considered a master and wanted to tell

"I don't want to be compared to anyone, and particularly Bruce Lee. As a martial artist he was a true philosophical, spiritual kind of guy, while I concentrated much more on the sport. My specialty was fighting."

everybody that he was my teacher. In fact, that's one of the reasons why we fall apart—I wouldn't say it because it wasn't true.

Q: Yet you have been compared to him many times.

A: I don't want to be compared to anyone, and particularly Bruce Lee. As a martial artist he was a true philosophical, spiritual kind of guy, while I concentrated much more on the sport. My specialty was fighting.

Q: Do you consider yourself a Bruce Lee student?

A: I did at one time. He was a very good teacher we had very good experiences together analyzing all boxing films, studying fencing and wrestling, and observing Ali's favorite strategies. Then I used to go to tournaments and find out whether it really worked or not.

Q: Did you spar with him?

A: Never. Our training workouts were teaching-exchange sessions. Sometimes we used to put on gloves and head gear and do some drills but not real sparring. Don't forget that he wasn't in my weight class. I always called it controlled or academic sparring, but not sparring in a real sense.

"The kind of training I was doing was very contact oriented. I decided to not compete anymore in point tournaments. I was sick of them. I knew that the only way I would fight was full contact. The ring announcer saw the boxing gloves and made up the term kickboxing."

Q: Why did you disassociate yourself from his followers and stay out of the picture?

A: Well, I didn't want my name associated with his anymore. I didn't want to lean on him and I didn't want him to lean on me. By kung fu standards, he was the superior master and I always tried to protect Bruce behind his back. But after he died a lot of people that had been nice to him began putting him down. I just didn't wanted to deal with the whole thing.

Q: In the early 1970s you introduced the sport of kickboxing. How did that come about?

A: The kind of training I was doing was very contact oriented. I decided to not compete anymore in point tournaments. I was sick of them. I knew that the only way I would fight was full contact. My student Lee Faulkner organized a karate championship and I became the attraction, fighting full-contact against Greg Baines. The ring announcer saw the boxing gloves and

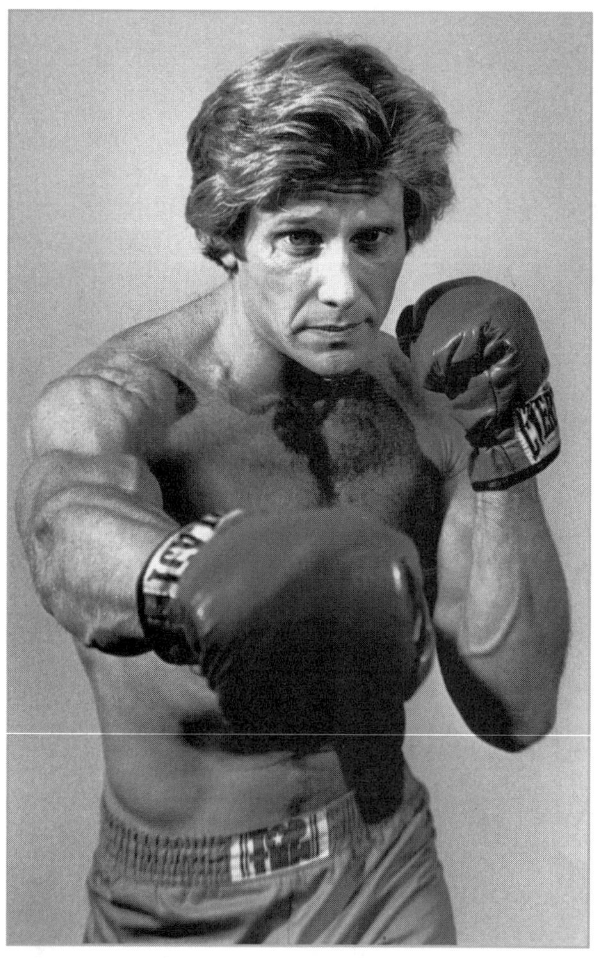

"Mike Anderson, in 1973, was the first promoter to make contact mandatory at his tournament. So everybody had to wear protective equipment. The plan for the full contact championships followed within the year."

made up the term kickboxing. That was the first time I ever heard the term. After that fight I couldn't find an opponent for my size so I retired. I said, "If I can't make any money, to heck with it." Mike Anderson, in 1973, was the first promoter to make contact mandatory at his tournament. So everybody had to wear protective equipment. The plan for the full contact championships followed within the year.

Q: In 1982 you were a karate legend and a movie star, why did you fight again?
A: Looking back, it was one of the stupidest things I ever did in my life. I tried to combine training, living, and thinking as a fighter with the movie business. They just don't mix. I really had no desire to fight anyone. My body had changed and I didn't have enough drive. The inspiration never came back.

Q: It is true that you trained at Hidetaka Nishiyama's JKA dojo for a while?
A: Yes. The only reason I did that was because I wanted to train with Nishiyama and spar with Frank Smith, who I considered one of the top guys ever. They told me I had to start as a white belt and I did.

Q: But you had already your own schools, right?
A: Yes! I had my own school and then would go to the other side of the city and put on a white belt! Anyway, I wanted to train with the competition

team and they told me I had to wait for six months. After two months I got tired of being used and I left.

Q: Did you had any problems there?

A: Well, there was 5th degree black belt who tried to made me look bad in front of everybody. We were supposed to be slow motion sparring and he came real fast and hard trying to sweep me. He couldn't and I got really pissed off and I picked up the little sucker and dumped him on his butt. He was really, really embarrassed but he asked for it.

"Combat is not a matter of how many combinations of techniques you know but rather one's manner of execution. It's not one's weapon, but rather one's tactical and strategic manner of delivering the technique that counts."

Q: Did you finally spar with Frank Smith?

A: I never did get a chance but I'm sure he would have been my meat the way they sparred in traditional shotokan karate.

Q: Neither as a fighter or an instructor were you ever known as a man of a thousand techniques. Why?

A: Because I'm a fighter I know that you'd better have a few good techniques that you can rely on that thousand of them fighting against you. Combat is not a matter of how many combinations of techniques you know but rather one's manner of execution. It's not one's weapon, but rather one's tactical and strategic manner of delivering the technique that counts.

There are teachers who like to go from style to style. I don't think this is because they want to enhance their knowledge, but because they have this

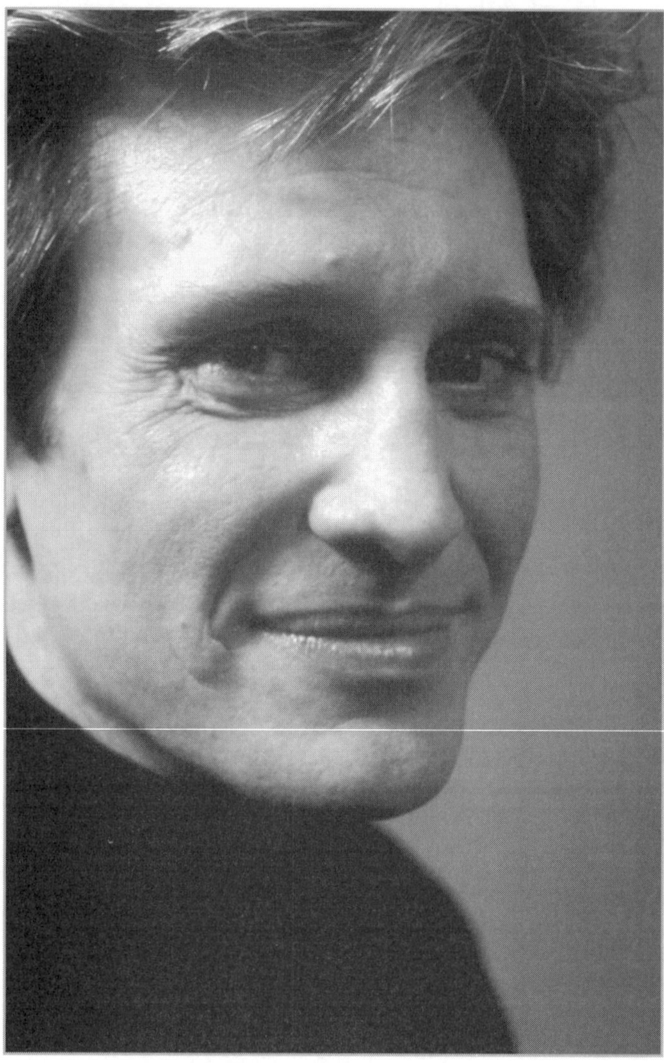

"When you have that tactical and strategic knowledge, you know you've got it. You know you can make anything work and you'll be able to cause anyone's stuff not to work against you."

basic innate sense that what they have been taught doesn't work. When you have that tactical and strategic knowledge, you know you've got it. You know you can make anything work and you'll be able to cause anyone's stuff not to work against you. Bruce Lee told me that the reasons he and other teachers would sometimes do this is to show you what not to do. The problem is that if you follow this kind of teacher you're gonna spend a great deal of time learning all the nonsense, simply learning what not to do.

Q: Do you think that money can be another reason?

A: Of course. The more stuff you teach, the more money you make and also the more you lead the student to believe that he doesn't know everything yet. The more he thinks this, the longer he's going to stay around hoping that one day he may have it.

"Competition was a way of improving myself. If you have no motivation and no inspiration then you have no sense of purpose. You die out. That's probably why most of the people involved in martial arts quit."

Q: What made Joe Lewis head and shoulders above everybody else?
A: I had a goal and my standards for physical aspects were higher than those of most people. By being able to improving myself, I felt proud. Competition was a way of improving myself. If you have no motivation and no inspiration then you have no sense of purpose. You die out. That's probably why most of the people involved in martial arts quit. They don't have a pathway to follow. This is why the spiritual aspect is very important in the long run.

Q: What are your feelings about ranking?
A: I only believe in the black belt. To me the ultimate achievement was and is the black belt. I've always believed that actions speak more strongly than words and I've always just worn a simple black belt. ↄ

Thomas B. Mitose

Carry On My Wayward Son

Separated at birth from his legendary, mysterious father, Thomas Mitose sought him out years later, learned his art of Shorei Ruy Kenpo, and became a great master himself.

Thomas Barro Mitose, son of the legendary James Mitose, is the 22nd Great Grandmaster of Kosho Shorei Ryu Kenpo. He inherited the system from his father and founded the International Kosho Shorei Association to help father James while he was in prison. In 1987 Thomas decided to reorganize the philosophies and techniques of kosho kenpo, as handed down from generation to generation, and come forward to preserve and teach his father's reorganized art in the traditional manner.

Many are the times Thomas thinks about what happened to his father, and what could have been had his father never been sent to prison. He carries on the family tradition because his father always talked to him about opening a family dojo where they could teach together. Thomas understand his responsibilities and is happy trying to fulfill his father's desires.

Adopted as a child, Thomas B. Mitose didn't get to see his real father until later in life. Once father and son were reunited, Thomas commenced his studies in the kosho ryu art. On October 1995, kajukenbo founder Professor Adriano D. Emperado wrote an statement proclaiming Grandmaster Thomas Barro Mitose as the rightful heir to the Mitose kosho ryu kenpo crown, according to James Masayoshi Mitose's last will and testament.

Q: Where did you father's system come from?
A: It was developed by the Koshogi monks of Japan. They combined jiu-jitsu and chuan fa Shaolin kung-fu and, of course, different traditions and cultural approaches from China.

Q: Is it a self-defense method?
A: Yes, it is. But you must remember that in 1953 my father, James Mitose, gave up teaching because he felt the students were leaning too much

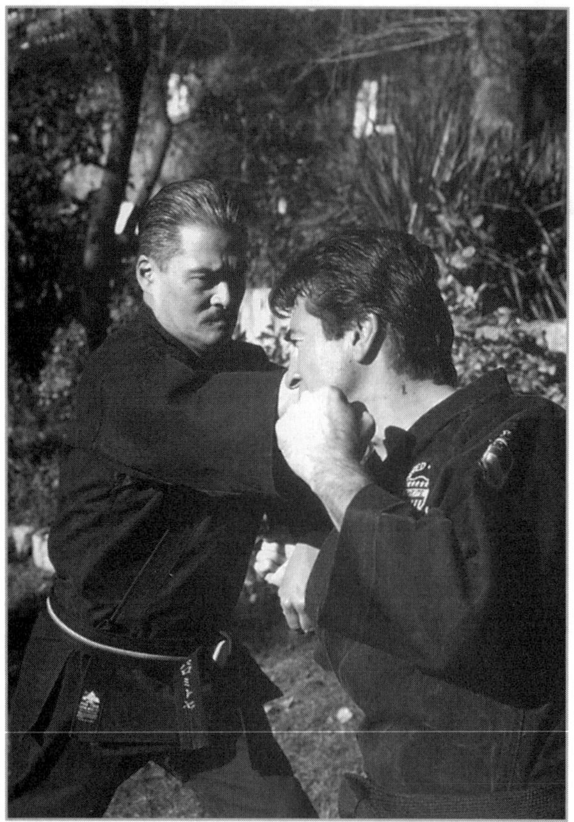

"Kosho shorei ryu is a philosophical and spiritual self-defense system where each physical techniques has a spiritual complement. It also uses meditation and yoga as vehicles for that."

toward the violent side of the art and not studying enough of the spiritual aspects. Kosho shorei ryu is a philosophical and spiritual self-defense system where each physical techniques has a spiritual complement. It also uses meditation and yoga as vehicles for that.

Q: You didn't get to know your father until much later in life, correct?
A: Yes. My parents weren't able to support me so they gave me up to adoption. Later on, my adoptive father and mother got divorced and I went to meet my real father in Los Angeles in the mid '60s. My adopted family name was Barro and I keep it out of respect for them, but I legally added the Mitose name to my own.

Q: Is that when you started to train under your real father?
A: Yes. The most important thing during the lessons from my father was to make sure that I gained the correct knowledge, techniques, and philosophies of kosho ryu as handed down from generations to generation. My father, James Masayoshi Mitose, was the 21st Great Grandmaster of Kosho Shorei Ryu Kenpo.

Q: Did he speak English?
A: He never felt very comfortable speaking in English. He liked to speak Japanese and even his way of reasoning was very Japanese. After all, that's the culture he grew up in.

Q: What was your first meeting with him like?

A: A relative of a close friend informed me that my real father was living in Los Angeles and I decided to go there. He opened the door looking really rough, saw me, and then closed it right away in my face. I was shocked. A few minutes later he reopened the door with tears in his eyes, and was washed and clean shaven! Even after all that time he had known who I was from the very first moment he saw me.

"I expect kenpo practitioners incorporate the kosho philosophy into their styles. It's not a matter of changing the technique but rather the attitude and the philosophy."

Q: Who was you first martial arts instructor?

A: Mr. Joe Halbuna, a kajukenbo teacher.

Q: It is true that your father never gave you any rank or certificate?

A: He always felt that I didn't need it. He said that I had his blood in me and also his name. He said that even if some people claim to be masters, I should not pay attention to them, because unless someone comes from the blood line of the grandmaster they will never have a full understanding and knowledge of the art.

Q: Did he ask you to change your name to Mitose?

A: Yes, several times. I guess it was away of apologizing for not taking care of me when I was young. A way of correcting something he felt he did wrong. That's why I changed my name. But I kept "Barro" out of respect for my adoptive family.

"Our goal is not to teach a devastating street fighting art but to teach a life philosophy which happens to also include a component for physical self-defense. Our primary goal is to teach our students how to live a good life and become valued members of society."

Q: Does your father's kenpo system agree with other kenpo styles' methods?

A: Well, there are continual arguments about who is representing the true art. It happens in every system or style. What I really want is for all kenpo people to look deeper into the art than just self-defense techniques and fighting. You see, after my father retired some students of kenpo liked to train very hard at the school. They were very intense about the physical and technical aspects of the art. To find out if the techniques was useful or not they used to get into several fights every day at bars, theatres, et cetera. This is what gave kenpo and other systems developed from my father's method such a violent reputation. This made my father very sad. I expect kenpo practitioners incorporate the kosho philosophy into their styles. It's not a matter of changing the technique but rather the attitude and the philosophy.

Q: Is the kenpo style that you teach similar to the one developed by the late Ed Parker?

A: Our own art of kenpo is very different from Ed Parker's kenpo in both its approach and its goals. Our goal is not to teach a devastating street fighting art but to teach a life philosophy which happens to also include a component for physical self-defense. Our primary goal is to teach our students how to live a good life and become valued members of society. Our definition of self-defense is quite broad and our goals guide the training our students receive.

One major difference between kosho-ryu and other kenpo systems is that our students begin learning the spiritual arts before they are taught to punch and kick. We believe that by learning the spiritual arts first, the stu-

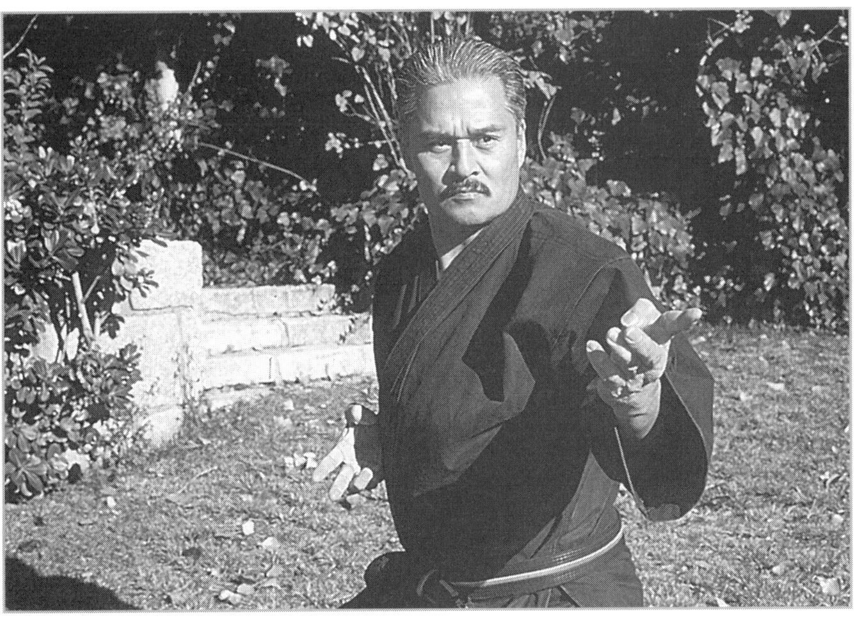

"The true art of self-defense—teaches you how to use jumping patterns to escape from danger by using no physical contact with the opponent whatsoever. For this reason is called the true art of self-defense."

dents who become proficient will revert to the spiritual side when threatened, rather than to the combative side.

Q: So the system is divided into spiritual and physical arts?
A: Yes. But these two aspects of the system cannot be studied separately and independently because they represent different aspects of one complete art. Also the physical art is divided in three systems. The first aspect of the fighting system teaches you to punch and kick, the kata forms, and so on. The second aspect is what we call the push-pull arts, and teaches you how to defend yourself by making use of push-pull patterns and strikes to the extremities. The third aspect—the true art of self-defense—teaches you how to use jumping patterns to escape from danger by using no physical contact with the opponent whatsoever. For this reason is called the true art of self-defense.

"Self-defense is not, strictly speaking, a fighting method. It is a life philosophy characterized by survival methods according to the universal laws of God."

Q: You mentioned once that the true kosho practitioner would never kick or punch on the street. Why?

A: Because he would never be caught in the street! We look at true self-defense as the art of anticipation rather than the art of reaction. By anticipating trouble, the practitioner would simply never be there when trouble arrived. Self-defense is not, strictly speaking, a fighting method. It is a life philosophy characterized by survival methods according to the universal laws of God.

Q: So what's the use of learning how to punch and kick?

A: The main purpose for kicking and punching is to strengthen the body and to remove any evil in oneself by mentally transferring it to the object being kicked or punched. The only exception to this principle is during times of war.

Q: How is the concept of anticipation taught?

A: The students are taught to use their awareness to deal with conflict. It means to understand their environment and when they are most vulnerable to attack. They are taught to interact with people so that a conflict never arises. They are taught to become aware of dangerous environments and situations where they can be assaulted. They learn how to understand the opponent capabilities of sight, hearing, touch, and movement so that an attacker will never reach its mark. If all else fails, they concentrate on attacking opponent's extremities in order to contain the attacker's ability to strike. Finally, they are taught the location of parasympathetic nervous system receptors in the body which, when activated, will counter the release of adrenaline from an enraged opponent.

Q: This is very different from other kenpo systems.
A: We work to make our more aggressive students softer and to teach our less assertive students self-confidence. It is the weakness that require practice, not the strengths.

Q: Do you think teaching martial arts is like coaching sports?
A: Not at all. Teaching martial arts is something very different than coaching ball games. Improper teaching of martial arts can turn students into predators. The students are taught how to defend themselves, but are also taught to avoid harming another human being.

Q: Is it correct to say that kenpo roots are Chinese rather than Japanese?
A: Yes. Kosho shorei kenpo traces its roots directly from China without the Okinawan link.

Q: It is said that your father was very skilled in jiu-jitsu and that he taught techniques resembling modern aikido.
A: It is true. My father was not an aikido man, but Morihei Ueshiba, the founder himself, specified in his will that James Mitose should be promoted to 10th dan in aikido and given the title of *remonstrant* for all aikido in America. My father was highly respected by O Sensei Ueshiba.

Q: How do you remember you father?
A: Many people think of my father, James Mitose, as a mysterious figure who taught early kenpo practitioners how to punch and kick in the kenpo way. I really do believe that all his teaching boils down to one single principle which is the essence of kenpo—live an ethical life, do justly, love mercy, and walk humbly with God. All the techniques, katas, forms, and strikes are just tricks. Ↄ

Master Mitose (left) squares off with his opponent (1) Aggressor attacks with a reverse punch that is nullified by Master Mitose's side step and body punch (2) followed by a replacement of his body position (3) to hit again with a backfist to the temple (4). This enables him to use his left arm to control the aggressor's right side (5) finishing him off with a groin kick (6)

Master Mitose squares off with his opponent adopting an "en guard" position (1). As his opponent executes a high roundhouse kick, Master Mitose blocks with his left arm (2) and simultaneously (3) delivers a front kick to the aggressor's groin (4) that finish him off (5).

Hiroo Mochizuki

The Master of Yoseikan Budo

Based upon human physiology, not animal movement, Master Mochizuki's eclectic style focuses on results not rank. The son of a Japanese martial arts legend, Hiroo Mochizuki received his training from the top masters in world. His practical approach and eclectic mentally enabled him to develop a new system called Yoseikan Budo, which combines traditional training aspects with modern views and a practical teaching methodology. After discovering what he called "the undulant movement," Master Mochizuki began to change and adapt the physical techniques to the human body, thereby creating a revolutionary martial arts method that is taking the traditional Japanese martial arts world by storm.

Q: Is yoseikan a sport or a martial art system?
A: Nowadays we have to balance both training aspects. If you train for sport competition there are some regulations that you have to consider, but if you talk about martial arts then you can use everything. Anyway, I don't think the practitioner has to focus on real fighting all the time. The sport aspect of the art enables the student to develop some important attributes—but these sportive shouldn't be mistaken for skills that you could use in a real confrontation.

Q: Do you think that by using the sport training as a practice guide, the real essence of martial arts can be understood?
A: I think so and that's yoseikan's goal. With proper training and diligent practice the student can understand some of the basic tenets of the old warrior. The yoseikan system strives to be a method for everybody who wishes to practice the martial arts in a safe way. Its approach is very eclectic and borrows from many different traditional systems.

Q: What is the technical structure of the yoseikan system?
A: Our eclectic approach supplies us with a great variety of combat techniques used in many combat methods. A yoseikan practitioner doesn't limit

"Because of my traditional background and the training under my father, I've been criticized by some of my peers. But they don't understand that the traditional principles are still in the Yoseikan method."

himself to punching or kicking techniques from this or that system. He tries to logically combine fighting structures in order to develop a wide spectrum of possibilities for any given situation. Because of my traditional background and the training under my father, I've been criticized by some of my peers. But they don't understand that the traditional principles are still in the Yoseikan method. Aikido founder Morihei Ueshiba's teachings are a very important part of the art. We also use some techniques and fighting principles of the shorin karate system combined with elements of the shorei method. The study of tai chi educates the yoseikan exponent on the understanding of the body balance and the inner energy. In short, we use different elements to develop certain aspects important for the martial artist.

Q: Does the yoseikan art involve weaponry training?

A: Yes, it does. We teach all the traditional Okinawa weapons as *tonfa, sai, nunchaku,* and *bo,* and all the ancient weaponry of the old Japanese warriors. This includes the *kenjutsu* (bow and arrow). My weaponry training mostly was under Koizumi sensei.

Q: It is true that the techniques have been developed based on an anatomical study of the human body?

A: Yes. The physical techniques are developed according to the very nature of the human body. Humans can't move like a leopard or a mantis. This is a very important consideration in the approach to martial arts training. We must learn to respect the human body because only by doing so will we understand our higher potential. It's true that there are some very effective techniques in some systems. But when studied in detail we discover that those techniques deform the human body. Therefore, their practice and training is detrimental for the student's health. In the yoseikan system we look for physical techniques that keep us in shape, give us self-defense resources, and help us avoid injuries in our bodies.

"The teaching ability to transmit and communicate with the practitioner is paramount in the educational process. Being a good practitioner or exponent in yoseikan is very different from being a good teacher or instructor. You can be one and not the other."

Q: What are the requirements for being an instructor in yoseikan kempo?

A: Of course the technical aspect is paramount, but teaching is a very important activity and some people forget this. Therefore, being an instructor is not an easy task. As a teacher you have to understand the student's goals and mentality and help him to achieve the former and strengthen the latter. The teaching ability to transmit and communicate with the practitioner is paramount in the educational process. Being a good practitioner or exponent in yoseikan is very different from being a good teacher or instructor. You can be one and not the other.

Q: Why are all the ranking belts in yoseikan the same color (white and blue)?

A: People look at the color of the belt to evaluate a practitioner's skill level and that's wrong. Some people are very good when performing physical

"You need to train in different systems to understand the different approaches to combat. Only by training in several and technically different methods the student can develop an understanding of what it is important and effective."

techniques but mentally they are very weak. Some student's techniques are not very sound but their attitude and will are superb. There's no reason to classify people. We don't like to compare people's skills. However, we accept the fact that a student coming from other different systems wants to keep his belt during training at any yoseikan dojo.

Q: How do you train for a real fight?
A: A lot of people like to talk about real fighting, but training for this kind of situation is very demanding both physically and mentally. In a real fight, the mind has to be free to react instantly and the physical technique is not all that important. In a real fight will power, determination, and spirit is more important than what technique you use.

Q: It seems lately that martial artist tend to use a more eclectic approach to the training, what do you think about this?
A: Well, I can't be against since this is pretty much what I have done with yoseikan budo. I can see the reason why practitioners are using this eclectic approach to their training and research; no martial art system is complete. You need to train in different systems to understand the different approaches to combat. Only by training in several and technically different methods the student can develop an understanding of what it is important and effective. Martial arts should care about self defense primarily and even if all the systems claim this to be their goal...I believe it would be great if they give it a little push.

Q: What do you think is your contribution to the martial arts world?
A: I truly believe everybody is in this world for a reason. I believe to be adding a 'new' approach to the most traditional arts of budo and I hope to leave an important legacy for my disciples to follow. In the world of Nature evolution and change are the leading elements, why should be that way in budo?

Q: Do you have any advise for the practitioners of martial arts?
A: One of the most important things these days for the practitioners to understand is martial arts is budo. There is a philosophy in the art that we should all try to keep and develop for the future generations. Respect is paramount in budo and respect is one of the basis of our society; no respect, no human relationships. Peace can only be achieved through mutual respect among human beings. Unfortunately the majority of martial arts practitioners today are more interested in develop their ability as fighters instead as skill as good human beings. And that's not the right way. All the traditional masters such as Funakoshi Gichin and Jigoro Kano tried to keep the traditional values in the arts they taught. Regardless of the type of physical technique we use, we must strive to keep these values in our lives and budo training. Ͻ

Andre Nocquet

Living the Dream

Sensei André Nocquet was a direct disciple of aikido founder Morihei Ueshiba. A native of France, Sensei Nocquet moved to Japan to be a real "uchi deshi" at the aikido honbu *dojo. His daily contact with the legendary martial arts master had a great influence on him. As he said once: "I am nothing, O Sensei is everything."*

During his training sessions he could constantly be heard making comments such as "Techniques are nothing," "Aikido is the moment," "5 percent philosophy, 95 percent training", et cetera. His style was very spontaneous and natural. Nocquet Sensei was an inspired teacher who also had a great sense of humor—something which comes out in his teaching. He was recognized around the world as one of the foremost authorities on the theory and practice of the art. Nocquet was a small man, but only in stature. In all other ways he was a truly the "gentle giant" of aikido.

Q: How did you begin your training in the martial arts?

A: I started at the age of 17 with Master Kawaishi, who was the founder of judo in France. He was a very great master. One day a man called Mochizuki Sensei arrived. His technique was not like judo. I understood that the aikido of Mochizuki sensei and judo could complement each other. In the street, if there is any aggression, the one thing you must not do is take hold of your opponent, you must guide him but never touch him. Because if he has a knife, he can beat you immediately, and you're dead. So I practiced with him, and this man stayed a year with us, then he had to return to Japan. But the creator of aikido, Morihei Ueshiba, sent another man, Tadashi Abe, and he started to teach Aikido to a few students. I practiced with him a lot. One day he said to me, "Monsieur Nocquet, you like aikido very much. You absolutely must go to Japan and meet O Sensei, the founder of aikido." At that time I had my own judo club with more than 300 students and I thought it was a good excuse for not going. Master Abe said, "You must go to Japan." After a lot of thinking, I decided go to Japan by boat.

"I stayed with him in his home. I was a real disciple of Master Ueshiba. I slept on the tatami *(straw mats) and ate with Master Ueshiba every day. I trained five hours a days. My ignorance of the Japanese language kept me in a state of isolation for three complete years!"*

Q: Why by boat?

A: I knew a man named Georges Duhamel, who was a writer of the Academie Francaise. He sent me to Japan to learn aikido and kinestherapy (Japanese physiological treatment methods). He said to me, "If you take the plane from Paris to Tokyo, you won't understand the Japanese. You must deserve Japan—earn it in small stages."

So I left for Japan and stayed there three years; I slept in the dojo and ate Japanese food, and I was with Tamura Sensei. Master Tamura practiced with O Sensei for more than 15 years. Every morning he did 200 forward break-falls! He is a great master. I went back by way of the United States, where I taught near Fresno, California. The Americans set up some tests for me to see if Aikido was effective. The Americans were very good to me—they called me "Little Father Christmas," and they wanted me to stay in the USA in 1958. They offered to give me a contract to open an aikido club in Los Angeles, because at that time there were no aikido clubs in the States, apart from Tohei—a great master. He was one of the greatest masters of aikido—he was my friend and also my teacher. He's very, very strong—he is extraordinary. When I stayed in Fresno I taught the police, and then I went to New York. I didn't want to stay any longer because my family wanted to see me. So I took a boat back to Europe.

Q: What was your first impression of O Sensei?

A: I stayed with him in his home. I was a real disciple of Master Ueshiba. I didn't have a hotel—I slept on the *tatami* (straw mats) and ate with Master Ueshiba every day. I trained five hours a days. My ignorance of the Japanese language kept me in a state of isolation for three complete years! This isolation led me to be more aware of myself, to meditate more about things and my own life. After a while I understood that I had many things in my life that were truly secondary to the essence of my very existence. I perceived day by day how they were dissolving away like sugar in water and the only interesting thing for me was my personal and inner liberation. I guess everything went OK because when I arrived I held the grade of 2nd dan in Aikido, and now I am an 8th dan.

"I formed the Union of Aikido, not so much for technique, but for fostering international friendship. I don't travel that much anymore. My wife says, "You're married to Aikido, not to me." But I love my wife very much."

Q: Do you still practice?

A: Of course! I formed the Union of Aikido, not so much for technique, but for fostering international friendship. I guess that's the best way to go. Of course, I still practice all the time. I have never retired. But at my age I do a bit less. I don't travel that much anymore. My wife says, "You're married to Aikido, not to me." But I love my wife very much.

Q: Did you ever meet the great karate master Mas Oyama?

A: Yes! We were pretty good friends and I trained with him a few times. I guess because Master Ueshiba knew that I went to see Oyama, he was a little jealous. O Sensei said to me, "Have you come for karate or for aikido?" But Oyama was a terrific person. He was very strong.

Q: What other martial arts systems have you practiced?

A: I did wrestling, jiu-jitsu and karate. And, of course, judo. In Japan I went to the Kodokan for some judo training under Master Uchijima, who was a great teacher. I did *ne waza* (ground techniques) with him for competition.

"It is important to understand that aikido is not simply a matter of techniques. I believe that the practice of martial arts, without all the emphasis on winning and competition against each other, is the basis for a very complete education of the population."

Q: Were there many differences between Western teaching methods and O Sensei's?

A: When I was in Japan, masters Tadashi Abe and Mochizuki developed a teaching method for Western students that was objective. But when I arrived at Ueshiba's it was a different method—it was subjective—for the body to understand. The Japanese teach us Westerners objectively, they teach us techniques separately, and that's not real aikido. Real aikido is to repeat the movements for a very long time, until you forget the mental aspect and it becomes part of your body. That's real Aikido. Karate is the same. You must repeat, repeat, and repeat. If you think during an attack, that's the end of your actions. Your body doesn't think, it just reacts. Master Ueshiba said, "the level of an aikidoka is not judged but the number of techniques he knows, but by the manner in which he uses them." It is possible to learn aikido through the study of a single technique. It is important to understand that aikido is not simply a matter of techniques. Don't forget that in Japan the training in martial arts is not an end unto itself, on the contrary. In the Western world, the practice of martial arts may be dangerous since it may constitute a certain danger due to the combat sports that are so popular these days. I believe that the practice of martial arts, without all the emphasis on winning and competition against each other, is the basis for a very complete education of the population.

Q: Is the subjective aspect you mentioned the same as the Japanese word *kan* (intuition)?
A: Yes, the same, because you must stop your opponent's attack when it is in his mind, but if the attack is carried out, it's too late. If a karateka wants to kick me, and I wait, it's too late—it's over. The adversary is not defeated by the physical technique but at the right instant the intention to attack rises up within him. Because he is already defeated it is possible to apply a technique on him in order to solidify his defeat. It is about mastering the attacker's intent. As an aikido practitioner, you must lead the adversary into a position where it is impossible for him to avoid your technique. Of course, we must use techniques, but this is the reason aikido is not found in physical techniques but rather the manner in which they are applied.

"The adversary is not defeated by the physical technique but at the right instant the intention to attack rises up within him. Because he is already defeated it is possible to apply a technique on him in order to solidify his defeat."

Q: So this is *sen no sen*?
A: Yes. Western people make *go no sen*—they go against an attack. If a man has a knife, and we wait for the knife to come, it's too late.

Q: Can you cultivate *ki*, or is it intrinsic within you?
A: Master Tohei is the master of ki. Master Ueshiba said that to really understand ki, you must be empty—empty yourself so ki can enter into you. But Master Ueshiba always spoke in parables. He said, "How do you want ki to enter in you?" I could also explain it like this. Your glass is full of coffee. You must empty your coffee first before I can penetrate with my tea. You must meditate, put the conscious mind on one side, forget to think, and maybe then ki will emerge naturally. There is no way for ki to enter into many people, because they are too pretentious, too full of

"He didn't want to make any kata in aikido, because he said if we do kata the forms are fixed, they stay like that, and there is no progress. By creating a kata you fix the form for all time. Monsieur Descartes didn't do us a great service!"

themselves. You must empty yourself, and after that ki is at your service. Ki does everything in a person except for the ordinary thing like eating, going for a walk, or going somewhere—for those I use my brain. It is necessary to use ki for important things. To believe in the presence of ki in us is also to persevere with confidence, to renew, each day, our good resolutions. Therefore, we are not controlled by the flesh but by the spirit.

Q: Did O Sensei favor kata training?
A: Not at all. He didn't want to make any kata in aikido, because he said if we do kata the forms are fixed, they stay like that, and there is no progress. By creating a kata you fix the form for all time. Monsieur Descartes didn't do us a great service!

Q: What advice would you give to a new aikido black belt?
A: Master Ueshiba said that *shodan* (1st degree black belt) is the beginning of aikido. When you're a shodan, you start to understand a little about aikido, that's how it is. When you are a *kuy* grade, it's like a primary school, when you're a shodan you enter high school. First dan is going to university. And if you make 5th or 6th dan, then you've graduated. The more martial arts you do, sometimes when you are a high grade you are still weak. And if you are weak, you can progress. But as soon as a man thinks he is strong, his way is blocked. That's why I prefer 2nd place to 1st. When a man is first he can't go any higher. But if he is second he can transcend the first without realizing it.

"Master Ueshiba said that shodan *(1st degree black belt) is the beginning of aikido. When you're a shodan, you start to understand a little about aikido, that's how it is."*

It is very important to practice martial arts without the intention of developing the aggressive instinct, but by creating an opposite mental attitude—directing the attention towards the partner and using one's energy with a brotherly intent. There are many kinds of forces within us, but they remain latent, asleep. The right practice of the martial arts helps the student to develop these latent energies within him without forgetting that the greatest art in the study of *Budo* is that of avoiding combat.

"Morihei Ueshiba was a genius. What fascinated me the most about his teaching is that he always wished to convey that all difficulties of man arise from a conflict between his heart and his ego."

Q: How do you remember O Sensei?

A: Morihei Ueshiba was a genius. Every day Ueshiba practiced alone, and I said to him, "But you are the great founder of aikido. Why do you do that?" And he said to me. "Monsieur Nocquet, I was given the gift of understanding, the spirit of non-violence and the love by God. There is some kind of ki within me, but my body is not supple and I practice every morning because I want my body to make progress." He was an amazing man, very modest. he said to me one day, "Monsieur Nocquet, the higher you go, the more you must humble yourself." I said to him, "But why

stay that low?" He replied, "If someone pushes you, you fall from lower down." What fascinated me the most about his teaching is that he always wished to convey that all difficulties of man arise from a conflict between his heart and his ego.

Q: What's your philosophy of teaching?

A: As student, you look after your master, you help him all the time. That's spirit. It's not a question of money; it's a question of the relationship between the disciple with the master. In seminars and at most of the schools, the people pay—they buy the teacher. That's not good. You buy the master. Where's the value in that? No, you must not buy the master. If you say to me, "I have a lot of money, and I'll give you the time"—if I accept the money, I cannot teach you. That's terrible. Aikido is about spirit and heart. Kisshomaru Ueshiba, son of the founder, stated: "It goes without saying that the physical aspect of Aikido is important, but if the spirit and the heart are absent in the movement of the body, then it is not truly aikido." The opening of the human heart to the divine is the essential and central message of the teaching I received from Morihei Ueshiba. Within men, there is a great power that resides within his heart. My only purpose is to help my students to discover this.

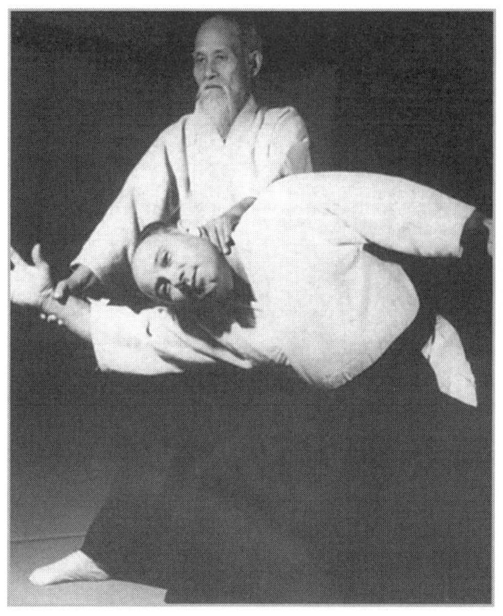

"Kisshomaru Ueshiba, son of the founder, stated: 'It goes without saying that the physical aspect of Aikido is important, but if the spirit and the heart are absent in the movement of the body, then it is not truly aikido.'"

Chuck Norris

Determination and Perseverence

Carlos Ray Norris began training in tang soo do in Korea in 1960, while in the Air Force. After returning from Korea, Norris began teaching and also training, learning from such world-class masters as Fumio Demura, Tsuomu Oshima, and Hidetaka Nishiyama. His reputation in the point-tournament karate circuit grew quickly. He became a world champion in 1968 and retired undefeated several years later. His determination to win led Norris to defeat every major competitor of his time with the exception of Mike Stone.

After dropping out of tournament competition, Norris made a name for himself in Hollywood, becoming one of the biggest action stars in the world. His fight in the final scene against Bruce Lee in The Return of the Dragon *has been described as the best martial arts fighting sequence of all time. At his 30th birthday party at a Chinese restaurant, his fortune cookie read, "Success should be a result, not a goal." When asked about his great success, he answered, "It just happened. I never planned it."*

Q: When did you decide to choose acting as a career?
A: I was teaching Steve McQueen and he said that I should try acting. He thought I had a presence that would be believable on the screen. I knew that nobody could fill Bruce's shoes as far as martial arts on the screen, but I felt that I could do something else that would work for me.

Q: Did you ever expect the kind of success you had?
A: To be honest I've never thought about it. As a karate practitioner I was never expecting to became a world champion—it just happened. I don't think you ever visualize these kinds of things. You work in a certain direction and you set realistic goals. Those things give you the chance to reach higher levels.

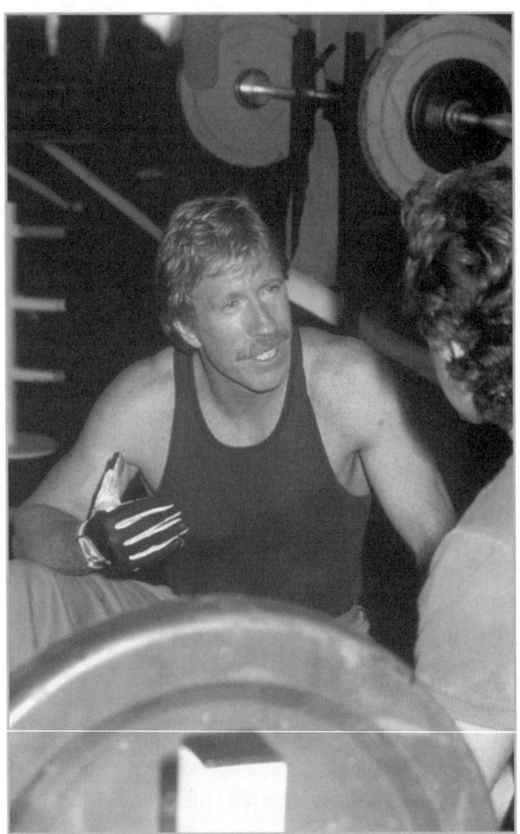

"I don't look at myself as a star, so I don't take it seriously. In the movie business you're up and you're down—it depends on a lot of things."

Q: Do you feel comfortable being a star?

A: I don't look at myself as a star, so I don't take it seriously. In the movie business you're up and you're down—it depends on a lot of things. That's why success, for me, means to be happy with your life and to be healthy. Money can't guarantee you happiness. I know a lot of very rich people who are very, very unhappy.

Q: Have you ever compared yourself to Steven Seagal, Jean Claude Van Damme, or other action stars?

A: I never felt like I had to be compared to anyone else—I do the best I can within myself. It's the old martial arts philosophy that the only person I'm competing against is myself. So I don't waste my energy looking outward.

Q: It is true that you began teaching karate in your parent's backyard?

A: Yes, it is. I did it because I had to support my family and there were no schools around. After that I opened a small school in Torrance, California. So when I was waiting to go into the LAPD, I decided to make my living teaching karate. I quit my job and opened a second school in Redondo Beach and began competing in tournaments. A little bit later I opened another school with my friend Bob Wall in Sherman Oaks.

Q: Why did you two decide to split?

A: We were planning to go nationwide so we sold our schools to a big corporation. It just didn't work out for whatever reasons, and Bob went into real estate and I went into films.

"I never felt like I had to be compared to anyone else—I do the best I can within myself. It's the old martial arts philosophy that the only person I'm competing against is myself."

Q: Who were the toughest competitors you ever fought in point tournaments?
A: Skipper Mullins, Joe Lewis, Ron Marchini, and Steve Sanders.

Q: You mentioned that you had a very good story about Skipper Mullins.
A: Yes, I do. It was Sunday night at the 1968 Grand Nationals. The next day I was going to make a movie with Dean Martin and I had to face Skipper Mullins in the finals. Skipper always left a mark on me. I might win but I was always bruised. Anyway, I went to him and said, "Skipper, don't hit me in the face, I have to do a movie tomorrow." He said OK. We bow in and the first thing he did was to fake a round kick, like he used to do all the time, but this one really hit me in the eye. As soon as I felt it, I knew it was going to swell. So when he was leading by three points he began running out of the ring to use up time. I went to him and said, "Why you don't stay

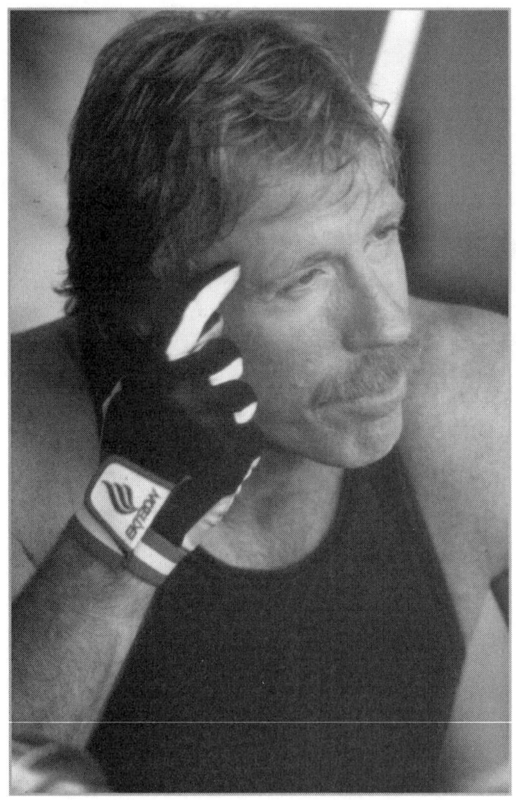

"First, you have to be in excellent physical shape—the top shape you can possibly be in. Then there is the mental aspect—intellectually, you have to know what to do at the right time. And the last aspect is your emotional balance—your psyche."

in the ring and fight like a man?" Boy, his pride got hurt. He didn't run out again and I wound up beating him! Afterwards, I told him that he was stupid. If he would have kept doing the same thing, he would have beaten me!

Q: Did you mind losing?
A: Yes, but as long as you learn from your mistakes you do OK. The only time you ever lose at anything is when you don't learn from the experience. Any experience, good or bad, is really not a failure.

Q: What your opinion on ranks?
A: Rank was never a big deal for me. Many people have been trying to exploit their ranks for years.

Q: What does it take to become a champion?
A: I believe there are three important aspects. First, you have to be in excellent physical shape—the top shape you can possibly be in. Then there is the mental aspect—intellectually, you have to know what to do at the right time. And the last aspect is your emotional balance—your psyche.

Q: You were one of the first practitioners to train under different teachers. Why?
A: Well, I realized that I had to pick up things from different instructors to enhance my fighting ability. That's why I trained under Fumio Demura, Tsuomu Oshima, Hidetaka Nishiyama, et cetera. To be honest, I think that was key that made me win. I was trying to unify their teachings under a system that would work for everyone. Fumio Demura was a very big influence in my life. He taught me a lot of things.

Q: What did you name your system?
A: Chun kuk do. One day I was trying to figure-out what my system was, because it definitely wasn't tang soo do anymore. My system is a mixture of many methods. In Korean it means "Universal System," because that's what I wanted to be, an all-encompassing system.

"I've always believed that when you're close-minded you stop learning. My martial arts training began in the Korean styles, but I also studied Japanese karate, Chinese kung fu, et cetera. I had no problem with learning different arts."

Q: Have you always had an open-minded approach to the arts?
A: I've always believed that when you're close-minded you stop learning. My martial arts training began in the Korean styles, but I also studied Japanese karate, Chinese kung fu, et cetera. I had no problem with learning different arts.

Q: What are your most memorable achievements in martial arts?
A: I always thought that my best achievement was to have some of the finest black belts ever. But to answer your question, I would say that tournament-wise I've won quite a few that were very satisfying. But the most prestigious tournaments at that time were the All-American Championships in New York under Mr. Cho and the Internationals in Long Beach, California under Ed Parker. I won the Grand Championship of them both in 1967 and 1968. I won the Tournaments of Champions from 1966 to 1968. Finally I won the World Middleweight title in November 1968, and held it until 1974 when I retired undefeated.

Q: How would you describe yourself as a martial artist—technically and philosophically?
A: Well that's a tough question. I consider myself a traditionalist as far as philosophy goes, but I believe each system has a lot to offer so I don't see why we can't blend systems and pick what we like of each. Other more modern versions of sport karate such as kickboxing or full contact karate are

"After all, fighting is just one aspect of the martial arts and not the only one. It's good to use competition as a learning tool and go out there and do your best. My advise would be to not take it so seriously that you get frustrated if you lose!"

second cousins to martial arts. I don't see anything wrong with them but I think more of them as professional sports and not an art and philosophy of life. After all, fighting is just one aspect of the martial arts and not the only one. It's good to use competition as a learning tool and go out there and do your best. My advise would be to not take it so seriously that you get frustrated if you lose!

Q: What do you think about fighters today?
A: They're more versatile. When I competed they were more stylized—they used to fight according to their styles. Anyone who could adapt a technique to a different style had an edge. Today, all the fighters are very well-rounded because they have seen and trained in several systems. They can adapt very easily and they have the understanding to refine what works and what doesn't in competition.

Q: You have also been involved in the grappling arts.
A: Well, being a friend with Gene LeBell is a great thing. I've also had a lot of training in Brazilian jiu-jitsu under the Machado brothers.

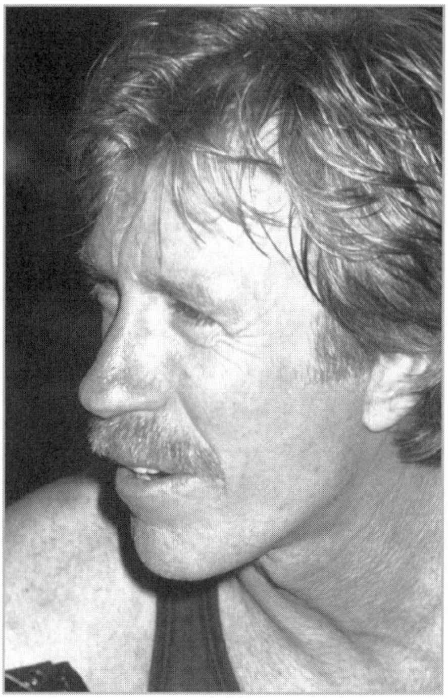

Q: How did you meet the Machados?
A: My good friend Richard Norton was talking a lot about his jiu-jitsu training, and he convinced me to go with him once and I really enjoyed it. That's why I decided to introduce Machado jiu-jitsu into my federation. Fighting on the ground is a whole different game and I wanted my UFAF instructors to get involved with the Machado system of jiu-jitsu.

Q: So you recommend grappling?
A: Of course! Punching and kicking are great, but many times you end up on the ground where your punches and kicks are no longer useful. To me this is not something new. I've been involved in judo and jiu-jitsu since the '60s. But I was fortunate enough to meet the Machado brothers, who have a more refined version that can be used on the street.

"Punching and kicking are great, but many times you end up on the ground where your punches and kicks are no longer useful. To me this is not something new. I've been involved in judo and jiu-jitsu since the '60s. But I was fortunate enough to meet the Machado brothers, who have a more refined version that can be used on the street."

Q: Do you follow any particular diet?
A: I believe in moderation in your eating habits. If you have to deprive yourself, then when you go off the diet, you'll put the weight back on.

Q: Why didn't you get involved with full-contact karate?
A: For me, full-contact kickboxing is a second cousin to true martial arts. There is nothing wrong with it, but it is a professional sport and not an art and philosophy.

"Priorities not only change in life but in training, too. The body is like an engine. Keep it finely maintained and tuned and you won't have problems with it. Just keep a high level of conditioning."

Q: How do you maintain a regular training schedule, being so busy filming?

A: It's hard—sometimes very hard. I like to do my cardiovascular training early in the morning, when I also do my flexibility training. For my kicking training, I do a lot of rehearsing so I kick a hundred times everyday. I used to weight train with Lou Ferrigno but my work schedule changed so much that I had to adapt. I still train with weights as my schedule allows. For me to be in shape—to be in good physical condition—is more important than kicking or punching 1,000 times everyday. I'm not competing anymore so my goals are different. Priorities not only change in life but in training, too. The body is like an engine. Keep it finely maintained and tuned and you won't have problems with it. Just keep a high level of conditioning.

Q: How did your training change after you got involved in movies?

A: You have to look for different things. When you're competing, all the training goes to the techniques you're going to use in the ring. But now, in my case, I have to be in good shape, I mean the look of my kicks has to be developed equally because of the camera angles. I have to be equally developed on both sides of my body—so in a sense I'm a better martial artist for it.

Q: What kind of training did you do when you had more time?

A: On Monday, Wednesday and Friday I used to do weight training with Lou Ferrigno. And then on Tuesday, Thursday, and Saturday I used to do all the cardiovascular training with karate punches and kicks for over an hour and a half. Then the treadmill, rowing machine, speed bag, and heavy bag.

Q: Did you ever feel weight training hurt your martial arts techniques?

A: Never. It made me stronger. Weights won't hurt your martial arts as long as you maintain your flexibility. If you maintain your stretching you can get

much stronger and faster. But you have to stretch daily.

Q: What has been the key to your success?
A: Determination and perseverance. You have to really believe in yourself to overcome all the obstacles that are going to be in your way because you can't avoid them. What makes you win or lose is your determination to overcome obstacles. I keep looking at myself in the mirror and thinking about where I came from and what I was able to do. To me, life is there to be able to have the excitement of accomplishing new things.

"Determination and perseverance. You have to really believe in yourself to overcome all the obstacles that are going to be in your way because you can't avoid them. What makes you win or lose is your determination to overcome obstacles."

Q: What was your relationship to Bruce Lee?
A: We were pretty good friends. We used to work out together. But I don't understand why people keep comparing us. My reputation came from fighting in tournaments and his came from *The Green Hornet* television series.

Q: How were your training sessions?
A: We never got competitive on a physical level. He used to show me things that he was using as close-in counters, and I showed him my kicking techniques. We were very different, physically speaking. He was small-boned and very thin. He trained with weights and put some weight on. I'm a little bigger-boned so our way of fighting was different.

Q: In "The Way of The Dragon" you and Bruce Lee created what some have called the best martial art fight of all time. What are your recollections of the day Bruce Lee killed you in the Roman Coliseum?
A: It was hectic. I have been told that the scene in the Coliseum was perhaps the most exciting fight sequence ever filmed. I guess you could say

"Bruce called me one day from Hong Kong and told me he had finished the script for a movie and then he asked me if I wanted the part. Of course, I jumped at the chance because I knew if Bruce Lee was involved in the film, it would not be a quickie, rip-off thing."

that the fight sequences in that particular movie were the ultimate in realism and detail that any martial arts movie fan had ever seen.

Q: Would you explain all the details of the process?

A: Sure! Bruce called me one day from Hong Kong and told me he had finished the script for a movie and then he asked me if I wanted the part. Of course, I jumped at the chance because I knew if Bruce Lee was involved in the film, it would not be a quickie, rip-off thing. I had always respected his manner of doing things, and I particularly admired his insistence on perfection and realism when it came to the martial arts. As far as the fight sequences go, they were very intricate. You definitely can't see anything amateurish about it. There is not a single white-belt-type technique in the entire thing. I think that anybody, whether he'd taken karate or not, would get the real idea of what fighting is all about. You see, when you go to a movie you tend to relate to the characters you see on the screen, whether it's Steve McQueen or whomever. And when fans see high levels of proficiency in combat against each other, like

Bruce and I in that fight scene, they have a tendency to overreact. I remember walking into one of my schools and all the students stared at me as if not really believing Bruce had not killed me. I found the while thing amusing, but you could tell they were obviously moved by what they had seen the previous night.

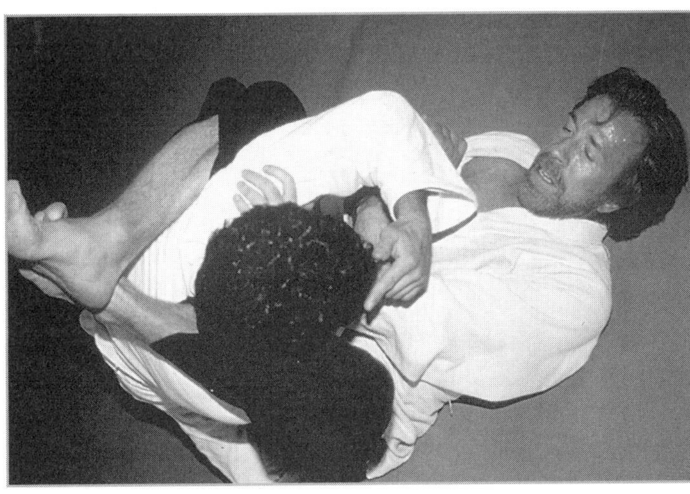

"The scene was full of difficult things. We had to redo the scene two or three times. It was amazing how hard it really was to realize I was doing nothing more than beating myself to death with all those hard falls."

Q: How many hours did Bruce and you work daily on that fight?

A: While the scene was being shot we didn't have too much time to socialize. The filming of the entire sequence took more than three full days. We worked and sweated for 14 to 16 hours each day and sometimes we would go about five or six hours without a break. The scene was full of difficult things. For example, once I had to throw a high roundhouse kick to his head and Bruce had to do a very low heel sweep to my supporting leg to knock me down. In the beginning Bruce came and said, "Let me just touch your foot, and then you jump up in the air and then fall to the ground." When the cameras started rolling, I brought my foot up a little slow and I had the other leg way up high in the air, so I couldn't get any real push from my supporting leg to get any height for my fall to the ground. I tried to kick as high as I could without any support and, naturally, what I did was nothing more than fall very hard to the ground. We had to redo the scene two or three times and I still couldn't get any height. It was amazing how hard it really was to realize I was doing nothing more than beating myself to death with all those hard falls.

"Physical training is only a vehicle to strengthen us mentally so we can develop character. If we don't respect ourselves, no one will. I would tell my students that martial arts are an avenue for us to grow in all areas of life."

Q: What is your opinion of how Bruce handled the filming of the scene and when was the last time you saw him?

A: Bruce had a keen talent for melodrama and it's never more evident than in this movie. I clearly remember the scene when Bruce was supposed to match his strength against mine. We broke for lunch and we laughed about the good times we had in California and, for a moment, it was the Bruce Lee I had always known. He loved life and enjoyed every minute of it. He was a very optimistic man, and never got pessimistic about anything—or, if he did, he never showed it. He was human and must have felt "down" at some moments in his life. He had a lot of energy that you seemed to sense. He never unwound.

I remember that last time when I finished my segment and he was still in Rome. He was still filming and he stayed there to finish. When I came back to United States, he was still in Europe. He went back to Hong Kong to wrap up the film. Bruce called me when he came back to Los Angeles. I talked to him on the phone. He had come in for a physical because he was feeling run down and over worked. He tried to call me back again before he went back to Hong Kong, but I was out of town. And yes, the last time I saw Bruce Lee was the time he killed me that afternoon in the Roman Coliseum.

Q: You have an anti-drug and anti-gang program. Why did you decided to start it?
A: Kids are the future. Do I need to say anything else?

Q: What does *Walker: Texas Ranger* mean to you, and why you did bring some of the good ol' boys of American karate to appear in the show?
A: *Walker* is a big part of my life. When we started, not too many people believed in the project. After a while it became a big success and look for how many years it lasted! In fact, four years was my goal. I always remember where I came from, and although from a business point of view you have to be very careful with the thing you do, I found places where I could use some of my friends and give them something back. It was great to have them in the show. We really had a great time. That's the spirit of martial arts, after all these years we still do things together. In the very end, trophies are not important; it is the camaraderie that really counts and that shows the real attitude of the true martial arts. It's a way of showing my loyalty to my friends and to the things that were important in my youth. That time of my life, when I was competing, is probably when I had the most fun. Many people think that making movies is more exciting, but all I can say is that at that particular time I really enjoyed it a lot.

"In the very end, trophies are not important; it is the camaraderie that really counts and that shows the real attitude of the true martial arts. That time of my life, when I was competing, is probably when I had the most fun. Many people think that making movies is more exciting, but all I can say is that at that particular time I really enjoyed it a lot."

Q: What would be your last will for your students?
A: Physical training is only a vehicle to strengthen us mentally so we can develop character. If we don't respect ourselves, no one will. I would tell my students that martial arts are an avenue for us to grow in all areas of life. Martial arts are the best avenue for gaining personal respect.

Richard Norton

Living in the Future, Looking to the Past

This Australian martial artist has come a long way since he first learned karate as a schoolboy. His friendly manner and infectious sense of humor belies the strength and skill that won him a notorious reputation as an elite bodyguard for Hollywood celebrities. Norton is not only a nice man, but a well-rounded one as well—and a man of many facets. Working in several movies and training in different martial arts systems, Norton never lost sight of his personal goals as a martial artist.

Norton makes his home in Los Angeles, where he enjoys every single day of his life, whether training, filming or having a relaxed chat with friends. Very few individuals conduct themselves the way this true gentleman does, not letting success go to his head while displaying the qualities of a true samurai. It all seems a far cry from his humble beginning as a 12-year-old neophyte at a modest suburban judo club in Nunawading, Victoria, but Norton takes it all in stride and one day at a time.

"If someone had told me that I'd end up where I am today, when I first started martial arts, I would have called them a damn liar and laughed in their face," Norton laughs. "But karate, just like life, doesn't happen all at once; you gain knowledge one day at a time, and you better yourself through loyalty, friendship, and hard work."

Q: How did you get involved in martial arts?

A: I started training when I was 12 years old, so that would make it 38 years of practice in various martial arts systems. I have trained in judo, karate, aikido, kendo, muay Thai, boxing, and jiu-jitsu. My first teacher in the arts was a judo sensei by the name of John Burge. He was a police sergeant in the Victoria police force and ran a dojo about 10 miles from where I was living in Croydon, a suburb of the city of Melbourne, Australia. He was a wonderful and caring instructor, the latter being important to me as I was small and skinny as a 12-year-old and realized that I would just have been cannon fodder for the older, more advanced students had it not been for the watchful eye of Sensei Burge.

"Most people don't really know a good instructor from a bad one when they first get into martial arts—and often it is only after wasting a lot of time and money that they come to the realization that what they are doing is not that good or doesn't have what they're really after in an art."

After training for approximately two years in judo I was introduced to goju-ryu karate. My instructors were Tino Ceberano and Sal Ebanez who had recently emigrated to Australia from Hawaii. Again, when I look back after all these years with the benefit of hindsight, I am so thankful that I was blessed with such wonderful instructors to start me on my martial arts journey. Most people don't really know a good instructor from a bad one when they first get into martial arts—and often it is only after wasting a lot of time and money that they come to the realization that what they are doing is not that good or doesn't have what they're really after in an art. Thankfully, this was definitely not the case for me. I still feel I have the whole essence of their teachings within me, and the rest that I now have is supplementation. I was taught not only the traditions and origins of the art of karate, but most importantly, the etiquette and disciplines that made what we did an art and not just a sport. This basis has held me in good stead the whole of my martial arts life.

The final instructor who had a huge impact on my early training, who started as a fellow student in goju-ryu and later became a life-long friend and partner, is Bob Jones. It was Bob who was instrumental in teaching me the realities of the street. Although only a beginner in karate, he was already a battle tested "black belt" when it came to real life street-defense due his many years of work as a bouncer and bodyguard. Bob was the one who got me into bouncing and bodyguard work and if that doesn't shape you in a certain way, nothing will. Bouncing taught me "real" techniques, not just those based on theory. On the doors, you have to be good at what you do and it has to work for you. That was a very big lesson for me. It made me realize that a lot of what we did in traditional karate training was nice, but it didn't always have a lot to do with the practical side of streetfighting. The environment Bob helped create back then with zen do kai was an ideal testing ground for measuring the effectiveness of a technique.

So I had the beginnings of the best possible traditional training in the arts with senseis Tino and Sal, along with the real-life practical teachings of my "street" sensei, Bob Jones. As far as my beginnings in America, Chuck Norris, of course, helped me tremendously. He introduced me to very effective training methods and a melting pot of eclectic instructors that I could only previously have dreamt about—wonderful teachers like Fumio Demura, Benny Urquidez, Bill Wallace, Tadashi Yamashita, and Pat Johnson to name a few.

Q: What are your most vivid memories of your early days in karate?

A: My early training years in Australia are full of fond memories. Most of all, I remember them being a lot of fun. Training back then was for a pure reason. You see, when I began training in 1964, karate was virtually unheard of in Australia. Sensei Ceberano was a karate pioneer in Australia and the school was run with no commercialism involved. It wasn't a matter of how much money Tino or the club was going to earn; we trained because we wanted to train, because in our hearts we were doing what we knew we had to do and we loved doing it, and all we wanted was to become martial artists. It other words, I feel our motivations were pure without regard for the commercial aspects so often seen in today's dojos. Training was full of camaraderie. The sense of belonging to the club was paramount. Tino, of course, instilled so much of that in us that the higher ranks would look after the lower ranks and the weaker students in our dojo. I remember the tournaments as days when there were no such things as gloves and protective equipment. There was a lot of contact. I used to get smacked around a lot in those days.

On weekends, Tino would have luaus at his house. A luau is a Hawaiian tradition that involves roasting a pig and everyone gorging themselves. Tino also had the first Australian martial arts training camp at a place called Falls Creek. Nobody had ever done something where you took a bunch of people away to the mountains and trained in martial arts. You took your own little makiwara pad, which was a small straw training pad and you would strap it to a tree and punch the crap out of it. It was just an amazing time; a time of introspection and a time of growing. We trained and Tino taught us because there was a common thread of instructors and students just wanting to be the best martial artists we could be. I will always treasure the memories of those early years in goju with Tino and Sal. One final and proud moment during my goju days was that I got to compete in the first-ever Australian Karate Championships, in which I placed 4th. Not bad for a skinny little asthmatic kid from Croydon.

My early years after leaving goju as a black belt and joining Bob Jones in starting-up a more eclectic system of martial arts we later called zen do kai were wrought with memories of a very different nature. You see, because of Bob's background in running a security business and providing security personnel for clubs and discos, our school was basically made-up of street-hardened bouncers. This made for, how should I put it, very "spirited" sparring or kumite sessions, to say the least. So here I was, still only a teenager and head instructor for a school basically made up of streetfighters and bouncers. Don't get me wrong. Bob and I ran our dojo with the utmost attention to respect, discipline, and traditional values, and all our students absolutely towed the line when it came to behavior in the dojo. But when it came to kumite, it was on. I can hardly remember a night when there wasn't at least one broken nose, split lip or what have you. Remember too, that protective equipment was also unheard of back then and these were the early days of this mysterious new fighting art of karate.

Also, back then I feel we didn't have to compromise our principles in what we wanted to teach or how hard we wanted to train people. If 10 students dropped out because it was too "hard", another 20 were waiting to join. These days I find that, due to the commercial aspects of the martial arts with so many schools around, you can't train people quite as hard now as you could then. The kata training was intense, the sparring was intense, the whole discipline was intense and the camaraderie was intense. I'm not saying that it doesn't exist in today's dojos, but I do feel it was a little different back then. We would usually spar around 30 rounds a class, and this after one full hour of conditioning exercises involving 100's of push-ups, squats and sit-ups, followed by literally sets of 200 of each and every basic block, strike and kick we knew. I have always said that back in those days, what we lacked in finesse, we certainly made up for in sweat and blood and tears.

One memory in particular that I'm not so proud of was back in the early days of zen do kai. One of the things Bob and I would do when a batch of students would be graded and receive a higher rank was to hold an initiation night. This basically meant that Bob and I would spar each and every student in the new class and basically beat the crap out of them, to kind of "introduce" them to their new rank and the hardships that would follow. Now again, remember that the majority of these students were bouncers and the like and would spar us with an almost street-ingrained mentality and intensity. Anyway, on one particular night I free-sparred with over 30 new brown-

belt students with the end result of 8 of them ending up in hospital, one with a cracked cheek bone, two with broken jaws, another missing some teeth and the rest with various injuries. This was a particular event that ended-up troubling me greatly and almost saw me giving up martial arts. I was suddenly struck with the feeling of such shame. I found myself severely questioning my values as an instructor and more importantly as a human being. I mean what right did I have to inflict such pain on other human beings, especially students under my care, regardless of the fact that this was the norm back then in our school and was almost "expected" by these street-hardened students of zen do kai. That period of time was one of great introspection for me and a real turning point in my development as a martial artist.

"When I look back on different periods of my training and life, I make no apologies for things that I may have done, good or bad, as I honestly feel that these were necessary life experiences for me. To me, life will always be full of trials and tribulations, as that is the reason we are here."

When I look back on different periods of my training and life, I make no apologies for things that I may have done, good or bad, as I honestly feel that these were necessary life experiences for me. The important thing is to have the wisdom to know that there are some things that one should never choose to repeat again as they were mistakes and should be used as tools to better oneself. To me, life will always be full of trials and tribulations, as that is the reason we are here. If my life was all-euphoric, I would have no reason to be here on earth. Dare to participate and make mistakes, but for God's sake give me the wisdom to learn from those mistakes.

Q: Did karate come easy to you?

A: No. I don't feel that I was so much a natural at karate, but more someone who was so driven and drawn to this mystical new art that I was going to succeed, no matter what. I honestly feel that I was drawn to martial arts because of this inner feeling that this is what I was supposed to do with my life. You see, aside from being very small at 14, I was also an asthmatic. For me to run a 100-yard dash would be all it would take to leave me gasping for air on the ground. My parents were worried about my martial arts training

"As I have gotten older and progressed, the main changes have been to cross over from a traditional base of martial arts to a more practical or 'hands on' type of training. I have often been described in Australia as a 'modern traditionalist.'"

until our family doctor, after a little research, recommended to my worried mother that I continue this new endeavor called goju karate, due to the *sanchin* and *tensho* kata that placed such an emphasis on diaphragmatic deep-breathing. He felt this would be a valuable exercise to develop and strengthen my lungs. Boy, was he right. The benefits of my goju karate training were a godsend to my asthmatic condition and before long I was on my way to becoming a competitive athlete. I was also not naturally flexible and had to work particularly hard at that aspect. Of course back then, no one really new that much about flexibility training. Stretching consisted of ballistic and hard movements that we now know to be the worst form of flexibility training. At least the goju system, with it's in-close system of kicks and strikes was, I realized later, more suited to me than say a Korean system would have been with it's long-range kicking and emphasis on flexibility. I also started weight training due to the prompting of my father, which was also the best thing that I could have been introduced to at that time due to my stature. So by the time Bob and I started zen do kai a few years later, I was almost cured of my asthma and was starting to put on some muscle and mature as an athlete.

Q: How have your personal martial arts developed over the years?
A: As I have gotten older and progressed, the main changes have been to cross over from a traditional base of martial arts to a more practical or "hands on" type of training. I have often been described in Australia as a "modern traditionalist." Now to many, those terms seem to be contradictory. But an important aspect of martial arts, when we talk about fighting, is that you are always taught to adapt to your environment. Like when we read about Miyamoto Musashi, the 16th century master of swordsmanship and combative strategy, and how he adapted to his particular environment in a duel by checking the position of the sun, so as to try to position his opponent so the sunlight would shine in his eyes and blind him. That sort of thing was his way of adapting and making effective use of his particular environment.

A lot of different martial artists have evolved through adaptation to their local environment. I mean I'm sure that back whenever some of our most esteemed martial arts legends were exposed to the superior technique of a wandering master that happened into their village or whatever, they would immediately seize the opportunity to improve their skills accordingly, and take advantage of this to add to their knowledge. I don't think it would have mattered whether that visitor was of a particular style, race, or whatever, What would have mattered is that here was a chance to improve one's skills and become a better martial artist.

I think that being a modern traditionalist involves having that same outlook—bringing the martial arts tradition into a more contemporary setting. That is adapting to today's environment. For me, that means muay Thai kickboxing and Brazilian jiu-jitsu. These arts represent today's environment. Nowadays we are living in cities—we are living in a modern age and we are part of today's social structure. So for me, I realized that the whole *bushido* spirit, that traditional samurai spirit, has got to be applied in a slightly different way—whether in the workplace, or at home, or in the street, or wherever. The stresses that are placed on us nowadays are different than those we would have encountered in say, feudal Japan. I think training as a modern traditionalist involves training in techniques that have been molded or adapted to today's realities. So for me, it just became a matter of looking at traditional ways of training and then adding or subtracting whatever I felt was applicable or valid. Of course, many of the traditional aspects of my early martial arts training are still very functional and applicable. This is part of the beauty of the martial arts—it is multi-faceted.

I want to consider as many of today's fighting specialties while never losing site of the wholistic ideal. Regardless of my traditional background, there was no way I could deny the amazing effectiveness of the Thai kickboxer or the incredible ground skills of the Brazilian jiu-jitsu practitioners. When I felt people like Benny "The Jet" Urquidez or Peter "Sugarfoot" Cunningham do their thing with me in the ring, or had a master like Jean Jacques Machado tie me up in knots on the mat, I could only bow my head and say, "Let me on board. These are skills I have to learn."

Q: Do you think there are still "pure" martial arts systems?
A: Well, it obviously gets down to one's definition of "pure." I do not think that any art I have been exposed to has been "pure" in the sense that it has not been a breakaway from some other system at some stage of it's inception. All traditional systems have gone through some modifications, even if just due to the inherent fact that each instructor cannot help but put his individual "stamp"on different techniques and kata within his system.

I was taught from a "pure" goju system headed by Master Gogen Yamaguchi. Yet within the goju system there is a wide variation of techniques between the goju that is taught in Japan and the goju that is taught in Okinawa. There are many well-meaning instructors who are representing their respective styles in the most traditional way, but I think that having different versions of the same style is almost unavoidable.

People talk about tradition and pure art—and that's fine but we have to realize that again, most of the "famous" martial arts leaders have broken away from one style or another and individualized. For example, the fact that Okinawa would maybe consider Yamaguchi a breakaway in no way detracts from what he has contributed to the essence of the same system that is goju. In fact, it is just the opposite. Being an innovator can be far more difficult than being an imitator. There are a lot of people following tradition and wanting things to remain unchanged, and I have no argument with that—but we each need to eventually get to choose how we wish to express our particular art. Because the problem with just being a follower, and by that I mean just mimicking one's parent style exactly, is that one can become a bit of a clone or a robot, and there are lots of them around. There must come a point where we realize that in order to express ourselves as artists, we must become individuals. Art has always been individual expression. It's like 10 painters following a particular style of painting—even if they were all to paint the same picture of say a tree, when it came down to what was on the canvas, each would be different. So what they have put on their canvas becomes art because of that individual expression.

Let me give you another analogy. If someone learns to say play the piano, they will, among other things, have to learn the musical scales. Now

"The ultimate expression of our artistry and individuality of those 'notes' comes when we free spar. Now we are composing our own music. The fact is, a student of any level, if he has a good instructor, will be encouraged to go out and seek more knowledge in his chosen style in order to become stronger and to grow."

the scales are the same for everyone. So you learn the scales and then maybe you learn to play a song that someone else has composed. Now you are at the stage where you dream of writing your own piece of music. So your ultimate expression as an artist comes when you take the same notes and write your own piece. You have become an innovator and not just an imitator. You are an artist. The martial arts to me are not much different to that. We have our music notes in the form of our basic blocks, kicks, and punches and we perform kata that we have been taught by our instructor. But don't tell me that each stylist will perform that kata in exactly the same way, even if taught these movements by the same instructor in the same school, let alone the same kata taught by another instructor of the same style another school in another country.

The ultimate expression of our artistry and individuality of those "notes" comes when we free spar. Now we are composing our own music. The fact is, a student of any level, if he has a good instructor, will be encouraged to go out and seek more knowledge in his chosen style in order to become stronger and to grow. Well, the only way I know how to grow is to find more knowledge and add to what I already have. Therefore, as a natural extension of this, the techniques I now teach will have a certain slant due to this added knowledge or growth. So I feel any advanced student of the arts will get to a certain point where they will need to individualize in order to become an artist and fully realize their own potential. That is what being a "modern traditionalist" means; taking the essence of a traditional style—the kata, basic movements, and philosophy—but then improving it with today's technology.

It's like when we look at swimming in the Olympic games. Although we see certain styles of swimming, the only way records have been broken by as many seconds as they have is largely due to an increase in our knowledge of sports medicine and improved training methods. We just know that

"One thing I feel combat sports does for the martial artist is provide a bridge between the dojo and the street. Feeling what it is like to go flat-out with someone for even 3 minutes with both of you throwing real, not theoretical, techniques is quite an eye opener for the average martial artist."

much more about our body now, how it works, why it works, and accordingly we re-adjust our training programs to get the most out of ourselves and improve our performance. Once again, the martial arts should be no different; science is constantly evolving and we have to change. For a martial artist to deny the value of today's technology and how it can be applied to his or her training would be a sad thing.

Q: What is your opinion of combat sports such as kickboxing and ultimate fighting?

A: I have no problem with these sports as an expression of athletic ability, and as an opportunity to display one's warrior spirit in a controlled and safe environment. I absolutely admire anyone who is willing to participate and put themselves on the line. It takes a lot of guts to climb into that ring and test one's technique and go one-on-one with another trained warrior.

One thing I feel combat sports does for the martial artist is provide a bridge between the dojo and the street. Feeling what it is like to go flat-out with someone for even 3 minutes with both of you throwing real, not theoretical, techniques is quite an eye opener for the average martial artist. A fight on the street often depends on that type of conditioning and often gets down to who is the fitter of the two. The better-conditioned fighter has a considerable advantage. However, you have to remember that not all street confrontations are anaerobic events. Often a situation will be resolved in a few seconds. But with that being said, in my own experience, this has not proved to be the case, especially in a multiple-opponent situation. Students must remember that they are very protected in the dojo. This is because the majority of students don't want to go home at night with teeth missing. The dojo fighter, though, if he wants to be considered a practical martial artist who is able to defend himself or others if it really came down to it, needs to know what impact feels like. He needs to know what it feels like to get knocked off his feet and have to get up again, because his very life may depend on it.

Those are often the very things that separate those that win in the street and those that lose. Kickboxing and full contact sparring gives you a way to find out exactly where you stand when it comes to experiencing impact, and also to experience dishing it out to the best of your ability. I'm not just talking about having to compete professionally in the ring—it can be in the dojo. In fact, I feel it can sometimes be more effective when you are in an environment where you are learning. Full contact fighting only in a tournament can put you in a one-dimensional mode and can detract from all the other things that the martial arts have to offer. Quite simply the important thing is to know what it feels like to be hit and to then acquire the ability to be able to come back rip into your opponent.

In full-contact training, however, we are usually limited because of safety factors—gloves, rules, ropes, rounds, a referee, no knees, head-butts, biting, et cetera. These are limitations that can hold us back, but at least it is a way to give us a feeling of what it is like to be hit and to come back under considerable pressure. I think it is important to not just be aesthetically pretty—there are lots of pretty martial artists around with great looking kicks; but a good ballet dancer makes a lot of those sorts of people look like cream puffs when it comes to dexterity and body control. So martial artists in the practical sense also have to be effective. Otherwise, why not just go out and take up ballet or gymnastics? There needs to be an intent and purpose to what we are doing that is just not based in theory, otherwise we become like little robots mimicking movements that have been robbed of their effectiveness.

I always remember Benny Urquidez saying, "How you train is how you react." In other words, don't think if you have never experienced pressure or pain, that your nervous system won't freak in some dive bar, when some gorilla has you nailed to a wall with a look in his eyes that says, "I'm going to kill you." You've got to be able to come up with the goods in a hurry and it's got to be totally reflexive; and that only comes from what you do in training. So again, any type of full contact sparring, even controlled, can at least be a valuable tool to help prepare you for that high-pressure situation.

I am reminded of a wonderful little paragraph called "The Peaceful Warrior," I read in a magazine: *Once, while training in the Chinese sword, I asked my teacher why, if I was striving to be inwardly calm and at peace, did I need to learn the ways of a warrior? "Would it not be more tranquil and serene to be a gardener and tend the plants?" I asked. "Tending the garden," my master replied, "is a relaxing pastime, but it does not prepare one for the inevitable battles of life. It is easy to be calm in a serene setting. To be calm and centered when under attack is much more difficult. So, therefore, I tell you that it is far better to be a warrior tending his garden, rather than a gardener making war"*

So my point is that you do not always get to choose when you may be confronted with violence. It sometimes chooses you, in which case you need to be ready. The UFC definitely shook-up the martial arts world in a good way, making us all realize the limitations of our respective systems. I mean, not all that long ago wrestlers or grapplers were never even mentioned in most martial arts circles. Boy, did the UFC ever change that. As I have said earlier, we as martial artists are products of our environments, good or bad. Now the stand-up fighters can stick their heads in the sand and rationalize why they would never get "taken" to the ground because of their deadly strikes, or they can smell the roses and seriously look at the merits of cross-training and the value of grappling in their martial arts arsenal. I, for, one left my ego at the door the first time I grappled with one of the Machado brothers due to the very obvious fact that once taken off my feet I was like a little baby in the hands of a skilled jiu-jitsu fighter. So I think that stand-up fighters shouldn't theorize about what they would do against a grappler, but rather learn grappling so they will know for sure. Then they will have a real game plan when they are taken off their feet and can't use their stand-up game.

Q: Do you like the current UFC rules?

A: I do. I am pleased that the rules of NHB have become more stringent and are geared towards an environment that protects the fighters a little more. I had a real problem with head butts for instance in the earlier years due to the damage and cuts they would cause to a fighters head and face. After all, it should be a sport that ensures some longevity for the careers and welfare of the warriors involved.

Q: Do you think the Western countries are reaching the same level of martial arts skill as the Eastern countries?

A: Yes, absolutely. This is evident from the worldwide results of international competition in the various arts, whether it be karate, judo, kickboxing or whatever. I think a lot of this "catching up" is due to the availability of technology that gives the word-wide practitioner of the arts a wealth of knowledge at the click of a computer button, and the availability of tapes and books written by masters of so many different arts and styles. Also, the world is such a smaller and more accessible place due to things like modern transport. When I was a kid the idea of getting to Japan would have been a monumental and expensive undertaking even from Australia. Now there are endless travel options available to the inquisitive martial artist.

Now, whether or not the West has caught up to the East in the philosophical aspects is open to discussion, but I tend to think it has. I'm also sure that this would get down to the individual practitioner and not the race or color of the artist. Remember, too, that the Western mind always questions everything we are told to do, as opposed to the Eastern mind where you don't ask any questions. Honestly, I think that this is due, in part, to the sensei himself not really knowing the answers to some of the probing questions—as he also learned his skills by imitating his senseis without too much introspective thought. I certainly know that if I wanted to know why a reverse punch should have a full rotation of the fist instead of a half rotation, and my instructor wouldn't tell me, I would go to the library and research books on kineseology and the like. Inquiring Western minds want to know. So I feel that the inquiring mind of the Westerner and the desire to always try to improve on something rather than just accepting it as is, is what has helped the Western martial artist to catch up and often surpass his Eastern counterpart.

"What the general public sees or knows of karate these days is tournaments based on "theoretical" damage caused by controlled strikes to the body and not actual knockouts, with a referee awarding points and a winner. Well, that is sport. That is fine and has it's place, and can be rightly called a sport."

Q: Martial arts are nowadays often referred to as sports. Is this correct?

A: I would think this definition could be applied to certain commercial schools, especially with the introduction of taekwondo into the Olympics and the resultant focus on schools readying their students for this type of competition. What the general public sees or knows of karate these days is tournaments based on "theoretical" damage caused by controlled strikes to the body and not actual knockouts, with a referee awarding points and a

"I realized long ago that life is all about the journey and not about the destination. The moment you think you know it all you stagnate and die. Life and the arts are all about bodies in motion."

winner. Well, that is sport. That is fine and has it's place, and can be rightly called a sport.

I honestly feel that what hasn't helped the status of certain martial arts schools, as far as teaching a fighting art, is that most schools are more interested in the appeasement of the student's ego in order to keep a student interested enough to come back and pay another month's fees. Belts are awarded for little effort and often with no regard for the student's real knowledge and philosophical understanding of the art he's involved in. There are still some schools with instructors whose goal is only to teach the karate or wushu or whatever, in the purist form they know, demanding excellence from their students. To those brave souls, I salute you for not succumbing to the pressure to water down something you wholeheartedly believe in.

Q: Do you still have room for growth as a martial artist?
A: Absolutely. I realized long ago that life is all about the journey and not about the destination. The moment you think you know it all you stagnate and die. Life and the arts are all about bodies in motion. I honestly believe that is the reason that when we are doing what we are meant to do with our lives, and we set goals and finally achieve them, it is suddenly not enough.

So we set new goals and away we go on a new journey of gaining knowledge and learning and understanding in order to achieve the newly set goal. This is what the human experience should be about. Anything in life that is motionless for any period of time is probably dead, or damn near it. I'm sure we all know some stagnant souls in our lives. That is not for me. I will always strive to be a student of the arts and of life in general and just keep searching.

Q: Do you think the practitioner's personal training should be different than his teaching schedule as instructor?

A: Yes, from the point of view that I believe an instructor should always be striving to better themselves in order to better serve their students. From my point of view as an instructor, I had to have a different training schedule. I always felt that I needed to be an innovator out of necessity. Bob Jones was instrumental in teaching me that when we started zen do kai, which we very loosely translated as being the "best of everything in progression." In the early days of ZDK, Bob would travel and look for ideas. He traveled to America and looked for ways to do things differently. So through that, Bob and I weren't content to do things the same as everyone else. It's easy to imitate, which is what a lot of students do for a long time under an instructor. They imitate, they do what they are told, they don't have a lot of room to be expressive on their own and creative in their own fashion. Mind you, that is absolutely necessary in order to establish a firm base of understanding within one's chosen style. I feel, though, that an instructor's job is to ultimately guide and lead the students to a point where they have the skills to become their own teachers.

My experience with zen do kai was that after leaving goju kai, Bob and I were suddenly head instructors of a huge school full of tough young students chasing us in every class, getting better and better and prompting us to get better. That made me very hungry for new knowledge out of necessity. I had to keep searching, as I now had no head instructor there to hand-feed me new techniques. I read books, I bought tapes, I went to look at other schools and I went to other tournaments—always with the thought of learning things that would help me instruct next week and keep the classes interesting. It was an incredible experience for me in that regard as I had to learn to think for myself, get new knowledge, internalize it, and make it my own so I could then pass it on to my students.

The best advice I can give to anyone is that the martial artist should always think of themselves as a student—never be content, keep searching, and never feel as though you have enough knowledge. Never be content with mediocrity. The world is full of mediocre people who are content to compare themselves with the average. Learn to only compare yourself with the best and then, when you have your goals set in the right direction, dare to be the best you can be.

Q: What are the major changes in the arts since you began training?
A: I think the major changes have been the inclusion of so many student options in the martial arts. Things like Thai kickboxing and jiu-jitsu are a result of the world getting smaller and more accessible through technology, providing better access to information. I see martial artists from different walks of life migrating to different parts of the world and thereby introducing their knowledge to a community that never had the opportunity to be exposed to this new art. I had never seen or heard of muay Thai when I started training. Now, instead of us just doing karate or just doing judo or whatever, we are totally into a world of cross-training with karate, jiu-jitsu, wrestling, muay Thai and so on. This is a whole new training environment than when I started as a 12-year-old in Australia in 1962.

Q: With whom would you like to have trained?
A: Perhaps with the legendary swordsman and combative strategist, Miyamoto Mushashi, and O Sensei Ueshiba in aikido. What wonderful teachers they would have been. The thing that fascinates me about masters like these is the total wholistic approach with which they lived their lives and spread their art.

Q: What would you say to someone who is interested in learning martial arts?
A: Do your research and trust your instincts when choosing your first discipline. It is an important decision as your first impressions can often dictate whether or not you become a martial artist, or quit before you really get started because of an inferior school or instructor. Go to as many different schools as you can and watch the classes and see how the instructor conducts himself and imparts his knowledge to his students. Also, try to honestly ask yourself why you are interested in the arts. Is it for meditative purposes, self-defense, to become a kickboxing champion or whatever? Because each of these questions will help you choose the right school, as each one can be very different in providing the end result of your desires.

Q: Can mixing styles be beneficial?
A: I think it all gets down to your reasons and goals for training. I feel it is absolutely beneficial to mix styles if, for instance, being a practical fighter is

"I feel it is very important though, if you are going to mix styles, to become proficient in at least one discipline or art to form your base. Then, after reaching a substantial level of expertise and understanding, I think it is definitely advantageous to supplement your base discipline with whatever it takes for you to grow and reach your goals."

your aim. In that case, I feel you can't go wrong by combining say muay Thai skills with jiu-jitsu. In fact, in today's environment, if you don't have skills in stand-up as well as grappling you will not be competitive in no-holds-barred. On the other hand, if your aim is to be a master of aikido, a total focus and concentration on that art is the best plan as you may find that art is totally inclusive on its own for all your martial and spiritual

"I still believe kata (forms) training to be the very essence of my karate. For me, it is like active meditation. It is a very personal thing. There is only you out there on the mat with no external influences."

desires. Again, it really gets down to your goals as a martial artist and why you are training in the first place.

I feel it is very important though, if you are going to mix styles, to become proficient in at least one discipline or art to form your base. Then, after reaching a substantial level of expertise and understanding, I think it is definitely advantageous to supplement your base discipline with whatever it takes for you to grow and reach your goals. I know that supplementing was important for me. Many masters of old became great by reaching out to other masters and styles, and endeavoring to become better and better as martial artists.

Q: What is the philosophical basis for your martial arts training?

A: To help me become a better person and be the best martial artist I can be—in the most wholistic way possible.

Q: What is your personal feeling on kata training?

A: I still believe kata (forms) training to be the very essence of my karate. For me, it is like active meditation. It is a very personal thing. There is only you out there on the mat with no external influences. This is when you really encounter the internal battle of the martial arts experience; this is the area from which you can derive the ultimate discipline. In sparring, for example, you can make a few mistakes. You just follow up fast with something better. But when you're out there by yourself performing kata, there's no covering-up a single error. It is very much an internal discipline experience. You've got to get your body to do precisely what your mind is directing it to do—not just what it feels like doing.

A lot of kata stances and basics might seem irrelevant from a practical point of view, but I don't think that's the point of kata. I think it's the idea that you can show, through your kata, that you are getting your mind centered. You are showing that all your movement is emanating from your center and your concentration is equally as intense in your big toe as it is at the top of your head. Every component of your body is aligned, unified, and working as one unit.

I sincerely believe that kata is an excellent method for developing complete control. If you see some people doing *kaku-suko* (pre-arranged sparring), and look at their stances and what their legs are doing—and they're all over the place—I think that indicates a lack of really meaningful kata training.

Kata represents my expression of what I feel as an individual. You see, everything is movement. A famous saxophone player by the name of David Sanborn once said to me in reference to his playing: "You don't create sound; you merely punctuate the quiet." That's how I like to think of my kata training—it's as if before I even walk out onto the floor to perform kata, I'm already doing it. So you don't create movement, you merely punctuate the stillness with your own expression of kata. So while at some point of the kata you may seem like you are not moving, you are moving—because there's this constant involvement of body and mind in that point, in that individual expression of your mood and temperament. Kata is always there; you are always doing it.

Q: How can one increase their understanding of the spiritual aspects of karate?

A: Get a copy of the D.T. Suzuki book, *Zen and Japanese Culture*. It is simply wonderful reading for any martial artist. The author addresses Zen and its whole relationship to the warrior. I still love the traditional aspects of the martial arts and that's probably the reason why I enjoyed reading it so much. The book goes right into Suzuki's ideas on where the mind is supposed to be when you are fighting and what happens between the thoughts and the actual execution of the technique. That's one book I truly recommend for any serious martial artist.

Q: Did your job as a bodyguard let you experience the samurai attitude of always living with the possibility of death?
A: I began working as a bodyguard in 1972 with the Rolling Stones, hooking up with Mick Jagger. It was just wild! I also worked with James Taylor, Fleetwood Mac, Linda Ronstadt, Joe Cocker, and David Bowie. Being a bodyguard involves being psychologically prepared to die. You have to prepare yourself for the inevitable. If you are not, you are living a lie and not really doing what you are paid to do. You can never deal with running away or bailing out. You always have to face the realization that this could be it. The samurai were bodyguards in the strictest sense of the word. They were hired to protect the shogun. If someone pulls a gun, you have to be resolved to take the bullet for the person who hired you.

My idea of security is that when you don't know you have got it, you don't even know you need it. That is perfect security. When I was doing that type of work I was really doing something which has been done for centuries, in the most traditional way; not abusing my art form by using other non-physical methods to dissolve the problem.

Q: What can you tell us about your friendship with Chuck Norris?
A: I have been fortunate to not only of work next to Chuck in movies and TV shows but also to train with him and hang out with him. When we met in Australia we hit off immediately. He is a very open and approachable person. He doesn't have an I'm-Chuck-Norris-so-kiss-my-butt attitude; he is just the opposite. He has been a personal inspiration to me and I truly believe he is one of the greatest role models in the history martial arts. When I came to America, we used to train together, and let me tell you that I was in very good shape. We went through three-to-four hour workouts that could kill a horse! He never misses his workouts—he is always there. As far as work is concerned, I decided to go on my own because I never, ever wanted to be Chuck's friend because I needed the work. If I felt I could be right for something, and it was an advantage for both of us, great. I like Chuck because he is Chuck, and because we train together. We have fun, we laugh together and there is just a lot of respect. Those are the reason why I like to be around Chuck and those are probably the reasons why our friendship has lasted.

Q: What is your most memorable moment as a martial artist?
A: That would have to be when I was on tour with Linda Ronstadt when she was touring with a top Mariachi band out of Mexico City. It was the tour when she was singing Mexican love songs and I was working as her person-

al bodyguard. We were backstage one day and the band was outside the dressing rooms warming up. One member of the mariachi band was at that time considered to be only one of two living masters of the Mexican harp, which is a quite large instrument made of wood. Anyway, I happened to ask this master to play a little bit for me. Now I have to tell you that he, and in fact all the members of the mariachi band, were the biggest rebel rousers when offstage when it came to drinking and partying. They were a far cry from one's image of a master of anything. So after some prompting he reluctantly picked up his harp and began to play. It was the most moving and memorable feeling of my life as a martial artist to watch this master do his thing. As I watched him play I was struck by the image of this man just seeming to observe his hands on the strings of this instrument, seemingly just moving by themselves. It was like he was outside of himself and just observing—with this totally peaceful smile and seemingly unconscious and totally in his moment.

"Suzuki describes "myoyu" *or simply* "myo" *as a certain artistic quality perceivable not only in works of art but anything in nature or life. The sword in the hands of a swordsman attains this quality when it is not merely a display of technical skill patiently learned under the tutelage of a good master."*

There is a truly wonderful quality described in *Zen and Japanese Culture* that I believe I witnessed that day. In his book, Suzuki describes *"myoyu"* or simply *"myo"* as a certain artistic quality perceivable not only in works of art but anything in nature or life. The sword in the hands of a swordsman attains this quality when it is not merely a display of technical skill patiently learned under the tutelage of a good master—

"Open your mind to any kind of supplementary training that may help your performance. If it helps you become a better martial artist, why not do it? I don't really know what the future holds for the martial arts, but whatever it is, I want to be there."

myo is something original and creative growing out of one's own unconscious. The hands may move according to the technique given to every student, but there is a certain spontaneity and personal creativity when the technique, conceptualized and universalized, is handled by the master's hand. An example of this in nature is the spider spinning its web, or the beaver building its nest. I am not ashamed to say that I was moved to tears by this moment—I was privileged to witness a true master displaying these qualities of *myo*. As martial artists, this is the absolute desired artistic quality to attain when performing our art.

Q: What do you consider to be the most important qualities of a martial artist?

A: To be forever humble, polite, and courteous; to always consider themselves as students of the arts and always strive to be the best role models possible, and never forget where they came from. He should take advantage of today's advanced knowledge and technology when it comes to sports training and conditioning. Open your mind to any kind of supplementary training that may help your performance. If it helps you become a better martial artist, why not do it? I am a firm believer in strength training with weights for instance. I realized that with weight training, my punches, kicks, and stances felt much stronger. Again, it may not be for everyone, but I received tremendous benefits from progressive resistance training.

I don't really know what the future holds for the martial arts, but whatever it is, I want to be there. When I look back on my own journey and evolution, I can only get excited at the prospects of what the future holds. I can only imagine what new and wonderful discoveries will unfold that will further our understanding of the martial arts as they continually shift and are redefined according to the ever-changing environment of the world we live in.

Q: Have there been times when you felt fear?
A: More times than I will probably ever admit to; but as my friend Geoff Thompson says in his book on fear, "Fear is the friend of extraordinary people." The people I have met in my years as a martial artist, who told me they never felt fear, were either very misguided or blatant liars. The feeling of fear is as natural as the feelings of hunger and thirst. It's a matter of what you do with it. Each time I approached a new situation at a higher level, and found myself in unfamiliar circumstances, I felt fear. For example, the first time I walked into the Jet Center, or my first jiu-jitsu encounter. What I realized though this, is that the only way to overcome the fear of doing something new or unfamiliar is to go out and do it. You will not learn to swim until you immerse yourself in water. Saying that you don't feel fear is the same as saying that you don't feel hunger, thirst, love, or hate, Everyone feels emotion—fear being one of the most powerful and primeval. Franklin D. Roosevelt said, "The only thing we have to fear is fear itself." As long as you continue to learn and grow, fear will never go away. I guess I just try to learn to confront my fears, because living with fear is probably more painful than confronting it.

Q: What keeps you motivated?
A: Learning. There's a world full of knowledge out there for the taking, by any individual driven enough to want it. ↄ

Ed Parker

The Father of American Karate

A traditionalist in spirit, but a modernist in technique, Ed Parker used the teachings of William K.S. Chow to create a unique fighting system that would revolutionize martial arts forever.

Edmund Kamehameha Parker, a native from Hawaii, was the turning point in the history of American martial arts. Called "The Father of American Karate," Parker began his martial arts studies at age 16 under William K.S. Chow. Parker received his black belt in 1951 and moved to Los Angeles when he opened one of the very first karate schools on the U.S. mainland. Soon, he began teaching some of Hollywood's biggest stars such as Blake Edwards, Robert Culp, and Robert Wagner. He also became a personal friend and teacher of the King of Rock and Roll, Elvis Presley.

In 1964 he created the Long Beach International Karate Championship and gathered names such as Bruce Lee, Tsuomu Oshima, Ben Largusa, and more to give demonstrations. During his life, Ed Parker continually studied new ways of improving his art. His personal philosophy was based on practicality, and still reaches thousands of instructors all over the world. Ed Parker helped martial artist as Tak Kubota, Chuck Norris, Joe Lewis, Mike Stone and the great Bruce Lee to achieve their full potential.

As a great innovator, Ed Parker wrote several books to educate people about the martial arts way as he perceived it. His International Kenpo Karate Association became one of the biggest martial arts organizations in the whole world with branches in the U.S., England, Ireland, Germany, Chile, and Spain. Although Ed Parker died suddenly in December 1990, at an early age, his spirit can be felt every time a kenpo practitioner puts on his gi.

Q: When did you start your martial arts training?

A: I met a man named Frank Chow in Hawaii. He was telling me how he beat a tough local bully and I didn't believe a word until he began to show all these movements he used. I started to train under him regularly and a little bit later he took me to his brother William K.S. Chow.

"The thing I liked about Professor Chow was that to a streetfighter like me, his concepts and ideas were better in terms of what was realistic. That's why I really went along with him."

Q: Did you have any experience in other fighting systems?
A: I was a street fighter already and my father was a boxing inspector so I had great chances to learn boxing which I eventually did. I was, I think, a fairly good street fighter. I discovered that a lot of the traditional techniques did not work in the street the way they were supposed to.

Q: What was Williams Chow's system like when you began to learn it?
A: Chow's father was a kung-fu man, but he also learned under a Japanese teacher, so William Chow had a very balanced system incorporating the linear and circular motion from both methods—although it was a little primitive when compared to the methods nowadays. The thing I liked about Professor Chow was that to a streetfighter like me, his concepts and ideas were better in terms of what was realistic. That's why I really went along with him. He led me toward the goal of logic and practicality. He used to tell me, "Come on, don't settle for less, you know what it's like on the street!"

Q: Is it true you started the first commercial school in the United States?
A: Yes, I did. At that time there was no other business like it so I had to listen to others as far as how to deal with certain things. I knew that I had to tailor the business concepts to whatever field I was getting into—that's why I decided to finish college and get my degree before going into business.

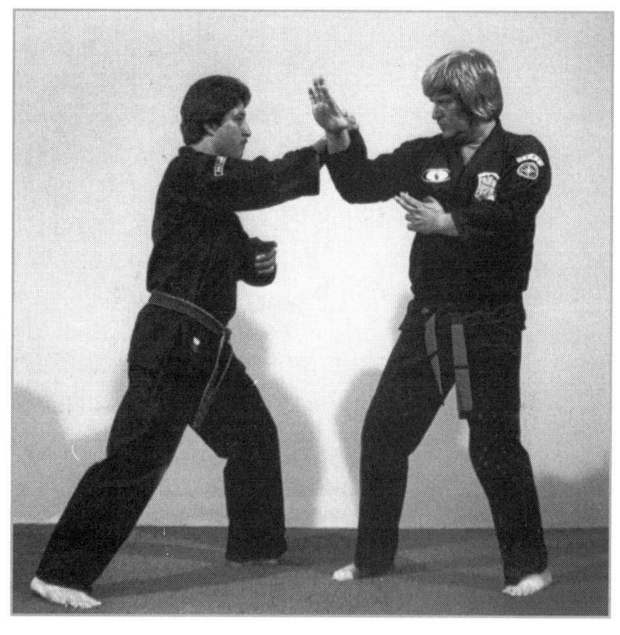

"I realized that I hadn't had the chance to do everything I could for martial arts and kenpo. So I began to be very active again and started really pushing the IKKA."

Q: You were franchising schools all over the United States and making plenty of money. All of a sudden, you came back and start traveling and teaching again. Why?
A: I was having a very relaxed life and all of a sudden I got the feeling that I was going to die—it really hit me—I had no doubt about it. I felt like I was running out of time. Right away I called my wife and my top black belts and told them how I wanted things done in case I died. The intensity of that feeling grew stronger every day. Two months later my brother called me and told me that my older brother dropped dead from jogging. The weird feeling left me immediately. I realized that I hadn't had the chance to do everything I could for martial arts and kenpo. So I began to be very active again and started really pushing the IKKA.

Q: How did you meet Bruce Lee?
A: Jimmy Lee was a good friend of mine and an expert in Chinese kung fu. He said that there was a guy I should see. So I went to see Bruce. He was a great person and very intelligent. He liked to say, "Never be like the man at the bottom of the well who, when looking up at the sky, thinks that the portion of the sky he sees is all there is to heaven." I remember him as a good friend.

"It started in 1960, when I was giving a demonstration at the Beverly Wilshire Health Club. Elvis was there—he was one of the spectators."

Q: Was Bruce a talented martial artist?

A: He was very good. When he punched, he could pop the air—he was very talented. He could copy in a minute all the movements you were practicing for ten years and duplicate them right away! We had long conversations about martial arts.

Q: Did you ever disagree?

A: Yes, sometimes! He liked to use all the Chinese philosophy and stories like the tale about the empty cup, and I kept telling him to not compare that to martial arts. He would just grumble back.

Q: Some people say he had a difficult personality.
A: Perhaps, but not with me. He was cocky—but the kind of cockiness that comes from being sure about what you know. Other than that he was clever, sharp, and he was joking all the time. I asked him if he'd like to perform in my tournament in Long Beach. He accepted right away and did an excellent job. Everybody was impressed with him. That demonstration was packed with great martial artists like Tsuomu Oshima, Bruce Lee, Ben Largusa, Tak Kubota, and more. Taky Kimura from Seattle was assisting Bruce Lee that day. It was 1964.

"He was already the King of Rock and Roll by then, but he was acting very humble. He mentioned his karate training in Germany and that he really liked the martial arts. He told me that I was a rebel, just like him."

Q: Did you still have the film?
A: Yes. We filmed in color and we used three different cameras. I took the film over to Willian Dozier, who at that time owned the *Batman* series and was planning on doing the *Green Hornet.* The rest, like they say, is history. Bruce became the greatest martial artist in the world and the greatest Chinese action movie star of all time.

Q: What was your relationship with Elvis Presley like?
A: It started in 1960, when I was giving a demonstration at the Beverly Wilshire Health Club. Elvis was there—he was one of the spectators. Once I finished he came and introduced himself saying, "I don't think you know me but my name is Elvis Presley." He was already the King of Rock and Roll by then, but he was acting very humble. He mentioned his karate training in Germany and that he really liked the martial arts. He told me that I was a rebel, just like him.

Q: When did you begin teaching him?
A: Just a little bit later. We hit it off right away. I really enjoyed his company. He was very respectful to me. He was the kind of guy that if he recognized

"I was going to see Elvis in Memphis a few hours later and was taking a flight from Los Angeles. All of a sudden, I had an empty feeling inside me and depression hit me like a sledgehammer. It was hard for me to accept that I was not going to see my friend anymore. I learned many things from him."

your knowledge in something, he'd keep his mouth shut and listen to you.

Q: Was he really a black belt?
A: Yes he was. I gave the black belt rank to him. He had the skill for that level and I didn't hesitate in doing it. But I didn't give it to him because he was Elvis Presley. He was a very dedicated student and he deserved it.

Q: You became his bodyguard, right?
A: Yes. At some point he discharged three of his bodyguards and he asked me to do it. I guess he felt very comfortable having me around, and I was happy doing that for a friend. I guess I was more like a protective companion than a true bodyguard. We had some great moments together.

Q: How did you feel when you learned that he was dead?
A: I was going to see him in Memphis a few hours later and was taking a flight from Los Angeles. All of a sudden, I had an empty feeling inside me and depression hit me like a sledgehammer. It was hard for me to accept that I was not going to see my friend anymore. I learned many things from him.

Q: Such as?
A: He told me that the audience, the public, must first be entertained then subliminally educated. I use that principle in everything in my life.

Q: What's your martial arts philosophy?
A: My main idea is that martial arts have to be used to build character rather than build fighters. I had to face different odds during my early days. In high school I had a teacher who told me once, "Ed, you'll never be a success in life." These words have been the driving force all my life.

"My main idea is that martial arts have to be used to build character rather than build fighters. In high school I had a teacher who told me once, 'Ed, you'll never be a success in life.' These words have been the driving force all my life."

Q: Did you ever see that teacher again?
A: No, but I was looking for him during one of the old student reunions. Unfortunately, I couldn't find him, because he had moved.

Q: What you were planning to say to him?
A: I wanted to thank him!

Q: Do you believe in breaking boards?
A: I have never heard of a board or a brick attacking anyone! I don't see the point in doing that.

Q: You are a innovative, driving force in American martial arts. Do you think anyone can create their own system like you did?
A: It depends on a lot of things. I've been criticized because I broke away and started changing the martial arts I learned from Professor Chow. Only certain individuals believe that they can create forms or make innovations in the arts. And this is not right. That's the reason my black belts are required to create a kata of their own and then write a thesis about the art. Kata is a mere notion, pure and simple. They are ideal situations for learning, and they are great as a method of practice. But you have to know how

"Traditionalists think they really know better, but it's going to be long time before they reach the true freedom and expression of self. I have no problem listening to somebody else if they know what they're doing."

to use them and add moves to them so they're worth something. Traditionalists think they really know better, but it's going to be long time before they reach the true freedom and expression of self.

Q: You sound like a very independent person.
A: I really am, but I listen to those who know how to do things better. I have no problem listening to somebody else if they know what they're doing.

Q: Dan Inosanto was one of your first students, is that right?
A: Yes, he was a black belt under me and used to teach for me. Then he met Bruce and became his student.

Q: It is true that you introduced him to the Filipino arts?
A: Well, I think so. He asked me about Filipino stick fighting and I told him there was much more than sticks in the Filipino martial arts. He is a humble man and wise enough to make room for progress.

Q: Do you consider yourself as a traditionalist?

A: If we talking about respect for the art or for your teacher, then, yes, I'm very traditional. But technique-wise I've always believed that the most important thing is to be able to adapt anything you learn to yourself. The teacher has to give the student a base, but not bind him. Things are much more sophisticated today that 30 years ago. We have to develop the ability to vary and change according to the times. John L. Sullivan was a great fighter, but he'd be wiped out if he were living today and kept fighting the way he used to. I don't think he would fare too well because now we have hooks, uppercuts, bob and weave, shuffling, et cetera. And he did not know about that.

"The teacher has to give the student a base, but not bind him. Things are much more sophisticated today that 30 years ago. We have to develop the ability to vary and change according to the times."

Q: You mean some traditional systems are like John L. Sullivan these days?

A: Yes, they definitely are. They don't want to change and they don't want to improve and evolve. I like to say, "Knowledge is bound when one is compelled to tradition—Knowledge is endless when tradition is bound." Unfortunately, I keep constantly hearing that this style is better than that style. It is not the style, it is the man. The style gives you the physical boundaries but you are the one who makes it work.

Q: What kind of training program do you recommend to students?

A: Every student is different so as far as physical conditioning goes, they need to evaluate what their needs are. For the kenpo karate techniques I'd recommend to train kata and the self-defense techniques for a couple of hours a day, at least three days a week. Of course, if they trains more, better off they are. I would also advise them to dedicate some time to deeply study

"I began to analyze the reverse motion of every offensive action. The reverse motion is the other half of the action and it shouldn't be wasted in offense. I learned what I call the "offensive defensive." No system has all the answers. Kenpo is a system that has answers coming in and coming out."

the concepts and principles behind the techniques so they can develop an in-depth understanding of what they are doing, so they can maximize their value.

Q: Do you think is beneficial to study other martial art systems besides your base system?

A: Yes, but let me elaborate on this. First you need a strong foundation—you shouldn't go jumping from one system to another every three months. Then, you have to analyze yourself and find out how your chosen art fits you, and how you can fill in the gaps and strengthen your weak points. Later on, you can look at other systems. Because even if you don't believe in something, you'd better know what others believe in. You can prevent defeat by knowing what the practitioners of a particular system are going to do if you face them.

Q: You've mentioned that the turning point in your research came one day you were viewing one of your films backwards.

A: Yes. I was watching myself on film because I liked to record demonstrations and training to analyze later on. I was so tired that instead of changing the reel, I flipped it in reverse and bam! There is was! It really hit me! I began to analyze the reverse motion of every offensive action. The reverse motion is the other half of the action and it shouldn't be wasted in offense. I learned what I call the "offensive defensive."

Q: Does the kenpo system have all the answers?

A: No system has all the answers. Kenpo is a system that has answers coming in and coming out. I keep researching in order to supply more scientific knowledge to the students. After all, human beings have two arms and two legs and there are definitely limitations in the way you can use them. By this I mean that the answers are in your own body and in knowing how to use it in a more efficient way. I want my students to become thinkers—to contrive answers on their own. I think I have developed a very complete system. Once the student has the very essence of the system he can develop their own style because my system has principals that can be tailored to any individual.

"I think I have developed a very complete system. Once the student has the very essence of the system he can develop their own style because my system has principals that can be tailored to any individual."

Q: What would be your last will for your students?

A: I would tell my students to make sure that their minds grow in proportion to their bodies.

Q: How would you like to be remembered?

A: As a happy person, and as someone who tried to help others—and I guess I did. Also as a good teacher, as a good husband, and as a good father. And also as the father of American karate.

Richard Rabago

A Higher Standard

High-ranking Shorin-ryu karate master Richard Rabago has the experience, training credentials, and budo skill to have earned the right to be called "master" several times over. If you call him that, however, you'll most likely get a roll of the eyes, a slightly embarrassed laugh, and the words, "Just call me 'sensei'—that is enough." A throwback to the age of budo and honor, where a karateka earned respect through skill and dedication, not by self-given titles, Rabago measures himself against a higher standard than is commonly used in martial arts today. Trained by two of karate's most famous masters, Nishiyama and Oshima, Rabago learned his most important lesson from them—the basics are everything. It wasn't until be met Terashi Imashda, though, and saw how the Shorin-ryu master generated tremendous power from flexibility and speed, that Rabago truly found his martial arts path in life.

Applying the karate lessons of commitment, perseverance, and mental training, Rabago also embarked on the dual careers of engineering design and acting. Appearing in numerous television and movie roles, while holding down a job as a digital chip designer, he became well-known for his part in VR Troopers. Still working, teaching, and pursuing his acting career, Rabago insists that the most important lessons he can teach his students are not the physical ones, but the mental. "I teach my students never to say the words, 'I can't do it.' Because this will help them for their entire life. If you have a positive attitude from a young age, and then become an adult, your positive thinking will push you to whatever goals you might have."

Q: How did you get involved in the martial arts?

A: I started in about 1955 where my uncle, when he was in the Air Force, took the martial arts from Professor Chow. So when he would come home on furloughs I would see him practice the art and this got me interested in kenpo area which led me to karate. I was already taking judo back in Hawaii at the time. From there I started to think that the art of kenpo was very useful and practical. It was similar to boxing, yet they were using their

"I was born on Honolulu but raised on Kuai. I told myself that when I found someone who had a really strong teaching foundation in karate that I would really apply myself to it."

feet and hands to fight. I was only about 12 then, but I still was very impressed by it.

Q: How long did you do judo before finding kenpo and karate?

A: Judo was basically done from around 8 years old on. All the kids in the area were doing it so I kind of followed in their footsteps. This was on Kuai, so there wasn't a lot to do besides judo, because it is a sleepy place. I was born on Honolulu but raised on Kuai. I told myself that when I found someone who had a really strong teaching foundation in karate that I would really apply myself to it.

Q: What did you like about karate as opposed to judo, that would motivate to make the vow?
A: Because of my size, basically. I didn't really want to hold onto people that were bigger than myself and try to throw them, or wrestle them to the ground. I wanted to hit and run in a fight, and use my speed to my advantage with my feet and hands. But I always wanted the art of karate. I always really like sports. And being a boy and having friends that played sports and did martial arts I said to myself that why not and go ahead and find an art you really like and then stick with it? So that is why I'm where I'm at today; I found an art that I really liked. I'm past 50 now, and still doing it. I started training shotokan with Sensei Nishiyama and then with Sensei Oshima—both great masters. Then, after a while, I switched to shorin-ryu, where I still am today.

Q: Was there a big difference between training with Nishiyama and Oshima?
A: Not really. They both leaned toward teaching the basics—punching and kicking—hundreds of each. There were no fancy punches or kicks, just the basics. That's where I think the martial arts have gotten a little lost today—they've forgotten the basics. People are not getting the basics. They're more into the real acrobatic techniques such as the high spinning kicks because they want to do things that they see on television. So they both just did the total basics. I don't think that people would like that kind of training today. To me, because of the early training, I like focusing on the basics.

Q: So you trained in shotokan but then switched to shorin-ryu. Why?
A: I did it when I saw my sensei, Terashi Imashda, do a couple of kicks and punches with my kid brother. Senseu was no bigger or heavier than I, but he would throw his punches with the force of a 250-pound person and with the speed of lightning. The same was true with his kicks—they were very crisp and powerful. So this showed me what the human body could do with very good training and proper technique. The shorin-ryu, to me, was not as hard as the shotokan that I learned. It was based on relaxation, which I felt developed more power from the techniques. Also, I think because of my personality, I think that being looser fit me better. But both styles had the same type of training mentality with the emphasis on the basics. The basics will work for you ninety-nine percent of the time.

Q: You don't spend a lot of time talking about your belt ranking. Why?
A: To me a ranking is something that should be kept within. But today I see a lot of people walking around with high ranking belts, calling themselves masters. I really hate that, for myself. I don't want to be called master. I'm just myself. Respect me as a sensei and I will be honored enough. But to call me master is something that should be reserved for the legends. Actions are a lot stronger than words and I see a lot of people with very high rankings who do kata, kumite, or bunkai that I would be ashamed to see a first degree black belt do. A true master doesn't think of himself as one. They don't seek to draw attention to themselves. They just want to be themselves.

Q: Do you feel weapons training is important to karate?
A: Yes, because if forces you to use the basic. The most important aspect of weapons training is first learning the basics of empty-hand karate. If you don't have the basics then you won't be able to control the weapon—any weapon. Because of my training in shorin-ryu under Sensei Imashda, who is know for his weaponry, he has given me some knowledge of his weapons' expertise. So I instill that same quality in my studio. My favorite weapon is the *bo*, or stick, because of the weapon control—you have both hands on the weapon so you get more control. I also like sai, tonfa, and kama. Sensei Imashda is one of the best weapons masters around; he brought the kama to California and today, I think every studio is using the kama, especially the version that has the rope tied around the end and swings free. He is most famous for that. But the weapons that he uses are no dull or fake—they are real. That is why one needs to work with the basics to control the weapon. If you can't control the kama you're going to have cuts all over your body because the kama is razor sharp. Of course, today, because of tournament competition, the real weapons are not used. I always start beginners with the bo because of the control factor.

Q: What are the most common questions you get from beginners?
A: Most people come into the dojo and first ask how long does it take to become a black belt—that's the number one question. Then they ask if we fight a lot. Then they ask what weapons do we teach. I tell them that we do, but that it takes time to get to where they can handle the training. So once they learn the truth about the martial arts—that it takes a lot of work—they usually shy off. I tell them they can come in and train and see if they like it.

"The most important aspect of weapons training is first learning the basics of empty-hand karate. If you don't have the basics then you won't be able to control the weapon—any weapon. I always start beginners with the bo because of the control factor."

Q: You're also well-known for your movie and television roles. How did you start to combine martial arts and entertainment?

A: Well, I was basically working at a company in 1964 in Los Angeles and one of my friends asked me if I wanted to be an extra in a movie. The movie was *Sand Pebbles* starring Steve McQueen. So they needed some younger looking Orientals to play some students in the movie. So I went down and auditioned for the part and got it. From there it was a stepping stone to other parts. I eventually wound up on the TV show *VR Troopers*, just a few years ago. For that, an agent called and asked for me to audition for the show. So I went down there and lo and behold, I got the job.

"Everything is beneficial in the martial arts in everything you do. You really can't separate the physical and the mental. If your mind is strong enough to overcome that negative thought then the physical will follow."

Q: Do you feel that the physical or mental part of karate helped you the most to get parts like this?

A: Everything is beneficial in the martial arts in everything you do. You really can't separate the physical and the mental. But most of the martial arts that I've really tried to strive and teach my students about is the mental area before the mental area. Because if your mind is not strong your physical skills will never follow. No matter how strong you are, if you get hurt what does you mind tell you? "I'm hurt—I don't want to do it anymore." But if your mind is strong enough to overcome that negative thought then the physical will follow. So you will never be weak in any of the areas: spiritual, mental, physical. So that is why I tell my students to work on their mental area. And by doing strong workouts, you will gather the mental areas. If your mind says, "The training is so hard that I can't do it: I can't do 50 punches, I can only do ten. Then you have negative thinking and will stop at that point. So even in school, if your teacher gives you a mountain of homework to do, your mind might say, "I can't do this. It's too much work." But by training your mind you'll be able to overcome those negative thoughts. So this mental aspect of karate applies to life as well as the martial arts. That is why I say you cannot separate the aspects. They all work together and are part of each other.

Q: So is the mental training just a part of doing the exercises?
A: Very much so. I'd say about 90 percent of the time. If you push your body to the limit, you've already gone a long way towards conquering the mental side of the art. But if you don't push your body to the limit, then you will have the negative part of human nature in control. You will always stop at the point that things get hard—in everything you do. So by helping the person to push themselves you have to be strict with them. You might tell them to do 10 push-ups at first; but in your mind you know that you're going to ask them to do 5 more after the 10 are finished. So by asking them to do 5 more than ten, this is where the training becomes stronger and their mind becomes stronger. Then from 15 you go to 20; and from 20 to 50—and they will never know the difference between 10 and 50. So now their minds become stronger and more positive. And they get stronger physically, spiritually, and physically. It all comes from going beyond yourself—pushing yourself into unknown territory. Not getting caught in a comfort zone where you never challenge what you know you can do. They never say, about anything, "I can't do it." They automatically assume that they can. And this is what helps everyone in life. Because if you start from a young age, and then become an adult, your positive thinking will push you to whatever goals you might have.

Q: Now you do other things besides karate, right?
A: Yes, and no matter what I do—my acting, my technical career, my whatever—I use those same principles to continue to move ahead and to not give up. Martial arts has a lot of good in it if you have a strong instructor that can set you on the right path. An instructor cannot live your live for you—they can only guide you. If you don't follow the example then you can easily lose sight of your goals. They can't stay with you 24 hours a day. They can't be there if you have a fight outside the dojo, or a test in school,

or a moral dilemma of whether to use drugs or not, or break the law, or whatever. At some point the student has to stand on their own.

Q: Do you encourage your students, then, to further their education? Do you focus on them winning a tournament to make you look good, or to practice hard to make them better people.

A: Education and becoming a better person is the number one goal I have for my students. Martial arts is second. Martial arts helps you do develop a winning attitude about yourself. Then I want them to take that attitude and move forward into life with it. Once you can focus, then you can focus on anything. I design integrated circuits, for example. Sometimes I will get to a layout or a problem area that requires me to set it aside for awhile so I can come back and approach it from a different angle or a different perspective. So this is the same thing with martial arts. If you're in a tournament and you get hit, you might say to yourself, "Man, I don't want to get hit anymore." Then you say to yourself, "That's my mistake. I need to analyze what happened and adjust accordingly, to make sure it doesn't happen again." So then you'll be able to defend it the next time. Life, as well as martial arts, is all about focus, attitude, and taking responsibility for your actions and for yourself.

Q: What is your favorite part of karate?

A: I don't really have a specialty. Every kata that I do is a favorite of mine. The most basic kata, actually, are my favorites. I want to use something that is natural and is second nature. You don't want to use something that you have to think about in your movement. If you think too muck about the kata, then you'll forget what the kata is about. So the simplest kata that you do every day becomes the one that does you the most good. It will become a natural movement. The most important thing about karate technique is making it reflexive where you don't have to think about it. You don't what to be thinking, "Okay, this guy is doing a straight punch so I'll do a fancy block." You'll get hit. But if you react without thinking then you'll always be able to defend yourself because there is no lag time.

I think that once you have a strong relationship with karate that you will have a strong relationship with the right way to live your life. That is why the traditional values of karate are so important to pass along. What you're trying to do with the training is to have total positive thoughts, not negative thoughts. I think, to a point, that the fighting part of the martial arts has become overemphasized today because of the entertainment factor. People who are not martial artists like to see blood and guts in events like the UFC, or other no-holds-barred shows. I don't think that there is a lot of respect for traditional values shown there because you're taking away the mental and spiritual part of the martial arts and emphasizing only one part—the fighting. But over the long run I think you'll see that the traditional arts will flourish and grow. Traditional martial arts have survived for thousands of years because there is much more to offer than just fighting.

Q: What would you tell a prospective karate student?
A: You'll get out of it what you put into it. What a student gets out of martial arts just depends on what attitude they have going into it. If they focus on fighting then all they'll get out of it is the ability to fight. But if they include other things then they'll get other things out of it. Basically, when you take karate you know what you could do to someone who has no knowledge of the martial arts. If he comes up to you and says, "I'm going to kick your butt." Already that guy has lost because that guy doesn't know what you know. You could have punched him right away but you have more self-control than that. So you try to avoid the conflict of a fight. By doing that you have learned something from martial arts—walking away from trouble. But if you're cornered you can also defend yourself because you have that knowledge of martial arts. You have the distance and the timing and you have the whole body to work with. Whereas the person who's trying to start trouble is just limited to trying to punch you. He doesn't know you have defenses with your feet, legs, elbows, palm, et cetera.

Q: So do you think of yourself as an actor, an engineer, or a martial artist?
A: I think of myself as an everyday person. I don't think of myself in any one sense. I try to be myself; I don't try to be what others think I am or what others want me to be. I believe in keeping everything in balance and that includes yourself. Never forget who you are and never lose your sense of self. People will always try to influence you to go their way. I don't want people to see me or think of me as anything other than who I am—which is myself. Karate is an anchor that keeps you from getting swept away by the tide of life.

Sensei Rabago faces a bo-wielding attacker (1). He blocks a low strike with his tonfa (2), strikes to the head, which is blocked (3) then finishes with a counter strike to the head (4).

Facing an attacker armed with nunchakus (1), Master Rabago blocks a high strike (2), blocks the opposite-hand attack (3), then steps outside an intended follow-up attack (4), secures the wrist (5), then blast a finishing kick to the midsection (6).

1

2

3

4

5

6

Surachai Sirisute

The World is his Gym

A natural fighter as a child who went on to become a champion in Thailand's toughest stadiums, Master Chai has spread the art of muay Thai around the globe, earning the respect and admiration of all he has come in contact with.

At only 4 years of age, Surachai Sirisute demonstrated a natural ability to kick. This piqued the curiosity of Thai boxing master Ajarn Suwan, who taught him the art of muay Thai. At twelve, young "Chai," as he was called, was fighting in amateur bouts at the local temple fair. After became a champion at the two most important stadiums in Thailand, Chai, now called "Master" himself, decided to change his life and begin a challenging quest to teach the art to the "Brown Hairs" (Americans). Since 1964, Ajarn Chai has been teaching the art of muay Thai in the United States and all over the world. His reputation has reached every corner of the globe and his training sessions became legendary for their intensity. He is a very hard trainer and time moves very slowly on the Ajarn stopwatch—three minute rounds on the Thai pads often stretch to five—for a minimum of 15 rounds!

The Thai people are very devoted to astrology, palmistry, and numerology. Ajarn Chai's ring name was Han Vattana, meaning "Strong Fighter." Many legendary instructors of other different martial arts systems have visited Ajarn Chai for instruction. His ability not only includes empty-hand methods, but also weaponry as well. Students from all over the world revere him like a father. He has earned that level of respect by sharing muay Thai with love, compassion, empathy, dedication—and lots and lot of endless and exhausting training sessions!

Q: Can you explain the history of muay Thai?

A: Thai boxing is one of the oldest martial arts in existence. Its origin dates back to 250 B.C., when the Thai clans migrated from central China on the banks of the Yangtze river to Thailand. The Thais began a military training regimen for their young men called *chupasart,* which dealt mainly with the use of swords, spears, and crossbows. In peacetime, legs and arms replaced

"Kickboxing is not Thai boxing. We say that kickboxing evolved from Thai boxing. In Thai boxing the whole body is fair game. You can use elbow and knee techniques which are illegal in many fighting competitions."

weaponry, and these movements became the basis of modern Thai boxing.

Q: When did you began your training in the Thai arts?

A: I started as a young kid training in the training camps in Huay Kwang-Dindang province in Thailand. Everybody knows this province for producing great champions. As a kid I was always ready to fight. I began fighting in the ring at 12 years old. I still remember the surprised faces of the Western tourist watching us fighting!

Q: When did you decide to move to the United States?

A: I came to United States in the early '60s, so I've been here for a long time. I wanted to light a candle where it was dark concerning to Thai arts. Ajarn Suwan told me to came here to teach the art and spread it all over the world.

Q: You are the president and founder of the USA Thai Boxing Association. Don't you also have different associations around the world?

A: Yes. We have Thai boxing associations operating in the United States, Mexico, Spain, Switzerland, Australia, New Zealand, and more. Some very dedicated students of mine came to United States to get their training and later on returned to open the associations. We keep in touch and I update their training constantly so they keep improving their techniques and understanding of the muay Thai art. Some of them have been with me for more than 15 years non-stop. We feel close to each other and are like a family now.

Q: Is muay Thai like kickboxing?

A: This is wrong. Kickboxing is not Thai boxing. We say that kickboxing evolved from Thai boxing. In kickboxing you have specific rules as to where you can kick and with what weapons. In Thai boxing the whole body is fair game. You can use elbow and knee techniques which are illegal in many fighting competitions.

Q: Someone said once that muay Thai boxing skills are very primitive and almost non-existent. What do you think about that?
A: Whoever said that had no idea of what he was talking about. The Thai boxer doesn't use boxing very much because in boxing distance the Thai arsenal includes the elbows and the knees. Both are much more damaging than punching with a glove on. So they prefer to use the elbow to the face and the knee to the ribs instead of boxing with gloves. This is just one thing of many. But it's nonsense to say that the Thais don't know how to box—this is a misunderstanding. Everybody knows that many world boxing champions from Thailand have been muay Thai champions that made a transition to Western boxing.

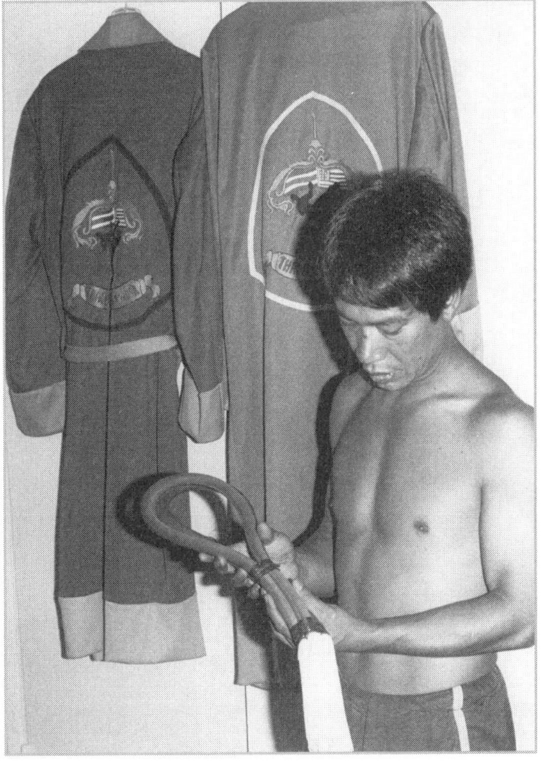

"If you work on your conditioning, run, skip rope, hit Thai pads, the heavy bag, spar and fight once a month, you can become a strong fighter in six months. Stamina, experience, and heart are the basics of Thai Boxing."

Q: How long does it take to become a good Thai fighter?
A: I know that I'm going say may be hard for some to accept, for it destroys the notion of that a practitioner must train for five or six years to attain the black belt rank. If you work on your conditioning, run, skip rope, hit Thai pads, the heavy bag, spar and fight once a month, you can become a strong fighter in six months. Stamina, experience, and heart are the basics of Thai Boxing. I believe that the one standing after the fight is the true expert.

Q: Due to the dangers of the muay Thai techniques, is hard sparring common in the training camps of Thailand?
A: They spar a lot but the hard sparring is kept to a minimum. To go all out, even with training equipment on, could be very damaging and non-productive. They do hard boxing sparring with gloves and headgear on but they go

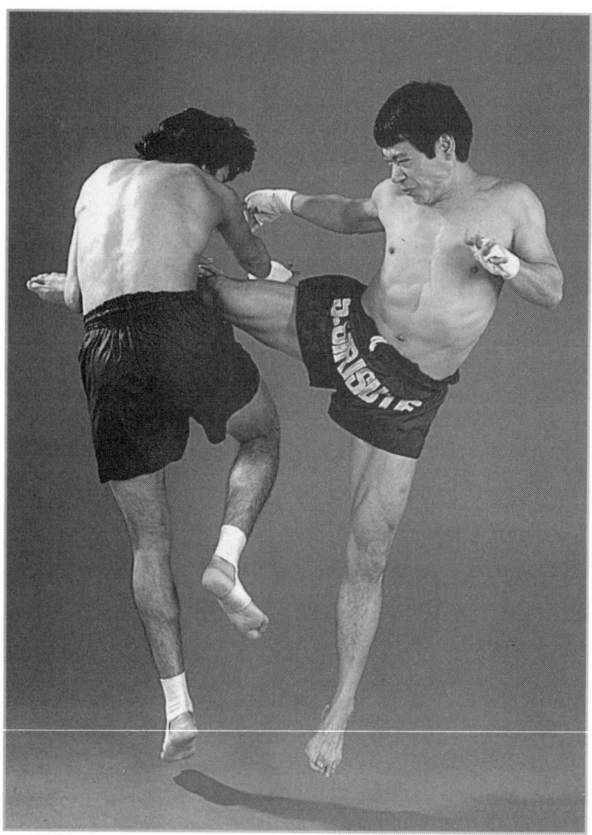

"Thai boxing teaching is very demanding. It's as exhausting to teach as it is to learn. The repetitions are murder but my students know what I expect from them. They are self-motivated. There's no need to tell them what to do."

light sparring with the legs and elbows, mainly for timing. Ring and sparring experience is very important. A good Thai fighter must learn certain timings in order to know the opponent's movements.

Q: How many hour of daily training do professional fighters Thailand do?
A: Somewhere from six to eight every day.

Q: How do you start training a beginner?
A: First of all, the beginner shouldn't be afraid of hard training. I usually start them off with basic footwork, basic punches, elbow, and knee combinations. Then they are taught the roundhouse kick, which for many is Thai boxing's trademark. It takes about two months for beginners to reach the conditioning level to be able to work in a continuos training circuit for two or three hours. You have to train like this for five days every week. Thai boxing teaching is very demanding. It's as exhausting to teach as it is to learn. The repetitions are murder but my students know what I expect from them. They are self-motivated. There's no need to tell them what to do.

Q: How you gauge a new student's heart?
A: After the student has built stamina on the roundkick, I ask him to kick the heavy bag 500 times. If he reaches 500 and keeps going I feel happy and I work harder on him. I know that his spirit is strong.

Q: Do you use any belt ranking?
A: No thanks! No belts here.

Q: Would you ever train a woman to fight in Thai boxing?
A: I did already. Even if she wanted to fight a man, I wouldn't stop her.

Q: You took an American team to Thailand, is that right?
A: Yes, I did. The first time was in 1982 and we stunned the Thai community by taking a third place team trophy at an international meet at Rajadamnern Stadium, one of the two biggest arenas.

Q: Did you countrymen advise you not to teach Westerners?
A: No, never. I always had a total support from my teachers and the government of Thailand, including the king and the queen, to spread the art around the world.

"I always had a total support from my teachers and the government of Thailand, including the king and the queen, to spread the art around the world."

Q: Thai boxing's low-line kicking method is devastating. How easy is to break a leg?
A: Well, it is not that easy if you're moving all the time. It may hurt real bad but it won't break your leg if you know how to deal with it. If you don't, then you're out with a broken leg, that's for sure. In kickboxing it's forbidden to kick to the inner part of the upper thighs because is where the sciatic nerve groups are located and it is very dangerous. In Thai boxing they love to kick there. The Thai boxer's primary objective is to numb the legs so the opponent can't move or evade blows.

Q: What's your philosophy of teaching?
A: I've come to realize how important it is to personally teach those students who are really serious and dedicated. But don't misunderstand me, I

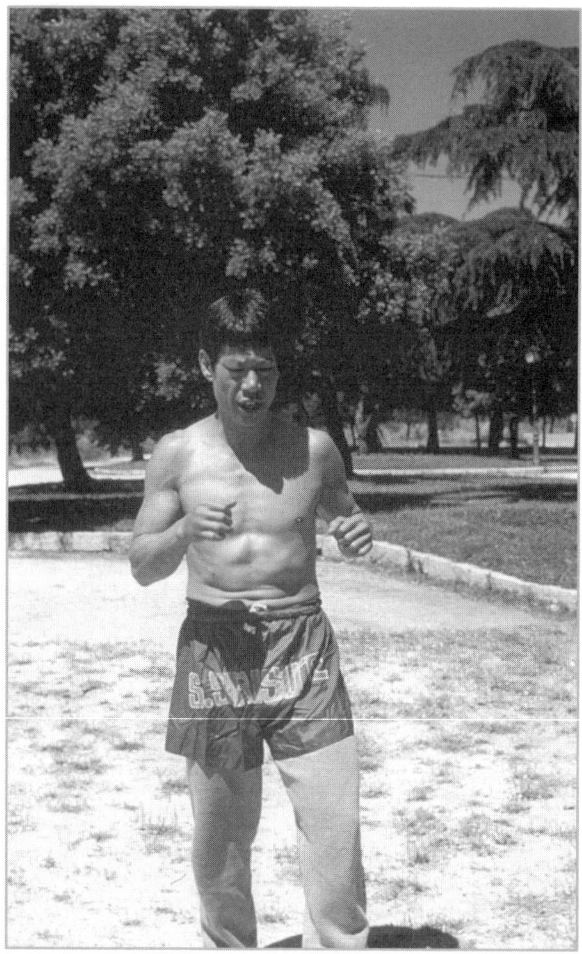

"In the ring muay Thai is a sport, a very hard sport, but a sport nonetheless. But in the street there are no rules. In muay Thai we have fighting techniques that are strictly used for self-defense and are forbidden in the ring."

don't try to withhold any knowledge from anyone. My teaching is for everybody.

Q: Do you use high kicking in Thai boxing?

A: Yes we do, but the Thai precept is "kill the body and the head dies." We begin killing the legs so the opponent can't move, then we go for the upper body and head. The opponent becomes a heavy bag to us.

Q: How do you transfer muay Thai ring skills to street self-defense?

A: Well, fighting in a ring is very different that fighting for your life on the street. In the ring muay Thai is a sport, a very hard sport, but a sport nonetheless. But in the street there are no rules. In muay Thai we have fighting techniques that are strictly used for self-defense and are forbidden in the ring.

Q: Do you know the art of krabi krabong?

A: Yes, I do. It's the ancient art and is not a sport. It's for military and fighting purposes only. They use sword, knife, spear, et cetera, and the techniques used in kabri kabrong are not allowed in Thai boxing.

Q: Did you train the Dallas Cowboys football team?
A: Yes. My student and friend Dan Inosanto introduced me to Dr. Bob Ward, who was an Inosanto student and a coach of the Cowboys. He was impressed with the training and conditioning methods so he arranged for me to go every year, for three months, to their pre-season training camp.

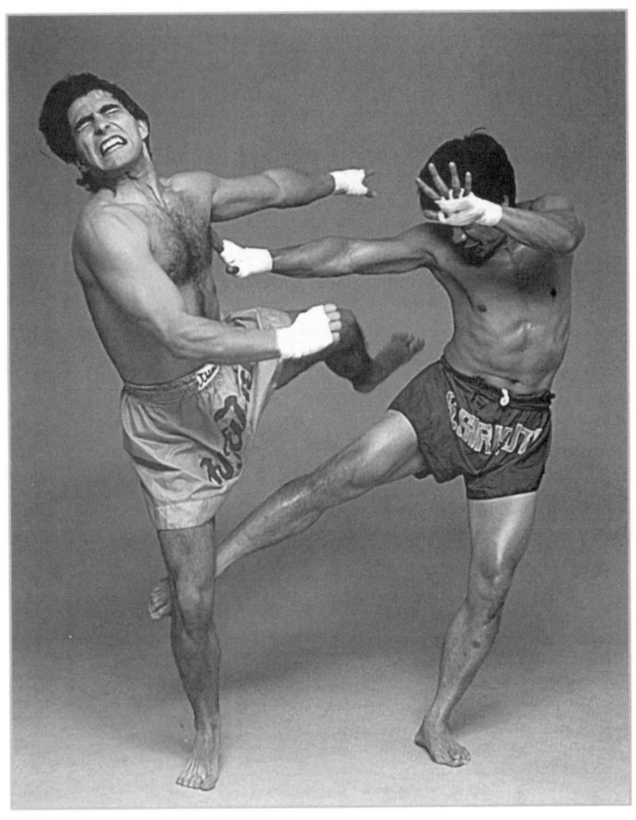

"I feel very grateful to all my students around the world. I always tell them, 'If I can do it, you can do it.'"

Q: What did you think of the Dallas players the first time you saw them?
A: They were great athletes but were lacking stamina. So I'd work them on the Thai pads. In the beginning they were huffing and puffing after only a couple of minutes. But after a few training sessions they really improved.

Q: Do you feel your teachings have been well-received?
A: Yes, I do. I feel very grateful to all my students around the world. I always tell them, "If I can do it, you can do it." Together, we have all been doing a great job spreading the art of Thai boxing.

Arjarn Sirisute faces his opponent (1). He closes the distance with a low kick to the inside of the leg (2) follows with a cross to the face (3), a left hook (4), and pushes the opponent away (5) to deliver a finishing low kick to the thigh (6).

Master Chai squares with his opponent (1). He block the punch to the face (2) entering inside of the line of attack (3) to deliver an upward elbow to the face (4) and finishes (5) with a downward right elbow to the head (6).

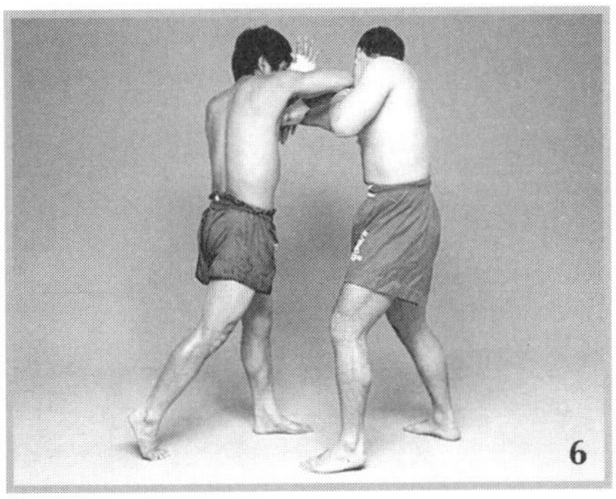

Edgar S. Sulite

A Legacy of Steel

He was one of a kind. A man who belonged to that special group of people who have such inner power and charisma that they touch the lives of all those around them.

Punong Guro Sulite was born September 25, 1957, in Tacloban City, on the Philippine island of Leyte. He was raised in a family of martial artists—his father, Hilacrio Sulite, was a professional boxer, arnis expert, and U.S. Army soldier, and his brother, Hilacrio Jr., was a karate expert. Since his childhood, having been born in a rural province where brawls between arnis experts were common, Edgar witnessed the deadly Filipino martial arts first-hand. His father began to teach him the arts of Western boxing and arnis at the age of 12. It was common for Edgar receive a constant battering on his hands and feet as a means to correct the technical mistakes he made in training, This crude, traditional method, although cruel, helped him to build-up resistance to pain and personal courage. While training under his father and mastering the family system known as "Sulite repelon," Edgar continually expanded his skill and combat knowledge by training with other masters and grandmasters all across the Philippine islands.

On April 8th of 1997, Pumong Guro Sulite passed away at the age of 39. Too strong and skilled to ever be defeated by an external opponent, he was felled by a stroke which surprised him while on a visit to the Philippines. Before leaving this world to pursue higher goals, though, Punong Guro Sulite left with us his legacy of steel.

Q: How did you begin training under the old escrima masters?

A: My family was transferred to Ozamis, where I was able to finish my Economics degree from Misamis University. Taking advantage of residing in the city, I furthered my knowledge by studying under different arnis masters such as Grandmaster Antonio Illustrisimo of Bag-on Bantayan, founder of kali illustrisimo, Leo Gaje of pekiti tirsia, Jose Caballero of de campo uno-dos-tres, and Jesus Abella of the modernos largos system.

"I founded the lameco system of arnis, which combines the different methods of "largo," "medio," and "corto." I didn't create a new system to become a grandmaster, per se. My intention in creating lameco eskrima was to properly organize, in a perfectly balanced synthesis, all the effective knowledge I had learned from my instructors."

Q: Did any of the old masters refuse to teach you because you studied so many arts?
A: Well, they were a little sensitive about someone from another system coming to their school to learn. For instance, Grandmaster Caballero was hesitant about teaching me his method because he felt I was going to steal his techniques! Fortunately, he saw the loyalty in me and began to trust me little by little.

Q: Your curriculum and skill is very impressive. Did any of the grandmasters ask you to be the successor to their system?
A: A few of them. But I did not want to stop teaching techniques from other methods which I consider very useful. So it was impossible to be somebody's successor and still teach others systems at the same time. It just didn't mix.

Q: You seem to be very committed to spreading the Filipino arts.
A: All I can say is that I devoted my entire life to the study of the ancient systems and masters—trying to refine my art and reach a physical embodiment of technical perfection.

Q: Did you ever think about creating your own system?
A: I founded the lameco system of arnis, which combines the different methods of "largo," "medio," and "corto." I didn't create a new system to become a

grandmaster, per se. My intention in creating lameco eskrima was to properly organize, in a perfectly balanced synthesis, all the effective knowledge I had learned from my instructors. My goal is to preserve the ancient teachings, but I came to understand that the old method of teaching—the bleeding forearms and the knots on top of the head—wasn't a good way."

"I do use some techniques for demonstrations. You have to have some of these if you want to give impressive displays. But the system I really teach is not meant for show. It is meant for real combat."

Q: How did you go about it, then?
A: I tried to systemize and present the arts in a modern context easily absorbed through a synthesis of multiple effective systems.

Q: "Kali," "escrima," and "arnis" are all names given to the Filipino martial arts. Which one is correct to use?
A: In Mindanao, "kali" was the term used, but that doesn't mean it is the only one. In fact, the three names mean the same. My first name is Edgar, my middle name is Gerez, and my last name is Sulite. The three of them describe the same person. So the three different named also describe the same art. We must remember that according to the region where you live, the terms change and others apply such as "estocada," "pagkalikali," and more.

Q: It seems that your art is not focused on demonstrations, and doesn't have very many flashy techniques.
A: Well, I do use some techniques for demonstrations. You have to have some of these if you want to give impressive displays. But you're right—the system I really teach is not meant for show. It is meant for real combat. The techniques that don't fit into this principle are immediately discarded.

"It is very different when you practice escrima for real fighting and self-defense rather than train just for fun or physical activity. Back in Philippines we used certain methods that wouldn't be fit the Western mentality."

Q: You have been living in U.S. since 1989 and visited other countries such as Germany, Australia, New Zealand, and more. How did you see the art being practiced there?

A: First of all, there are some people that only have been to a few of seminars and claim to have credentials to teach. This is wrong. It doesn't matter who gave those certifications. This is not good for the art, the students, or for the instructor giving the credentials! Their reputation and credibility are on the line. My advise for these practitioners is that they should keep training and going back to the basics. The basic techniques are the platform to achieve higher levels of proficiency—not only in escrima but in every martial art.

Q: What are the differences in the way the art is practiced outside the Philippines?

A: I can't talk about every country because I haven't visited them all—but I guess that the major difference is the mentality the art is practiced with. It is very different when you practice escrima for real fighting and self-defense rather than train just for fun or physical activity. Back in Philippines we used certain methods that wouldn't be fit the Western mentality. I would run all the students out of the school right away!

Q: What's your opinion on modern arnis sport tournaments?

A: They're OK, but a lot of important things are missing. If we really hit the hand holding the weapon, in the most "real" situations the fight is going to be over—but in a tournament this action is not that relevant. The environment and experience that you can get from a tournament can be deceiving if you don't know how to properly "read" what you're doing. This is the reason why, in the Philippines, we have two different kind of tournaments—with safety equipment and without.

Q: Do the Filipino martial arts have any spiritual aspects?
A: Of course there are religious aspects involved. The Filipino Christian people believe in God and the Muslims in Allah. These are different conceptions of a higher being. But it is only when you have reached a high level of physical proficiency that your instructor introduces you to the spiritual levels. Traditionally, it is your teacher who gives you an *oracion* to help you pray.

"The art has to be practiced the right way. Don't play with the art—give it the credit it deserves. Develop the art of escrima properly, with the right attitude and training to apply it to real situations. Kali is not a game."

Q: It is true that Grandmaster Caballero asked you to *not* teach his art to the public?
A: Yes. He sent me a letter three months before he passed away.

Q: Did you keep that promise?
A: Yes and no. I broke it and I kept it out of love for my teacher. I teach his method but I teach it in my own way within the lameco system. I do not teach it as he taught it to me. I wanted to keep his art alive but at the same time keep the promise I made to him.

Q: What is the right way to learn kali?
A: The art has to be practiced the right way. Don't play with the art—give it the credit it deserves. Develop the art of escrima properly, with the right attitude and training to apply it to real situations. Kali is not a game. ↄ

The assailant indicates something to Master Sulite (1). Suddenly he attack with a punch that is blocked (2). Master Sulite uses his right hand to control the aggressor (3-4), and delivers a strike to his elbow (5) putting pressure to take him down to the ground and apply a control (6).

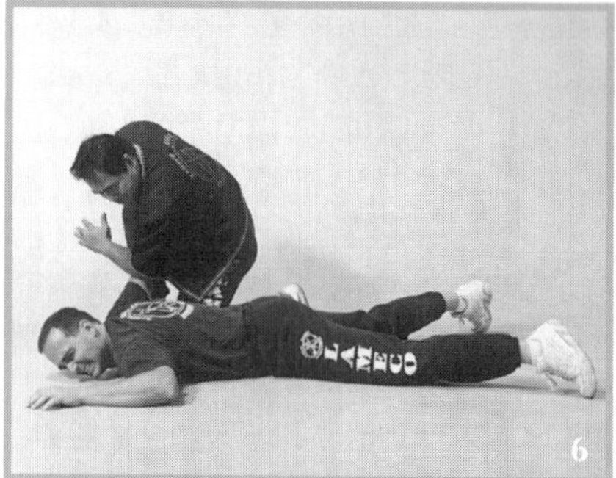

The aggressor approaches Master Sulite (1) and bearhugs him (2). Master Sulite reacts by hitting the aggressor's groin (3-4) and pulling him with his right hand (5) all the way to the ground (6) where he applies an armlock (7).

Master Sulite faces his opponent (1). The attacker throws a front kick that Master Sulite blocks to the outside (2) and circles his arm around, controlling the leg (3). He simultaneously grabs the aggressor's right hand (4), kicks his leg with to unbalance him (5) and takes him to the ground (6) where he applies a knee-bar lock.

1

2

3

4

5

6

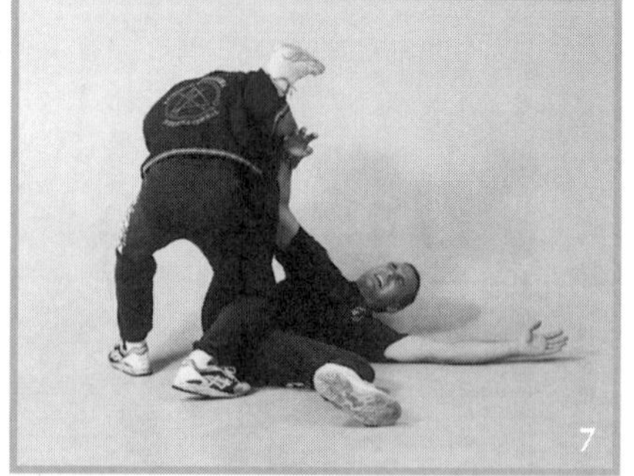
7

The aggressor is mounted on Master Sulite (1). Master Sulite grabs his aggressor's left hand (2) and twists his wrist (3) to hit the left arm (4) unbalancing and reversing the position (5) so he can apply a combination of writs and elbow lock (6).

1

2

3

4

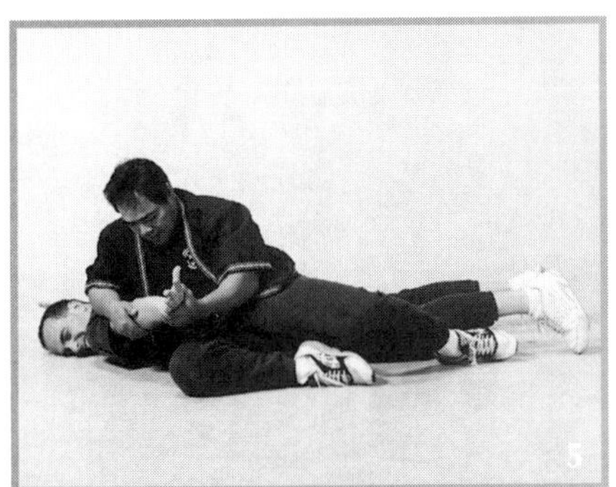
5

6

Benny Urquidez

The Ultimate Warrior

The name "Benny The Jet" is as much a part of American Pop Sports Culture as "Magic Johnson," "Tiger Woods," or "Hammering Hank." But the real Benny Urquidez is even more interesting than the legend he represents.

By the time he was 5, Benny Urquidez was already boxing before a crowd at the Olympic Auditorium in Los Angeles. The son of a professional boxer (his father) and a professional wrestler (his mother), he began to study martial arts at 8 years of age. He learned from his brother, Arnold Urquidez, as well as with such masters as Tak Kubota, Bill Ryusaki, Ed Parker, and Mas Oyama. At age 14 he earned his black belt despite the unwritten rule that you had to be 18 years of age to earn that rank.

After years of fighting in point tournaments, Benny Urquidez decided to compete in full contact karate. He was one of the few point fighters make the transition successfully. When Elton John released the song Benny and the Jets, *a kickboxing legend was born. Benny "The Jet" Urquidez never lost in 100 kickboxing matches. He has been featured in several documentary films and appeared in action movies with Jackie Chan, Patrick Swayze, Sylvester Stallone, and John Cusak. He is the author of great books about kickboxing, including* Training and Fighting Skills *and* King of the Ring. *He is more than just the result of successful hype and good public relations—he is a true champion who has conquered whatever challenge is placed before him.*

Q: You have been called a rebel. Why?

A: Well, I guess my motivation pushed me to find the best way of doing things, so I never took anything for granted and never followed anyone blindly.

Q: Why did you go from point tournament to full contact karate?

A: I was quite successful in point tournaments. But I had the problem of hitting my opponents too hard. This was the way I trained and so I went hard from the neck down. I couldn't believe that some fighters were scoring points

"There's a learning curve that you have to force yourself to go through, before you catch on and start to enjoy something. Successful people are the ones who stick it out through the learning curve. Most people quit."

just things like a really weak back-fist. I felt that every punch had to be real. You have to have a certain degree of reality in everything you do in life.

Q: Who introduced you to karate?

A: My brother Arnold. He used to take me to class by the ear! I didn't enjoy karate. I really hated it so he forced me to go there and train every day. Then one day, just from training so much, I found out that I was really good at it. So then I started to like it. Most things in life are like that. There's a learning curve that you have to force yourself to go through, before you catch on and start to enjoy something. Successful people are the ones who stick it out through the learning curve. Most people quit.

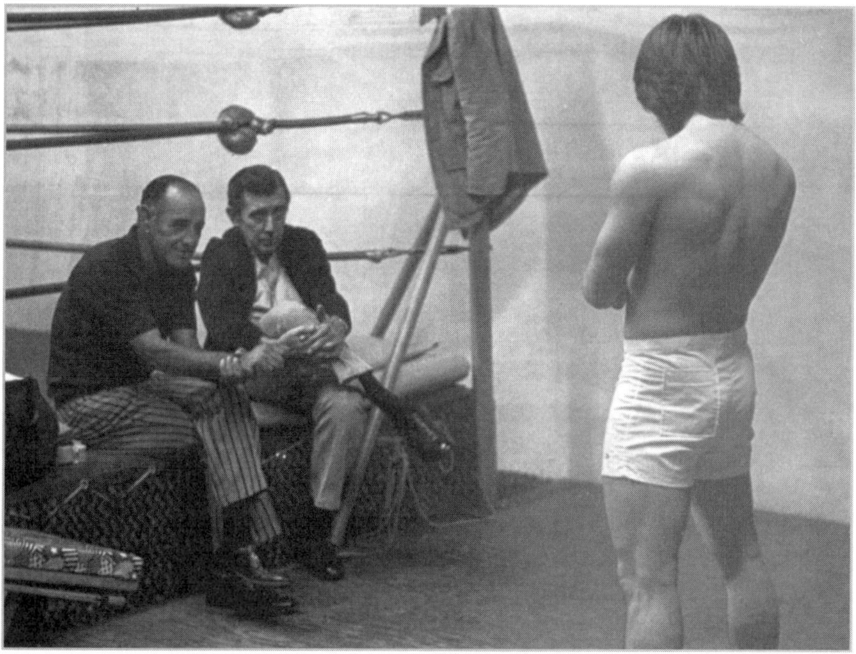

"I entered full contact—but only after trying boxing first. I was very happy when full contact started because I could finally use everything I had learned in martial arts."

Q: When did you hear about full contact karate?
A: I boxed as a teenager, so contact was not strange to me. That's probably the reason I couldn't deal with point tournaments. Anyway, in the early '70s, full contact began as a sport and I felt that was for me. I entered full contact—but only after trying boxing first. I was very happy when full contact started because I could finally use everything I had learned in martial arts.

Q: What do you think about the way martial arts are taught today?
A: To be honest, there are many things out there that won't work on the street or in the ring. I mentioned that on television one time and I received a lot of negative calls. I feel bad if I hurt some people's feelings by saying that, but I'm just being truthful.

Q: How do you think Bruce Lee would have done in full contact karate?
A: To me, Bruce Lee is number one. Unfortunately, he's gone forever, so we can only speculate. But he will always be the best in my heart.

"Many people thought that if you changed a few things you could easily move from point to contact. But reality is a different thing. The attitude has to be different and the training is much more demanding."

Q: What do you think some point champions never made it in full contact?

A: It takes a lot to change over—it's not easy. Many people thought that if you changed a few things you could easily move from point to contact. But reality is a different thing. The attitude has to be different and the training is much more demanding. You have to change your whole combat conceptions and your fighting spirit has to fit into the warrior environment. A few great fighters—such as Joe Lewis, Bill Wallace, David Moon, my brother Arnold—made it. But it wasn't easy.

Q: Why did you create your own style Ukidokan?

A: For many years I gathered a lot of information and knowledge so I decided put it together. It is a combination of nine different hard and soft styles. What was good for the '70s won't work now because the fighting level has risen in the last 25 years. Of course we modified certain things and I still change things in order to improve the training methods and the fighting techniques.

Q: So you want your students to be well-rounded.

A: Yes, because you need to be able to fight against anyone. That's why you need muay Thai, jiu-jitsu, judo, savate, boxing, karate, et cetera. I've also seen a change in myself. I'm a better teacher now than a fighter, and this is because I really love people. I like to help people to become good martial artists and what I do I do from the heart. If you ask what Benny is all about,

I'd say Benny is about teaching. I can teach anybody.

Q: Have you taught many celebrities?
A: Yes, I've worked with big names such as Silvester Stallone and Patrick Swayze.

Q: What is the secret of your success
A: I don't think there is any secret but there are a lot of different factors working together. I was hungry and I had the desire to be the best. I was crazy enough to get into many types of fighting and above all I loved what I was doing. You can't ask for anything more.

Q: It is true you went to train under Mas Oyama?
A: Yes. When I was in Japan I decided to visit his school and train there. He was a legend and a great teacher.

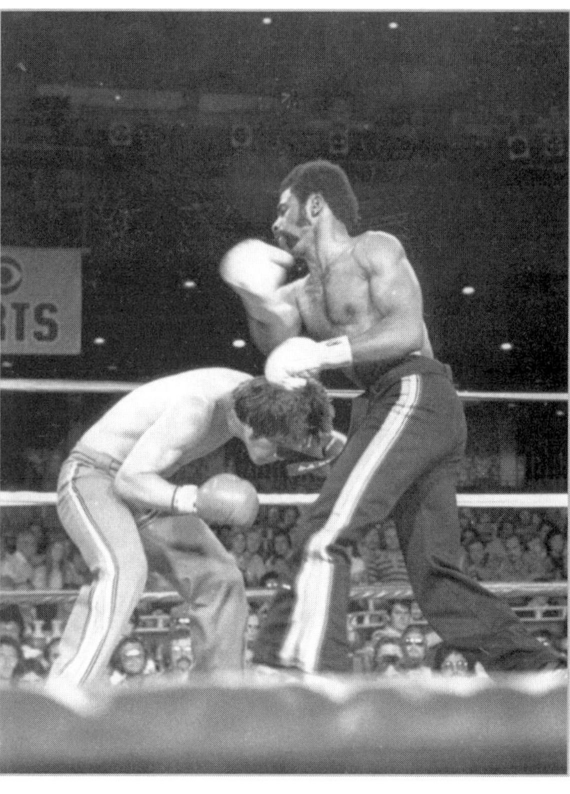

"I was hungry and I had the desire to be the best. I was crazy enough to get into many types of fighting and above all I loved what I was doing. You can't ask for anything more."

Q: Who influenced you as a martial artist?
A: I guess you receive influences from everybody. I do believe in learning from everybody who has something to teach. But to answer your question I would say Tak Kubota, Mas Oyama, Bill Ryusaki and of course, my brother Arnold.

Q: What do you think about the grappling arts?
A: Well, grappling has always been around. It is not something new. After the Ultimate Fighting Championship everybody wanted to learn submission but there were a few great teachers sharing the art with us already, like Gene LeBell.

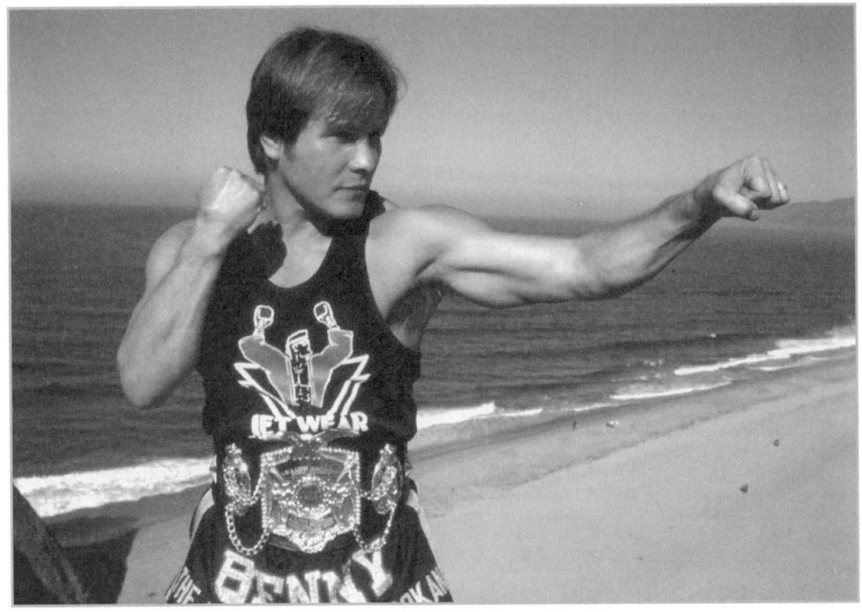

"I don't want to teach people just how to fight. What I teach is a way of life. Knowledge is power and I try to teach my students a desire to be the best at whatever they do."

Q: What do you think of "Judo" Gene LeBell?
A: I consider him "The" grappler. He's just it. He is a master class fighter and teacher. In fact when I was challenged by Rorion Gracie, I started training with Gene LeBell.

Q: What do you think about the UFC?
A: In the beginning was very revealing. It proved to everybody that the grappling arts were here to stay and that if you wanted to be a well-rounded fighter you needed to have an understanding of groundwork. Now is no longer a sport or an art—it is just a brawl. I completely disagree with it because I don't think it teaches anything at all, and martial arts are supposed to be a way of life, teaching humbleness, discipline and above all, respect for other people.

Q: How have you changed your training compared to when you were fighting?

A: When I was fighting I was younger and I did a lot of things wrong. I didn't allow the muscles tissue to heal and recover because I used to train too much. More doesn't always means better. When you get older you can still do the same things you used to but you have to rest more and not workout as hard. You have to get wiser and listen to your body.

Q: What's your teaching philosophy?

A: I don't want to teach people just how to fight. I want them to learn how to eat properly, and how to train the right way. What I teach is a way of life. Knowledge is power and I try to teach my students a desire to be the best at whatever they do.

Q: And your fighting philosophy?

A: The way you train is the way you react. Don't pull your punches or kicks. Hit hard.

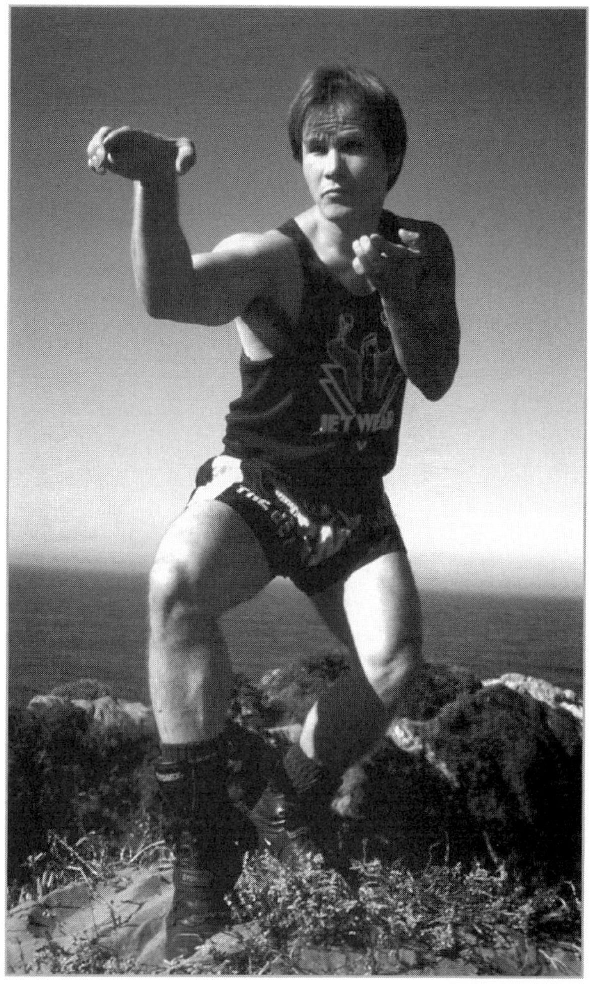

"I became a product of the countries I traveled to, to fight. I didn't know how lethal an elbow to the face could be until I fought in Thailand."

Q: What are the most important things you learned as a professional kickboxer.

A: I became a product of the countries I traveled to, to fight. I didn't know how lethal an elbow to the face could be until I fought in Thailand. In Mexico I perfected my punches, and in Japan I learned a different way of training. So the number one thing I learned is to have an open mind.

"If you are a pro, I recommend that you workout for over four hours everyday but it should be spread out, not four hours in a row. If you're not a professional fighter, two hours per day is good."

Q: How many hours do you recommend people to train?

A: Well, it depends on if you are a professional or not. If you are a pro, I recommend that you workout for over four hours everyday but it should be spread out, not four hours in a row. If you're not a professional fighter, two hours per day is good.

Q: Do you follow any particular diet?

A: I eat a lot of fish, turkey and chicken. Turkey is very good, specially if you want to lose weight. Forget about fried foods and salt and eat a lot of vegetables and fruit. Take vitamins like B complex, C, and E. I also indulge myself on Sunday just to keep my sanity. On that day I eat anything I want.

Q: What is the most important thing you want your students to never forget?

A: I would like them to be humble and quiet. If you're quiet, you only have time to look for knowledge—and knowledge is power. I also want them to be good listeners, because listening creates all sorts of reflexes. Unfortunately most people like to listen with their eyes, not their ears.

Q: How do you want to be remembered?

A: My life has moved onto the movie screen now, but as a martial artist I want people think of me not only as a champion but as somebody who really cared about people.

"My life has moved onto the movie screen now, but as a martial artist I want people think of me not only as a champion but as somebody who really cared about people."

Benny Urquidez faces his opponent (1). As soon as the opponent starts to move in, Urquidez jumps in the air (2), applying a devastating (3) downward flying punch to the face (4).

1

2

3

4

Urquidez squares off with his opponent (1). He closes the distance with a left punch to the face and simultaneously switches leg stances (2) to apply a left upward knee to the stomach (3) followed by a downward right elbow to the face (4).

1

2

3

4

Benny faces his opponent in matched leads (1). He closes the distance using a left jab (2), follows with a low kick to the inside of the shin to open the angle (2) for a side kick (3, 4-5), followed by a new back kick to the stomach (6-7).

Bill Wallace

With the Right Foot

William Louis Wallace began training in judo while practicing the ouchi gari throw. His partner took a straight downward plunge onto his right knee, severely tearing the ligaments and rendering it all but useless. This tragic and yet fateful incident helped to fashion the man that would one day be known as "Superfoot." Retired as the undefeated Professional Karate Association Middleweight World Champion in 1980, and a living legend in the full contact karate circles around the world, Wallace began his training in shorin ryu karate under Michael Gneck and George Torbett. People from all over came to personally train with him, like great European karate champion Dominique Valera, who introduced full contact karate in Europe after being tortured by "Superfoot" during a match.

Before entering the full contact scene, Bill Wallace was rated among the top point fighters in America. His left kick has been clocked in excess of 60 mph—he uses his foot as others use their hands. In sparring, his kicking precision is amazing and his faking techniques for setting-up kicks are astounding. In 1973, one of his famous friends, the late Elvis Presley, flew in a Los Angeles acupuncturist to treat "Superfoot" at Graceland Manor due to a leg injury. He became a bodyguard and personal friend of the late John Belushi being the one who found the great actor dead on his bed. He authored three great books, Karate: Basic Concepts and Skills, Dynamic Stretching and Kicking, *and* The Ultimate Kick: The Wallace Method (Unique Publications). *Simplicity is his hallmark—from the food he eats, to the clothes he wears, to the punches and kicks that made him a karate living legend.*

Q: How did you make your transition from point karate to full contact?
A: I won several national point tournaments. Then in 1973, Mike Anderson was putting a full contact team together that later on went to Paris. For me was an extension of what I was already doing.

"My whole strategy was to let my opponent walk into the technique. I used to throw kicks until the opponent got used to the block, then it was easier for me to score."

Q: How much did you have to modify your techniques?
A: My kicking was the same. I always believed in snapping the kicks, so I didn't train very differently for my leg techniques. Of course, I improved what I had and I changed a few things from the tactical and strategic point of view. For punching I began to train in boxing.

Q: Some people say that your punching techniques are not that powerful.
A: Well, neither are my kicks. My whole strategy was to let my opponent walk into the technique. I used to throw kicks until the opponent got used to the block, then it was easier for me to score. That was pretty much what I was doing with me hand also. My best techniques were the jab and the lead-hand hook. But for me, karate is kicking. I had always wanted to be able knock somebody down with a kick in the head!

Q: What about the rear hand?
A: I didn't use that much. I used about as often as I used my right leg!

Q: Is it true that you fought two professional boxing matches?
A: Yes, I did but very few people know. For the pure hell of it I fought two pro bouts down South. I knocked them both out with the left hook. I trained really hard to get good boxing techniques and I was lucky to train under great coaches and spar against great boxers. I learned a lot.

Q: Your style was very personal because you only used one side for kicking. How did this affect your overall fighting strategy?

A: To be honest, I think it really made me better because I was focused the 100 percent of my time on only one leg. While other people were kicking 50 times with the right leg and 50 times with the left leg, I was kicking 100 times with the left. Some people say that's bad, but everybody has a preference when they fight so, why not concentrate on one side and make it much better? Of course, I had to learn to be more unpredictable in my actions.

"I really enjoy sparring but I realize that your body doesn't heal the same way after you reach a certain age. I like to spar with the students at the seminars but the problem is that they like to go heavy and then I have to go heavy. I don't feel like taking chances anymore."

Q: Why are you still fighting in exhibitions?

A: I really enjoy sparring but I realize that your body doesn't heal the same way after you reach a certain age. I like to spar with the students at the seminars but the problem is that they like to go heavy and then I have to go heavy too. I don't feel like taking chances anymore. It's not worth it because I don't have anything to prove to anyone. I really just never wanted to be the kind of guy that teaches seminars and tells you that the techniques works but never shows you how.

Q: What was your toughest fight?

A: The one with Blinky Rodriguez. He got me with a left hook that I still remember. In point fighting it was Jeff Smith.

"Joe Lewis was the best that's ever been. His strong points were explosiveness, power and great speed—he was ahead of his time. I really think he was too soon with too much."

Q: You were fighting point-tournament during the karate's "Golden Age" with people like Chuck Norris and Joe Lewis. What do you think of them?
A: Joe Lewis was the best that's ever been. His strong points were explosiveness, power and great speed—he was ahead of his time. I really think he was too soon with too much. Chuck Norris was one of the reasons I started kicking. He's a great guy and we worked together in the movie business.

Q: You have fought in so called "point tournaments"—traditional and open versions—and in full contact. What are the major differences you perceived?
A: Well, let me explain this. Traditional karate tournaments and Open tournaments were two different things for obvious reasons. In a traditional tournament the event is an extension of the Japanese and Korean culture with respect, manners, self-discipline, etc. Technique wise, they punch and kick very hard but the technique has to be perfect, precise. During my time in the traditional tournaments, you had to score with a perfect movement because

otherwise the judges could never call the point. Simply touching was not enough. You had to give a solid blow but with control, although sometimes "control" meant different things to different judges!

"Because of my background in kinesiology and physical education I was able not only to demonstrate the techniques, but I also knew exactly what muscles were doing what."

For instance, in a traditional tournament like the J.K.A., a fast technique like the backfist would never score, but in an open tournament with safety equipment and a different approach to the rules, it is a fast and effective technique to use.

Tactics and strategies changed depending on where you were competing. In a traditional tournament you are better off counterpunching or counterkicking. It's the nature of the game.

In open competition the emphasis was on speed. The quickest technique, not necessarily the best, is the one that gets the flag. When fighting open, the all-out blitz works best. Throw a lot of techniques and one of them is bound to earn a point. A quick backfist is probably one of the best techniques to be used in open tournaments. In a traditional competition, stick to your reverse punch and front kick...keep it simple and direct. The interesting thing is that traditional teachers like Hidetaka Nishiyama have an amazing selection of kicks. For instance, his roundhouse kick was incredible but I wondered why his guys never threw one.

I truly believe that competitors should get into both types of tournaments because you can learn a great deal if you know how to adapt. This will make your game more versatile. No competitor should be afraid to enter in a lion's den of an opposing system. Just reach out and kick someone; you just may learn something new!

"I know that there is always somebody out there who is faster or stronger than you but there never has to be someone sneakier than you."

Q: You have a Master's degree in kinesiology. Has that helped your karate?
A: Because of my background in kinesiology and physical education I was able not only to demonstrate the techniques, but I also knew exactly what muscles were doing what. So in my seminars I can scientifically explain what it takes to develop speed, flexibility, or power in kicks or punches.

Q: You were one of the first fighters to weight train. Do you still lift?
A: Yes. I did lift weights, not heavy weights but lightly. I used to do it basically to keep up the tone and to work the opposing muscle groups. I never wanted to be bulky but I wanted to still have the strength. Also I had to stay flexible.

Q: What's your philosophy of fighting?
A: I'd rather hit you than you hit me because it hurts. I know that there is always somebody out there who is faster or stronger than you but there never has to be someone sneakier than you.

Q: You used to work out with Hollywood personalities as Elvis Presley and John Belushi. Both of then passed away. What are your feelings about them?
A: I can't even think about it. They were great friends, and that's why I try to not think about it anymore.

Q: What do you think about events like the Ultimate Fighting Championship?
A: I was at the first one as a commentator. I guess it was good in the beginning to educate people about how important the grappling arts are. When I began training the only guy that was doing some grappling was Joe Lewis,

because he was a wrestler before becoming a karate champion. I got my knee injured playing judo. I guess we were the only two that knew about grappling. I really don't think these kind of events are positive anymore.

"John was a great guy. He asked me to go with him and Dan Aykroyd during The Blues Brothers Tour. When he was with me he was a very, very wonderful person. If he liked you, he'd do the world for you."

Q: Did the grappling interest affect your kickboxing seminars?
A: Not at all. In fact I recommend that people study the grappling arts for self-defense because you don't know what kind of situation you'll find yourself in. There are aspects of grappling that I think are really fantastic, and I'm sure every martial artist can benefit from them. But also you have to be careful because usually a self-defense situation involve more than one opponent.

Q: How was your experience working in a movie with Jackie Chan?
A: Jackie Chan is a great guy! He is one of the bravest and most meticulous people I've ever met and his stunts are the best ever. We were shooting a fighting scene and after I don't remember how many takes he still wasn't satisfied so we kept doing it until he almost got hurt and said, "OK. This one is good!" I missed him by maybe half an inch and it scared the shit out of me. He said to me: "That's great, Bill." I answered, "You´re sick Jackie, really sick!"

Q: Do you like working in the movies?
A: Yes, I do. There's a good money in it and it's fun, but my life is karate.

"Stretching is the first part of my workout. When you stretch you open up the blood flow, your muscles become more elastic, and you get your heart pumping faster. Just think that if your muscles are loose and warm you can punch and kick faster."

Q: Can you talk about the great Blues Brother, John Belushi?

A: Listen, John was a great guy. He asked me to go with him and Dan Aykroyd during The Blues Brothers Tour. When he was with me he was a very, very wonderful person. If he liked you, he'd do the world for you. We used to workout all the time. Many times Dan Aykroyd joined us in the training. He was the kind of guy that if he ate a piece of cake he would gain 10 pounds. His metabolism was very slow.

Q: What were the workouts?

A: He would do three rounds on the heavy bag, three rounds shadowboxing, and three rounds skipping rope. Then we would weight train.

Q: Can you describe a typical Bill Wallace training session?

A: Stretching is the first part of my workout. When you stretch you open up the blood flow, your muscles become more elastic, and you get your heart pumping faster. Just think that if your muscles are loose and warm you can punch and kick faster because there is less resistance to the movement. My stretching program includes the whole body not only the legs. Then I skip rope for few rounds, somewhere between five-to-eight three-minutes rounds. The heavy bag is the next station. I go for five or six rounds and I never tape my hands. After that I shadowbox for five rounds, hands only. Then another five rounds shadow kicking. I don't like to kick the heavy bag because you get used to always kicking something and if you're fighting, and miss, the resulting momentum will make you lose your balance. If I have a partner, then I spar for eight-to-ten three-minute rounds.

After that I go to the weight room and I do bench press, dips, chin-ups, pull-ups and lat pulldowns. I do three sets of 10-12 reps. I don't believe in lifting very heavy because it slows the muscle contraction time, therefore you lose some speed. And I am after speed, not brute strength.

Q: How would you like to be remembered?

A: As someone who at a certain time was the best in the world at what he did. There was a time that nobody in the whole world was better than me. "Superfoot" is part of karate history and nobody can change that. I'm happy.

Q: What are your immediate plans?

A: I'm going for hamburgers. You buying?

"There was a time that nobody in the whole world was better than me. "Superfoot" is part of karate history and nobody can change that."

"A true martial arts practitioner—like an artist of any other kind—be this a musician, a painter, a writer or an actor, is expressing and leaving part of himself in every piece of his craft. The need for self-inspection and self-realization of "who" he is becomes the reason for a journey in search of that perfect technique, that great melody, that inspiring poetry, that amazing painting or that Academy Award performance. It is this motivation to reach that "impossible dream," that allows a simple individual to become an exceptional "artist" and "master" of his craft."

—Jose M. Fraguas